Lone Pine Publishir

Tree & Shrub
Gardening
for
OHIO

Fred Hower
Alison Beck

© 2004 by Lone Pine Publishing
First printed in 2004   10 9 8 7 6 5 4 3 2 1
Printed in Canada

All rights reserved. No part of this work covered by the copyrights hereon may be reproduced or used in any form or by any means—graphic, electronic or mechanical—without the prior written permission of the publishers, except for reviewers, who may quote brief passages. Any request for photocopying, recording, taping or storage on information retrieval systems of any part of this work shall be directed in writing to the publisher.

The Publisher: Lone Pine Publishing

10145 – 81 Avenue
Edmonton, AB, Canada T6E 1W9
Website: www.lonepinepublishing.com

1808 – B Street NW, Suite 140
Auburn, WA, USA 98001

National Library of Canada Cataloguing in Publication

Hower, Fred, 1937–
    Tree & shrub gardening for Ohio / Fred Hower and Alison Beck.

    Includes index.
    ISBN 1-55105-402-7

    1. Ornamental trees—Ohio. 2. Ornamental shrubs—Ohio.
I. Beck, Alison, 1971– II. Title. III. Title: Tree and shrub gardening for Ohio.
SB435.52.O34H68 2004   635.9'77'09771   C2003-905807-7

Editorial Director: Nancy Foulds
Project Editor: Dawn Loewen
Illustrations Coordinator: Carol Woo
Photo Editor: Don Williamson
Production Manager: Gene Longson
Book Design, Layout & Production: Heather Markham
Cover Design: Gerry Dotto
Illustrations: Ian Sheldon
Scanning, Separations & Film: Elite Lithographers Co.

Photography: all interior photos by **Tim Matheson** or **Tamara Eder,** except **Agriculture & Agri-Food Canada (Morden Research Station)** 151a, 336b&c; **Alison Beck** 80b, 324a; **Janet Davis** 90, 269a, 339a; **Dean Didur** 338a; **Don Doucette** 78, 81b, 201a, 204a, 264, 265a, 266a, 314; **Derek Fell** 211b, 291b, 293a, 320; **Anne Gordon** 339b; **Lynne Harrison** 99a&b, 155b, 199b, 335b; **Saxon Holt** 135b, 137b, 263d; **Linda Kershaw** 135a, 243c, 336a; **Dawn Loewen** 162, 165b, 225b; **Heather Markham** 296a; **Steve Nikkila** 154a, 220a, 270b, 271a&b, 335a, 340a; **Kim O'Leary** 10, 56a&c, 85a, 227b; **Allison Penko** 120, 121b, 123a, 126, 143a, 175b&c, 188, 212, 224b, 229b, 260, 280, 297a, 306, 307a, 308, 319a&b; **Robert Ritchie** 23a, 28a&c, 42b, 66c, 70, 72, 82, 83a&c, 89c, 91a&b&c, 98b, 97a&c, 100, 101b, 153a, 155a, 165a, 172, 173a&b, 191a&b, 230, 241b, 242b, 243a, 259a, 263b&c, 295b, 297a, 325a, 326, 327a&b, 334; **Royal Botanical Gardens/Chris Graham** 205a; **Mark Turner** 84, 115b, 119b, 219a&b, 290a, 291a, 318; **Tim Wood** 14a, 22b, 25b, 26, 32, 60a&b, 75, 77a, 79a&b, 81a, 83b, 85b, 86b, 88, 89a&b, 101a, 104a, 105b&c, 108a, 109a, 113a&b, 116, 117a, 119a, 123b&c, 129b&c, 131b, 133a&b, 137a, 140a&b, 141a, 144a&b, 147b, 149b, 150, 151b, 157b, 161a, 163a&b, 164a&b, 167a&b, 169b, 179b&c, 181a&b, 182, 183b, 189b, 195b&c, 196, 197b&c, 198, 199a, 202a, 209a, 213a, 214b, 215a, 223a&b, 224a, 235a, 249b, 251b, 253b, 255a, 263a, 265b, 266b, 267b, 270a, 272, 273a&b, 275a, 281a&b, 283a&b&c, 289a, 290b, 299a&b, 302, 303a&b, 309a, 310, 311, 312a&b, 313a&c, 315b, 316, 317a&b, 323a, 329c, 330a, 331b&c, 333a, 337b, 341a

Front cover photos (clockwise from top left): elm, maple, viburnum, oak, silverbells, euonymus. All photos by Tim Matheson, except for viburnum by Tamara Eder.
Back cover author photos: Fred Hower by D.K. Photographic, Alison Beck by Alan Bibby
Map: based on USDA plant hardiness zone map (1990)

We acknowledge the financial support of the Government of Canada through the Book Publishing Industry Development Program (BPIDP) for our publishing activities.

PC: *P1*

CONTENTS

ACKNOWLEDGMENTS

Fred Hower would like to acknowledge the following:
- Klyn Nurseries, Acorn Farms, Herman Losely & Sons and Lake County Nursery, whose catalogs I consulted in writing this book
- My mentor, Dr. Louis Charles 'Chad' Chadwick, whom I knew from 1959 until his death in 1993 at the age of 91
- Dr. D.C. 'Kip' Kiplinger, Dr. Kenneth Reisch and Dr. Fred Hartman—teachers as well as friends
- Mr. William Collins and Mr. William Hendricks—adventurous and enthusiastic horticulturists
- Mr. Carlton B. Lees and Professor Clancy E. Lewis—teachers, photographers, authors and lecturers who helped me see the total beauty of plants
- My mother, who made me work in the garden as a child
- My wife, Jo'Del, and our children, Tamara, Michael, Matthew and Tara, who encouraged me to write down my observations.

Alison Beck would like to express her appreciation to all who were involved in this project. Special thanks are extended to Debra Knapke, Tim Wood and Spring Meadow Nursery.

The Trees & Shrubs at a Glance

A Pictorial Guide in Alphabetical Order, by Common Name

Aralia
p. 76

Arborvitae
p. 78

Aronia
p. 82

Barberry
p. 84

Beautyberry
p. 88

Beauty Bush
p. 90

Beech
p. 92

Birch
p. 96

Black Jetbead
p. 100

Boxwood
p. 102

Butterfly Bush
p. 110

Buckeye
p. 106

Caryopteris
p. 112

Cherry
p. 114

Cotoneaster
p. 120

Crabapple
p. 124

Deutzia
p. 132

Dogwood
p. 134

Elder
p. 138

Dawn Redwood
p. 130

Euonymus
p. 142

False Cypress
p. 146

False Spirea
p. 150

Firethorn
p. 156

Flowering Quince
p. 160

Filbert
p. 152

Forsythia
p. 162

Fothergilla
p. 166

Ginkgo
p. 170

Golden Rain Tree
p. 172

Fringe Tree
p. 168

Hawthorn
p. 174

Hemlock
p. 178

Honeysuckle
p. 186

Hornbeam
p. 190

Holly
p. 180

Hydrangea
p. 192

Japanese Hydrangea
Vine, p. 198

Kerria
p. 208

Juniper
p. 200

Katsura-Tree
p. 206

Linden
p. 218

Larch
p. 210

Lilac
p. 212

Magnolia
p. 222

Maple
p. 226

Mock-Orange
p. 232

Mountain Laurel
p. 236

Ninebark
p. 238

Oak
p. 240

Oregon-Grape
p. 244

Potentilla
p. 252

Privet
p. 256

Pieris
p. 246

Pine
p. 248

Redbud
p. 258

Rhododendron
p. 260

Rose-of-Sharon
p. 264

Serviceberry
p. 268

Seven-Son Flower
p. 272

Silverbell
p. 274

Smokebush
p. 276

Snowbell
p. 278

Spirea
p. 280

Spruce
p. 284

Stewartia
p. 292

Sumac
p. 294

Summersweet
p. 298

St. Johnswort
p. 288

Sweetgum
p. 300

Sweetspire
p. 302

Weigela
p. 314

Thornless Honeylocust
p. 304

Tulip Tree
p. 306

Viburnum
p. 308

White Forsythia
p. 316

Witchhazel
p. 322

Yellowwood
p. 326

Wisteria
p. 318

Yew
p. 328

Yucca
p. 332

Zelkova
p. 334

INTRODUCTION

Trees and shrubs are woody perennials. They maintain a permanent live structure above ground year-round, and they live for three or more years. In cold climates, a few shrubs die back to the ground each winter. The root system, protected by the soil over winter, sends up new shoots in spring, and if the shrub forms flowers on new wood it will bloom that same year. Such plants act like herbaceous perennials, but because they are woody year-round in their native climates they are still classified as shrubs. Butterfly bush falls into this category of perennial-like shrubs.

A tree is generally defined as a woody plant having a single trunk and growing greater than 15' tall. A shrub is multi-stemmed and no taller than 15'. These definitions are not absolute because some tall trees are multi-stemmed, and some short shrubs have single trunks. Even the height definitions are open to interpretation. For example, some Japanese maple cultivars may be multi-stemmed and grow only about 10' tall, but they are still usually referred to as trees. Furthermore, a given species may grow as a tree in favorable conditions but be reduced to a shrub in harsher sites. It is always best to simply look at the expected mature size of a tree or shrub and judge its suitability for your garden accordingly.

Some vines are also included in this guide. Like trees and shrubs, these plants maintain living woody stems above ground over winter. They generally require a supporting structure to grow upon, but many can also be grown as trailing ground-covers. Again, the definition is not absolute. Some of the vines, such as wisteria, can be trained to grow as free-standing shrubs with proper pruning. Conversely, certain shrubs, such as firethorn, can be trained to grow up and over walls and other structures.

Woody plants are characterized by leaf type, whether deciduous or evergreen, and needled or broad-leaved. Deciduous plants lose all their leaves each fall or winter. They can have needles, like dawn redwood and larch, or broad leaves, like maple and dogwood. Evergreen trees and shrubs do not lose their leaves in winter. They can also be needled or broad-leaved, like pine and rhododendron, respectively. Semi-evergreen plants are generally evergreens that in cold climates lose some or all of their leaves. Some viburnums fall into this category.

The climate of Ohio is continental, which means that winters are

Yellow-cedar, a large evergreen tree
Smokebush as a multi-stemmed shrub

cold and summers are hot, though winters aren't as cold as those farther north and summers aren't as hot as those farther south. Rainfall is plentiful, but not as consistent as some gardeners might like in mid- and late summer. In general, the climate of Ohio is great for growing a wide variety of woody plants. The cold winters allow a good period of dormancy for plants that need cold in order to produce flowers. The summers are warm and long enough to give plants plenty of time to grow.

The geography of Ohio is diverse, providing gardeners with a wide range of soils and topographies. The Appalachian Plateau dominates eastern Ohio, creating terrain with rolling hills and rocky ridges. Soils tend to be acidic and fairly well drained. The terrain in the west of the state tends to be flatter, with the soil consisting mainly of alkaline clays deposited during the last ice age. The state is intersected throughout with creeks, streams and rivers.

Temperature and precipitation patterns in Ohio vary from area to area. Gardens in the south and those close to the shores of Lake Erie experience the warmest weather in winter, but lakeshore gardens aren't as warm as southern gardens in summer. Precipitation is fairly consistent throughout the year, but periods of extended drought in mid- and late summer through to fall are likely in all Ohio gardens. Our winter weather, with its characteristic freezing and thawing cycles, creates one of the biggest challenges for gardeners. Frequent warm spells in winter can spell disaster if plants break dormancy too early, only to be frozen again. As well, rainfall when the ground is still mostly frozen can cause roots to rot.

No matter what challenges you face in your garden, you will find a tree, shrub or vine that will thrive in your space. Hardiness zones (see map, p. 15), though not the final word on what will or will not grow, are a useful tool in helping decide what plants to put in the garden as well as where to put them.

Don't be put off because a catalog or book says a plant is hardy to only a certain zone. Part of the fun and challenge of gardening is experimenting with unusual and out-of-zone plants. Keep in mind that local topography in the garden creates microclimates, small areas that may be more or less favorable for growing different plants. Buildings, hills, low spots, drainage patterns and prevailing winds all influence your garden and the microclimates that occur in it (see Getting Started, p. 24, for more information on assessing conditions in your garden). Pick the right spot in your garden for that tender shrub, and you just may be surprised at how well it does.

Lilac needs cold winters to set its flowers.

Rhododendrons & azaleas thrive in a sheltered woodland garden.

Yew prefers some shelter from the wind.

You'll find a trip to a nearby park or botanical garden, where trees are labeled and unusual specimens grown, invaluable for showing you outstanding trees, shrubs and vines that thrive in Ohio. Keep your eyes open when walking through your neighborhood. You may see a tree or shrub that you hadn't noticed before or that you were told would not grow where you live. What is actually growing is the best guide.

Many enthusiastic and creative people garden in Ohio. From across the state, individuals, growers, societies, schools, publications and public and private gardens provide information, encouragement and fruitful debate for the novice or experienced gardener. Ohio gardeners are passionate about their plants and will gladly share their knowledge and opinions about what is best for any little patch of ground.

Outstanding garden shows, public gardens, arboretums and show gardens in Ohio attract gardeners

Well-maintained public garden

and growers from all over the world. Seek them out as sources of inspiration and information. Open yourself to the possibilities, and you'll be surprised by the diversity of woody plants that thrive here. At least initially, you may want to plant mostly tried and true, dependable varieties, but don't be afraid to try something different or new. Gardening with trees and shrubs is fun and can be a great adventure if you're willing to take up the challenge.

Flowering quince and other Asian natives can be grown in Ohio.

HARDINESS ZONES MAP

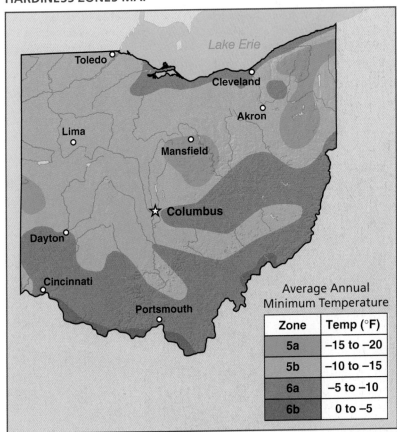

Average Annual Minimum Temperature

Zone	Temp (°F)
5a	−15 to −20
5b	−10 to −15
6a	−5 to −10
6b	0 to −5

Woody Plants in the Garden

Trees and shrubs create a framework around which a garden can be designed. These permanent features anchor the landscape, and in a well-designed garden they create interest all year round. In spring and summer, woody plants provide shade and beauty with flowers and foliage. In fall, leaves of many tree and shrub species change color, and brightly colored fruit attracts attention and birds. In winter, the true backbone of the garden is revealed; the branches of deciduous trees and shrubs are laid bare, perhaps dusted with snow or frost, and evergreens take precedence in giving the garden color. Stem and trunk character becomes important in the winter garden, along with the color and texture variations of exfoliating and shaggy bark.

Carefully selected and placed, woody plants are a vital and vibrant element of any landscape, from the smallest city lot to the largest country acreage. They can provide privacy and keep unattractive views hidden from sight. Conversely, they can frame an attractive view and draw attention to particular features or areas of the garden. Trees and shrubs soften the hard lines in the landscape created by structures such as buildings, fences, walls and driveways. Well-positioned woody plants create an attractive background against which other plants will shine. Trees and shrubs can be used in groups for spectacular flower or

fall color shows, and a truly exceptional species, with year-round appeal, can stand alone as a specimen plant in a prime location.

Woody plants also help moderate the climate in your home and garden. As a windbreak, trees provide shelter from the winter cold, reducing heating costs and protecting tender garden plants. A well-placed deciduous tree keeps the house cool and shaded in summer but allows the sun through in winter, when the warmth and light are appreciated. Woody plants also prevent soil erosion, retain soil moisture, reduce noise and filter the air.

Attracting wildlife is an often overlooked advantage of gardening. As cities expand, our living space encroaches on more and more wildlife habitat. By choosing plants, particularly native plants, that are beneficial to local wildlife, we provide food and shelter to birds and other animals, thereby helping fulfill our obligation as stewards of the environment. We can bring nature closer to home. Unfortunately, the local wildlife may so enjoy a garden that they consume it. It is possible, though, to find a balance and attract wildlife while protecting the garden from ruin.

When the time comes to select woody plants, think carefully about the various physical constraints of your garden and the purposes you wish the plants to serve. First and foremost, consider the size of your garden in relation to the mature size of the plants in question. Very large plants are always a bad idea in a small garden. Remember, too, that trees and shrubs not only grow up, they also grow out. Within a few years what started as a small plant

Pieris as a specimen plant (above)

Birds and squirrels are frequent garden visitors.

may become a very large, spreading tree. Spruces are often sold as very small trees, but most eventually grow too large for a small garden.

Another consideration that relates to size is placement. Don't plant trees and shrubs too close to houses, walkways, entryways or driveways. A tree planted right next to a house may hit the overhang of the roof, and trying to fix the problem by pruning will often spoil the natural appearance of the tree. Plants placed too close to paths, doors and driveways may eventually block access completely and will give the property an unkempt appearance.

Consider, too, the various features of trees and shrub species. A feature is an outstanding element, such as flowers, bark or shape, that attracts you to the plant. Decide which of the features that follow are most important to you and which will best enhance your garden. Many plants have more than one feature, providing interest over a longer period. A carefully selected group of woody plants can add

Large trees provide shade for a resting place.
Prostrate cotoneaster

beauty to the garden all year. Whether you are looking for showy flowers, fall color, fast growth, unique bark or a beautiful fragrance, you can find trees or shrubs with features to suit your design. Consult the individual plant entries and the Quick Reference Chart at the back of the book.

Form is the general shape and growth habit of the plant. From tall and columnar to wide and gracefully weeping, trees come in a variety of shapes. Similarly, shrubs may be rounded and bushy or low and ground hugging. Form can also vary as the year progresses and leaves are developed and lost. Often a unique winter habit makes a tree or shrub truly outstanding.

You should be familiar with some growth form terminology when contemplating a purchase. A *shade tree* commonly refers to a large, deciduous tree but can be any tree that provides shade. An *upright, fastigiate* or *columnar* plant has the main branches and stems pointing upward and is often quite narrow. *Dwarf* properly refers to any variety, cultivar or hybrid that is smaller than the species, but the term is sometimes mistakenly used to mean a small, slow-growing plant. The crucial statistic is the expected size at maturity. If a species grows to 100', then a 30–50' variety would be a dwarf but might still be too big for your garden. *Prostrate* and *procumbent* plants are low growing, bearing branches and stems that spread horizontally across the ground. These forms are sometimes grafted onto upright stems to create lovely, weeping plant forms.

'Skyrocket' juniper has a fastigiate form.

Dwarf Colorado blue spruce

Norway maple showing fall color

Needles of 'Emerald Sea' juniper

Magnolia blossoms (below)

Foliage is one of the most enduring and important features of a plant. Leaves come in a variety of colors, shapes, sizes, textures and arrangements. You can find shades of green, blue, red, purple, yellow, white or silver. *Variegated* types have two or more colors combined on a single leaf. The variety of shapes is even more astounding, from short, sharply pointed needles to broad, rounded leaves the size of dinner plates. Leaf margins can be smooth, like those of many rhododendrons, or so finely divided the foliage appears lacy or fern-like, as with some Japanese maple cultivars. Foliage often varies seasonally, progressing from tiny, pale green spring buds to the vibrant colors of fall. Evergreen trees provide welcome greenery even when winter is at its snowiest and coldest.

Growing plants with different leaf sizes, textures and colors creates contrast and makes your garden more interesting and appealing to the eye. An entire garden can be designed based on varied foliage. Whether it forms a neutral backdrop or stands out in sharp contrast with the plants around it, foliage is a vital consideration in any garden.

Flowers are such an influential feature that their beauty may be enough reason to grow a tree or shrub, such as forsythia, that is dull or even unattractive the rest of the year. Flowering generally takes place over a few weeks or occasionally a month; only a few woody plants flower for the entire summer. Keep this limitation in mind when selecting woody plants. If you choose species with staggered flowering periods, you will always have some plants in bloom. You can achieve different but equally striking effects by grouping plants that flower at the same time, or by spreading them out around the garden. An easy, effective way to create a garden with a season-long progression of blooms is to visit your garden center on a regular basis. Because many people shop for plants only in spring, their gardens tend to be dominated by spring bloomers.

Fruit comes in many forms, including winged maple samaras, spiny buckeye capsules, dangling birch catkins and the more obviously fruity serviceberries and crabapple pomes. This feature is often a double-edged sword. It can be very attractive and provides interest in the garden in late summer and fall, when most plants are past their prime. When the fruit drops, however, it can create quite a mess and even odor if allowed to rot on the ground. Choose the location of your fruiting tree carefully. If you know the fruit can be messy, don't plant near a patio or a sidewalk. Most fruit isn't all that troublesome, but keep in mind that there may be some cleanup required during fruiting season.

Bark is one of the most overlooked features of trees and shrubs. Species with interesting bark will greatly enhance your landscape, particularly in winter. Bark can be furrowed, smooth, ridged, papery, scaly, exfoliating or colorful. A few trees valued for their interesting bark are birch, cherry, ninebark, paperbark maple and lacebark pine.

Oakleaf hydrangea blossoms

Winged fruit of silverbell

Paperbark maple bark (below)

Armed stem of aralia

'Cardinal' dogwood

Fragrance, though usually associated with flowers, is also a potential feature of the leaves, fruit and even wood of trees and shrubs. Flowering quince, summersweet, witchhazel, arborvitae, viburnum and of course lilac are examples of plants with appealing scents. Site fragrant plants near your home, where the scent can waft into an open window.

Branches as a feature combine elements of form and bark, and, like those two features, they can be an important winter attribute for the garden. Branches may have an unusual gnarled or twisted shape, like those of Harry Lauder's walking stick; they may bear protective spines or thorns, like those of firethorn; or they may be brightly colored, like those of red-twig dogwood and kerria.

Growth rate and **life span,** though not really aesthetic features of woody plants, are nonetheless important aspects to consider when planning a garden. A fast-growing tree or shrub that grows 24" or more a year will mature quickly and can be used to fill in space in a new garden. A slow-growing species that grows less than 12" a year may be more suitable in a space-limited garden.

A short-lived plant appeals to some people because they enjoy changing their garden design frequently or aren't sure exactly what they want in their garden. Short-lived plants, such as sumac, usually mature quickly and therefore reach flowering age quickly as well. A long-lived tree, such as a sugar maple, on the other hand, is an investment in time. Some trees can take a human lifetime or more to reach their mature size, and some may not flower for 10 years after you plant them. You can enjoy a long-lived tree as it develops, and you will also leave a legacy for future generations—your tree may very well outlive you.

Fast-Growing Trees & Shrubs

- Birch
- Black jetbead
- Butterfly bush
- Cherry ✓
- Dawn redwood
- Elder
- Forsythia ✓
- Golden rain tree
- Hydrangea (except *H. quercifolia*)
- Lilac ✓
- Red-twig dogwood
- Staghorn sumac
- Thornless honeylocust
- Willow
- Wisteria

Slow-Growing Trees & Shrubs

- Beech
- Black tupelo
- Boxwood
- Burning bush ✓
- Enkianthus
- Fothergilla
- Fringe tree
- Ginkgo
- Holly
- Maple (not all species)
- Mountain laurel
- Oak (not all species)
- Pieris
- Rhododendron
- Yew ✓

Forsythia

Hybrid yew

Getting Started

Before you fall in love with the idea of having a certain tree or shrub in your garden, it's important to consider the growing conditions the plant needs and whether any areas of your garden are appropriate for it. Your plant will need to not only survive, but thrive, in order for its flowers or other features to reach their full potential.

All plants are adapted to certain growing conditions in which they do best. Choosing plants to match your garden conditions is far more practical than trying to alter your garden to match the plants. Yet it is through the use of trees and shrubs that we can best alter the conditions in a garden. Over time a tree can change a sunny, exposed garden into a shaded one, and a hedge can turn a windswept area into a sheltered one. The woody plants you choose must be able to thrive in the garden as it exists now, or they may not live long enough to produce these changes.

Light, soil conditions (including moisture) and exposure are all factors that will guide your selection. As you plan, look at your garden as it exists now, but keep in mind the changes trees and shrubs will bring.

LIGHT

Buildings, trees, fences, the time of day and the time of year influence the amount of light that gets into your garden. Light levels are often divided into four categories for gardening purposes: full sun, partial shade (partial sun), light shade and full shade. Some plants adapt to a variety of light levels, but most have a preference for a narrower range.

Full sun locations receive direct sunlight most of the day—a minimum of six hours. An example would be an open location along a south-facing wall. **Partial shade** locations receive direct sun for part of the day and shade for the rest. An

east- or west-facing wall gets only partial shade. **Light shade** locations receive shade most or all of the day, but with light and some direct sun getting through to ground level. The ground under a small-leaved tree is often lightly shaded, with dappled light visible on the ground beneath the tree. **Full shade** locations receive no direct sunlight. The north wall of a house is usually in full shade.

Heat from the sun may be more intense in one spot than another. A west-facing wall, for example, will be warmed in the afternoon and can radiate this retained heat until well after dark. Shelter from wind also influences the heat in a given area.

Spirea (above) prefers full sun.

SOIL

Plants have a unique relationship with the soil they grow in. Many important plant functions take place underground. Soil holds air, water, nutrients and organic matter. Plant roots depend upon these resources for growth, while using the soil to anchor the plant body. In turn, plants influence soil development by breaking down large clods with their roots and by increasing soil fertility when they die and decompose.

Soil is made up of particles of different sizes. Sand particles are the largest. Water drains quickly from a sandy soil, and nutrients can be quickly washed away. Sand has lots of air spaces and doesn't compact easily. Clay particles are the smallest, visible only through a microscope. Water penetrates clay very slowly and drains away even more slowly. Clay holds the most nutrients, but there is very little room for air and a clay soil compacts quite easily. Most

Sweetspire grows well in full sun or full shade.

soils are made up of a combination of different particle sizes and are called loams.

Particle size is one influence on the drainage and moisture-holding properties of your soil; slope is another. Knowing how quickly the water drains out of your soil will help you decide whether you should plant moisture-loving or drought-tolerant plants. Rocky soil on a hillside will

Summersweet thrives in moist or wet gardens.

sandy or rocky soil can also be improved by adding organic matter.

Another aspect of soil that is important to consider is the pH, or the measure of acidity. Soil pH influences the availability of nutrients for plants. A pH of 7 is neutral; lower values (down to 0) indicate acidic conditions; and higher values (up to 14) indicate alkaline conditions. Most plants prefer a neutral soil pH, between 6.5 and 7.5. Soils in Ohio tend to be alkaline in the western half to two-thirds of the state and acidic in the eastern half to one-third. Ask your Ohio cooperative extension agent about the local soils. The agent can make general recommendations or instruct you on getting your soil tested.

If a soil test reveals a pH problem, your soil can be made more alkaline with the addition of horticultural lime or more acidic with the addition of horticultural sulfur. The test results should include recommendations for quantities of additives needed to adjust your soil pH.

Keep in mind that it is much easier to amend soil in a small area than in an entire garden. The soil in a raised bed or planter can be adjusted easily to suit a few plants whose soil requirements vary greatly from your garden conditions. It is also easier to make amendments when the soil is first being prepared than it is after plantings are made. Easiest of all is to choose plants adapted to your garden's conditions.

probably drain quickly and should be reserved for those plants that prefer a very well-drained soil. Low-lying areas tend to retain water longer, and some areas may rarely drain at all. Moist areas suit plants that require a consistent water supply; constantly wet areas should be reserved for plants that are adapted to boggy conditions.

Drainage can be improved in very wet areas by tilling and adding organic matter to the soil, or by building raised beds. Avoid adding sand to clay soil, or you may create something much like concrete. Working some organic matter into a clay soil will help break it up and allow water to penetrate and drain more easily. Water retention in

EXPOSURE

Exposure is a very important consideration in all gardens that include woody plants. Wind, heat, cold, rain and snow are the elements to which your garden may be exposed, and some plants are more tolerant than others of the potential damage these forces can cause. Buildings, walls, fences, hills and existing hedges or other shrubs and trees can all influence your garden's exposure.

Wind can cause extensive damage to plants, particularly to broad-leaved evergreens in winter. Plants can become dehydrated in windy locations because they may not be able to draw water out of the soil fast enough to replace that lost through the leaves. Evergreens in areas where the ground freezes can often face this problem because they are unable to draw any water out of the frozen ground. This is why it is important to keep them well watered in fall until the ground freezes. Because the broad-leaved evergreens, such as rhododendron and holly, are most at risk from winter dehydration, grow them in a sheltered site.

Holly (above) needs shelter from drying winds.

Strong winds can cause physical damage by breaking weak branches or by blowing over entire trees. However, woody plants often make excellent windbreaks that shelter other plants. Hedges and trees temper the effect of the wind without the turbulence created on the leeward side of a more solid structure, such as a wall or fence. Windbreak trees should be able to flex in the wind or should be planted far enough from buildings to avoid extensive damage should branches or trees fall.

Hardiness zones (see map, p. 15, and Quick Reference Chart, p. 342) give an indication of whether a species can tolerate conditions in your area. But these zones are only

Hedges are excellent windbreaks.

guidelines that consider the coldest temperatures a plant is expected to survive. The health and vigor of a plant as well as degree of shelter can influence its ability to survive in a location considered out-of-zone. Don't be afraid to try species that are not listed as hardy for your area. Plants often adapt to varying conditions and just might surprise you.

Black jetbead (above) tolerates wet soil and shade.

St. Johnswort is drought tolerant when established.
Rhododendron prefers shelter from drying winds.

Here are some tips for growing out-of-zone plants:

- Before planting, observe your garden on a frosty morning. Are there areas that escape frost? These are potential sites for tender plants. Keep in mind that cold air tends to collect in low spots and can run downhill, through breaks in plantings and structures, the same way that water does.
- Shelter tender plants from the prevailing wind.
- Plant in groups to create windbreaks and microclimates. Rhododendrons, for instance, grow better if planted in small groups or grouped with plants that have similar growing requirements.
- Mulch young plants in fall with a thick layer of clean organic mulch, such as bark chips, shredded wood and bark, composted woodchips, composted leaves or compost mixed with peat moss. Insulating blankets are also available at garden centers. Organic mulches should be applied about 2–4" deep for good winter protection. Mulch over at least the first two winters.
- Water thoroughly before the ground freezes and again if needed during mid-winter thaw periods.
- If you have plenty of snow, cover an entire frost-tender shrub with salt-free snow for the winter. You can also cover or wrap it with burlap or horticultural cloth. If the plant is being grown in a container or planter, place it under shelter, or half bury and half mulch the container.

Purchasing Trees & Shrubs

Now that you have thought about the features you like and the range of growing conditions your garden offers, you can select the plants. Any reputable garden center should have a good selection of popular woody plants. Finding more unusual specimens could require a few phone calls and a trip to a more specialized nursery. Mail-order nurseries are often a great source of the newest and most unusual plants.

Many garden centers and nurseries offer a one-year warranty on trees and shrubs, but because trees take a long time to mature it is always in your best interest to choose the healthiest plants. Never purchase weak, damaged or diseased plants, even if they cost less. Examine the bark and avoid plants with visible damage. Check that the growth is even and appropriate for the species. Shrubs should be bushy and branched nearly to the ground, while trees should have a strong leader. Observe the leaf and flower buds. If they are dry and fall off easily, the plant has been deprived of moisture. The stem or stems should be strong, supple and unbroken. The rootball should be firm and moist when touched. Do not buy a plant with a dry rootball. Ask for the help of store personnel to inspect the root systems of container-grown plants.

Woody plants are available for purchase in three forms:

Bare-root stock has roots surrounded by nothing but moist sawdust or peat

Avoid purchasing root-bound plants.

Purchasing container stock in fall lets you see the fall color.

moss within a plastic wrapping. The roots must be kept moist and cool, and planting should take place as soon as possible in spring. Avoid stock that appears to have dried out during shipping. Bare-root stock is the least expensive type, but in part because of its short season of availability, it is becoming less common.

Balled-and-burlapped (B & B) stock comes with the roots surrounded by soil and wrapped in burlap, often secured with a wire cage for larger plants. The plants are usually field grown and then dug up, balled and burlapped the year they are sold. It is essential that the rootball remain moist, unbroken and in close contact with the plant's roots. Large trees are available in this form, but be aware that the soil and rootball can be very heavy and there may be an extra expense for delivery and planting.

Container plants are grown in pots filled with potting soil and have established root systems. This form is the most common at garden centers and nurseries. Container stock establishes quickly after planting and can be planted almost any time during the growing season. It is also easy to transplant. When choosing a plant, make sure it hasn't been in the container too long. If the roots densely encircle the inside of the pot, then the plant has become root-bound. If not properly handled at planting time (see Planting Container Stock, p. 37), a root-bound tree or shrub will not establish well. As the roots mature and thicken, they can choke and kill the plant. Be aware that sometimes field-grown stock is dug and sold in containers

Winter storage technique for container plants

instead of burlap; ask if you aren't sure. Such plants must be treated like balled-and-burlapped stock when planting (see Planting Balled-and-Burlapped Stock, p. 35).

Bigger is not always better when it comes to choosing woody plants. Research and observation have shown that small stock often ends up healthier and more robust than large stock. The smaller the plant, the more quickly it can recover from the shock of being uprooted.

Woody plants can be damaged by improper handling. You can lift bare-root stock by the stem, but do not lift any other trees or shrubs by the trunk or branches. Instead, lift by the rootball or container, or if the plant is too large to lift, place it on a tarp or mat and drag it.

Care during transport is also critical. Even a short trip home from the nursery can be traumatic for a plant. The heat produced in a car can quickly dehydrate a tree or shrub. If you are using a truck for transport, lay the plant down and cover it with porous burlap or similar material to shield it from the wind. Avoid mechanical damage such as rubbing or breaking branches during transport.

Once home, water the plant if it is dry and keep it in a sheltered location until you plant it. Remove damaged growth and broken branches, *but do no other pruning.* Plant your tree or shrub as soon as possible. A bare-root tree or shrub should be planted in a large container of potting soil if it will not be planted outdoors immediately. If you must store container plants over winter before planting, bury the entire container until spring or keep it in a very sheltered location.

Planting Trees & Shrubs

Before you pick up a shovel and start digging, step back for a moment and make sure the site you are considering is appropriate. The most important thing to check is the location of any underground wires or pipes. Call the Ohio Utilities Protection Service (1-800-362-2764) before you dig. Even if you don't damage anything by digging, the tree roots may in the future cause trouble, or if there is a problem with the pipes or wires you may have to cut down the tree in order to service them. Prevent injury and save time and money by locating utilities before you dig.

Check also the mature plant size. The plant you have in front of you is most likely small. Once it reaches its mature height and spread, will it still fit in the space you have chosen? Is

it far enough away from the house, the driveway and walkways? Will it hit the overhang of the house or any overhead power lines?

If you're planting several shrubs, make sure that they won't grow too close together once they are mature. The rule of thumb for spacing: add the mature spreads together and divide by two. For example, when planting a shrub with an expected spread of 4' next to another shrub with an expected spread of 6', you would plant them 5' apart. For hedges and windbreaks, the spacing should be one-half to two-thirds the spread of the mature plant to ensure there is no observable space between plants when they are fully grown.

Finally, double-check the conditions. Will the soil drainage be adequate? Will the plant get the right

Nicely planted and well-maintained shrub beds

amount of light? Is the site very windy? It's important to start with the plant in the right spot and in the best conditions you can give it.

WHEN TO PLANT

For the most part, trees and shrubs can be planted at any time of year, though some seasons are better for the plants and more convenient than others. Preferred planting times are indicated at the beginning of each plant entry in this book.

Spring is a very good time to plant. It gives the tree or shrub an entire growing season to become established and gets it started before the weather turns really hot. Many gardeners avoid planting during the hottest and driest part of summer, mainly because of the extra work involved with supplemental watering. However, even a spring-planted tree or shrub will require watering during hot, dry weather.

Bare-root stock must be planted in spring because it is generally available only at that time, and it must be planted as soon as possible to avoid moisture loss.

Balled-and-burlapped and container stock can usually be planted at any time, as long as you can get a shovel into the ground. They can even be planted in frozen ground if you had the foresight to dig the hole before the ground froze and to keep the backfill (the dirt from the hole) in a warm place. Most plants do, however, benefit from having some time to become established before a cold winter sets in.

The time of day to plant is also a consideration. Avoid planting in the heat of the day. Planting in the morning, in the evening or on a

Sizing up the hole (above), digging the hole (center)

Adding organic matter to backfill (below)

cloudy, calm day will be easier on both you and the plant.

It's a good idea to plant as soon as possible after you bring your specimen home. If you have to store the tree or shrub for a short time before planting, keep it out of direct sun and ensure the rootball remains moist.

PREPARING THE HOLE

Trees and shrubs should always be planted at the depth at which they were growing, or just above the root crown flare for bare-root stock. In dense soils, where drainage can be a problem, plant 1" higher. The depth in the center of the planting hole should be equal to (or 1" less than) the depth of the rootball or container, whereas the depth around the edges can be greater than this. Making the center higher and leaving the soil there undis-turbed prevents the plant from sinking as the soil settles and encourages excess water to drain away from the new plant.

Be sure that the plants are not set too deep. Planting even 1–2" too deep can cause problems. Most pot-ted field-grown trees are planted deeply in the pot in order to help keep the freshly dug tree from tip-ping over, and there may be mulch on top of the ball as well. Planting such a tree to the same depth as the level in the pot may not be a good idea. Scrape off the soil until you find the top flare of the root mass, and then plant at or 1" above grade. Balled-and-burlapped stock may also have excess soil collected at the top of the ball. Open the burlap and remove any excess soil above the root mass in order to determine the proper planting depth.

Make the hole for bare-root stock big enough to completely contain the expanded roots with a bit of extra room on the sides. Make the hole for balled-and-burlapped and container stock about two or three times the width of the rootball or container.

The soil around the rootball or in the container is not likely to be the same as the soil you just removed from the hole. The extra room in the hole allows the new roots an easier medium (backfill) to grow into than undisturbed soil, providing a transition zone from the rootball soil to the existing on-site soil. It is good practice to rough up the sides and bottom of the hole to aid in root transition and water flow. Smooth hole walls can increase water retention, possibly drowning the plant.

PLANTING BARE-ROOT STOCK

Remove the plastic and sawdust from the roots. Soak the roots in water for several hours or overnight, to be certain the new plant is fully hydrated before planting. Fan the roots out and center the plant over the central mound in the hole. The mound for bare-root stock is often made cone shaped and larger than the mound for other types of plants. Use the cone to help spread out and support the roots. Make sure the hole is big enough to allow the roots to fully extend.

PLANTING BALLED & BURLAPPED STOCK

Burlap was originally made from natural fibers. Though never recommended, it could be loosened and left wrapped around the rootball to eventually decompose. Modern burlap may or may not be made of natural fibers, and it can be difficult to tell the difference. (Try burning a small piece: synthetic fibers will melt rather than burn.) Synthetic fibers will not decompose and will eventually choke the roots. To be sure your new plant has a healthy future, you must remove the burlap

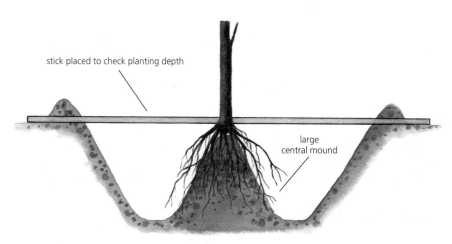

stick placed to check planting depth

large
central mound

Planting bare-root stock

from around the rootball, to at least two-thirds of the way down the rootball. If roots are already growing through the burlap, remove it anyway by cutting around and releasing as many roots as possible. Complete removal is best to maximize contact between the rootball and backfill.

If a wire basket holds the burlap in place, it should also be removed. Strong wire cutters may be needed to get the basket off. If the tree is very heavy, it may not be possible to remove the base of the basket, but cut away the sides at least two-thirds of the way down the rootball, where most of the important roots will be growing.

With the basket removed, set the still-burlapped plant on the center mound in the hole. Or, when possible, set and block the plant in place,

then remove the wire and burlap. Lean the plant to one side and roll the burlap down to the ground. When you lean the plant in the opposite direction, you should be able to pull the burlap out from under the roots. As with the basket on a heavy tree, just remove as much burlap as you can if the tree is difficult to move once in the hole. If you know the burlap is natural and decide to leave it in place, cut it back from the stem and ensure no burlap extends above ground level. Exposed burlap can wick moisture out of the soil, robbing your new plant of essential water.

Past horticultural wisdom suggested removing some top branches when planting to make up for the roots lost when the plant was dug out of the field. The theory was that the roots could not provide enough

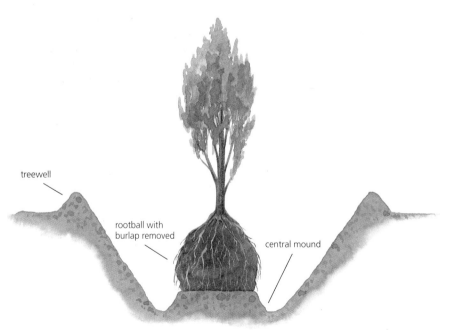

treewell

rootball with
burlap removed

central mound

Planting balled-and-burlapped stock

water to the leaves, so top growth had to be removed to achieve 'balance.' We now know that the top growth—where photosynthesis occurs and thus where energy is produced—is necessary for root development. The new tree or shrub might drop some leaves, but don't be alarmed; the plant is doing its own balancing. A very light pruning will not adversely affect the plant, but remove whole branches and only those branches that have been damaged during transportation and planting. Leave the new plant to settle in for a year or two before you start any formative pruning or branch spacing.

PLANTING CONTAINER STOCK

Containers are usually made of plastic or pressed fiber. Both kinds should be removed before planting. Although some containers appear to be made of peat moss, they do not decompose well. The roots may have difficulty penetrating the pot sides, and the fiber will wick moisture away from the roots.

Container stock is very easy to plant (see photos, p. 38). Gently remove or cut off the container and observe the root mass to see if the plant is root-bound. If roots are circling around the inside of the container, they should be loosened and/or sliced. Any large roots encircling the soil or growing into the center of the root mass instead of outward should be removed before planting. A sharp pair of hand pruners (secateurs), a pocket knife or a utility knife will work well. Since the lowest roots don't usually survive transplanting, many gardeners split the root mass one-third to one-half of the way up from the bottom and 'butterfly' or spread out the roots over the mound of soil in the bottom of the hole.

BACKFILLING

With the plant in the hole and standing straight up, it is time to replace the soil. About one-quarter to one-third of the backfill should be organic matter. This amount, well mixed with the rest of the backfill, encourages the plant to become established. More than this can create a pocket of rich soil that the roots are reluctant to move beyond. If the roots do not venture outside the immediate area of the hole, the tree or shrub will be weaker and much more susceptible to problems, and the encircling roots could eventually choke the plant. Such a tree will also be more vulnerable to blowdown in a strong wind.

Backfill should generally reach the same depth the plant was grown at previously. If planting into a heavy soil, raise the plant about 1" to help improve surface drainage away from the crown and roots. Graft unions of grafted stock are generally kept at or just above ground level to make it easy to spot and remove suckers sprouting from the rootstock.

It is important to have good root-to-soil contact for initial stability and good establishment. Large air pockets remaining after backfilling could result in unwanted settling and excessive root drying. Use water to settle the soil around the roots and in the hole, being careful not to drown the plant. It is a good idea to backfill in small amounts rather than all at once. Add some soil, then gently water it down, repeating until the hole is full.

1. Gently remove container.

2. Ensure proper planting depth.

3. Backfill with amended soil.

4. Settle backfilled soil with water.

5. Ensure newly planted shrub is well watered.

6. Add a layer of mulch.

Stockpile any soil that remains after backfilling and use it to top up the soil level around the plant as the backfill settles.

If you are working with a heavy clay soil, ensure that the surface drainage slopes away from your new transplant. Build a temporary 2–4" high, doughnut-like mound of soil around the perimeter of the buried rootball. Water into this reservoir for at least the whole first season. Doing so ensures that water will percolate down through the new root mass. The ring of soil, sometimes called a **treewell,** is an excellent watering tool for conserving moisture, especially during dry spells. Once the tree or shrub has become established, after a year or two, the treewell will no longer be needed and should be permanently removed.

To conserve water, mulch around the new planting. Composted wood chips or shredded bark will stay where you put them, unlike pebble bark or peat moss. Two to four inches of mulch is adequate. Do not use too much, and avoid mulching directly against the trunk or base of the plant; otherwise, you may encourage disease problems.

STAKING

Some trees may need to be staked in order to provide support while the roots establish. Staking is recommended only for bare-root trees; for tall, top-heavy trees over 5' tall; and for trees planted in windy locations, particularly evergreens because they tend to catch winter winds. Any stakes should be removed as soon as the roots have had a chance to become established, which normally takes about a year.

Young tree in its new home

Growing trees and shrubs without stakes is preferable because unstaked trees develop more roots, wider flares at the trunk base and stronger trunks. Most newly planted trees will be able to stand on their own without staking. You can always stake later if you find it's needed.

Two common methods are used for staking newly planted trees. For both methods you can use either wood or metal stakes.

The **two-stake** method is used for small trees about 5–6' tall, and for trees in low-wind areas. Drive stakes into the undisturbed soil just outside the planting hole on opposite sides of your tree, 180° apart and in line with the prevailing wind. Driving stakes in right beside the newly planted tree can damage the roots and will not provide adequate support. Tie string, rope, cable or wire to the stakes. The end that goes around the trunk should be a wide, belt-like strap of material that will not injure the trunk. Your local garden center should have ties designed for this purpose. Attach the straps to the tree about 3–4' above the ground.

The **three-stake** method is used for larger trees and for trees in areas subject to strong or shifting winds. This technique is much the same as the two-stake method, but with three thicker, shorter stakes driven nearly all the way into the ground. One of the stakes should be in line with the prevailing wind, with the other two stakes evenly spaced around the tree. Attach heavy wire or cable to the stakes and up to the wide strapping that goes around the tree trunk, positioned just above the lower branches to hold it in place.

Here are a few points to keep in mind, regardless of the staking method used:
• Never wrap a rope, wire or cable directly around a tree trunk. Always use a wider, softer material. Reposition the straps every two to three

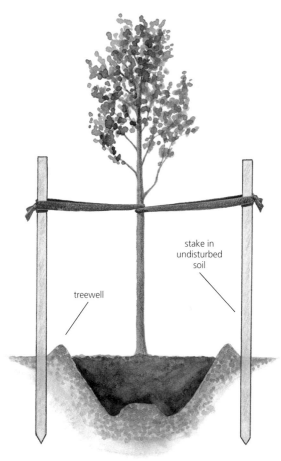

stake in undisturbed soil

treewell

Two-stake method

months to prevent any rubbing or girdling injury.

• Never tie trees so firmly that they can't move. Young trees need to be able to move in the wind to produce strong trunks and to develop roots more thickly in appropriate places to compensate for the prevailing wind.

• Don't leave the stakes in place too long. One year is sufficient for almost all trees. The stakes should be there only long enough to allow the roots some time to grow and establish. The tree will actually be weaker if the stakes are left for too long, and over time the ties can damage the trunk and weaken or kill the tree. Under no circumstances should a tree be left staked for more than two years.

TRANSPLANTING

If you plan your garden carefully, you should only rarely need to move trees or shrubs. Some woody plants (indicated as such in the individual species entries) resent being moved once established, and you should avoid transplanting

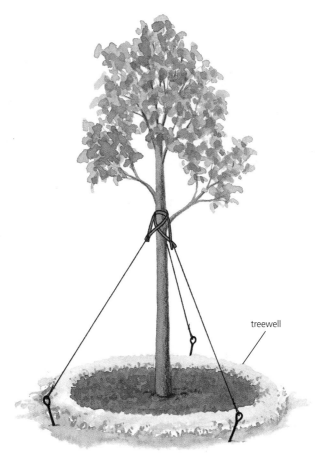

treewell

Three-stake method

Magnolia (above) and redbud (below) dislike being transplanted.

are bare of leaves: in spring, fall or early winter. Plants with specific preferences outside these general guidelines are indicated as such in the species entries.

When woody plants are transplanted, they inevitably lose most of their root mass. Care should be taken to dig a rootball of the appropriate size. The size of the tree or shrub will determine the minimum size of the rootball that must be dug out in order for the plant to survive. As a general rule, for every 1" of trunk or main stem width, measured 6–12" above the ground, you need to excavate a rootball at least 10" wide for deciduous plants, and at least 8" wide for evergreens. Even larger rootballs are preferable. Trees with trunks more than 2" wide should be moved by professionals with heavy equipment. When transplants are properly proportioned and carefully handled, they should suffer limited setback.

Follow these steps to transplant a shrub or small tree:
1) Calculate the width of the rootball to be removed, as described above.
2) Water the proposed rootball area to a depth of 12". Allow about 24 hours for excess water to drain away. The moist soil will help hold the rootball together.
3) Gently bend the branches up and toward the center, as much as possible, and wrap or tie them in order to minimize branch damage and to ease transport from the old site to the new one.
4) Slice a shovel or long spade into the soil vertically, cutting a circle around the plant as wide as the calculated rootball width. Cut down to about 12". This depth

these species whenever possible. For all species, the younger the plant, the more likely it is to reestablish successfully in a new location.

Generally, you can transplant evergreens in spring before growth starts or in fall after it stops, as long as you don't transplant during a spell of hot weather. Deciduous plants should be transplanted only when dormant, when the branches should contain most of the roots for the size of tree or shrub that can be transplanted manually.

5) At this point, most small, densely rooted trees and shrubs can be carefully removed from the hole by leaning on the spade or shovel and prying the plant up and out. If you encounter resistance, you may have missed some roots and should repeat step 4. Once the plant has been freed, place it on a tarp and continue with step 10.

Larger trees and shrubs will require additional steps; continue with step 6.

6) Cut another circle one shovel-width outside the first circle, to the same depth.

7) Excavate the soil between the two cut circles.

8) When the appropriate rootball depth is reached, carefully cut horizontally under the rootball. When you encounter a root, cut it with a sharp pair of hand pruners. The goal is to sculpt out a rootball that is standing on a pedestal of undisturbed earth.

9) Spread a tarp in one side of the hole. Gently remove the pedestal and lean the rootball over onto the tarp. Carefully cut any remaining roots in the pedestal. Lift the tree and rootball out of the hole with the tarp, not by the stem or branches.

10) Lift or drag the tarp to the new location and plant immediately. See planting instructions given in preceding sections for information on when to plant, how to plant, staking, etc. Transplanted trees and shrubs can be treated as balled-and-burlapped stock.

European beech (above) and mock-orange (below) tolerate transplanting well.

Caring for Trees & Shrubs

The care you give your new tree or shrub in the first three years after planting is the most important. During this period of establishment, it is critical to remove competing weeds, to keep the plant well watered and to avoid all mechanical damage. Be careful with lawn mowers and string trimmers, which can quickly girdle the base of the plant. Whatever you do to the top of the plant affects the roots, and vice versa; you won't see good results above ground until the roots are in good shape.

Once woody plants have established, they generally require minimal care. A few basic maintenance tasks, performed regularly, will save time and trouble in the long run.

WEEDING

Weeds can rob young plants of water, light and nutrients, so keep weeds under control to encourage optimum growth. Avoid deep hoeing under woody plants because it may damage shallow-rooted shrubs and trees. A 2–3" layer of mulch is a good way to suppress weeds.

MULCHING

Mulch is an important gardening tool. It helps soil retain moisture, it buffers soil temperatures and it prevents soil erosion during heavy rain or strong winds. Mulch prevents weed seeds from germinating by blocking out the light, and it can deter pests and help prevent diseases. It keeps lawn mowers and line trimmers away from plants, reducing the chance of damage. Mulch can also add aesthetic value to a planting.

Organic mulches can consist of compost, composted wood chips, bark chips, shredded bark, composted leaves and dry grass clippings. These mulches are desirable because they add nutrients to the soil as they break down. Because they break down, however, they must be replenished on a regular basis.

Inorganic mulches, such as stones, crushed brick or gravel, do not break down and so do not have to be replenished. These types of mulches don't provide nutrients and they can also adversely increase soil temperature. Some older books recommend using black plastic or ground cloth under the mulch. These products should be avoided with organic mulches, but a porous ground cloth can be used under stone and rock mulches to keep them from sinking into the soil.

For good weed suppression, the mulch layer should be 2–3" thick during the growing season, and no more than twice that for winter protection. Thicker layers of mulch can suffocate plant roots in our heavy clay soils. Always maintain a mulch-free zone immediately around the trunk or stem bases to prevent fungal decay and rot.

Keep mulch from the base of your tree or shrub.

WATERING

The weather, type of plant, type of substrate and time of year all influence the amount of water your shrubs and trees need. If your area is naturally dry or if there has been a stretch of hot, dry weather, you will need to water more often than if you garden in a naturally wet area or if your area has received a lot of rain recently. Pay attention to the wind; it can dry out soil and plants quickly. Different plants require different amounts of water. Some, such as willows and some birches, will grow in a temporarily water-logged soil; others, such as pines, prefer a dry, sandy soil. Heavy, clay soils retain water much longer than light, sandy soils. Plants need more water when they are on slopes, when they are flowering and when they are producing fruit.

Plants are good at letting us know when they are thirsty. Wilted, flagging leaves and twigs are a sign of water deprivation, but excessive water can also cause a plant to wilt. Test for soil moisture by checking at least 3" down with your fingers or with a soil probe (see sidebar). If you feel moisture, or see it on the soil probe, you don't need to water.

Make sure your trees and shrubs are well watered in fall. Continue to water as needed until the ground freezes. Fall watering is very important for evergreen plants because once the ground has frozen, the roots

You can make a soil probe from a 3/8" to 1/2" diameter wooden dowel. Carve one end into a point, then cut a groove or paint a mark 12" up from that end. Do not finish the wood, because you want it to discolor as it absorbs the soil moisture. Push the rod into the soil 12" deep, leave it for up to a minute then remove the stick. If it has darkened with moisture, you don't need to water. If it is still dry, water immediately. It is quite possible for our heavy clay soils to be dry down to 3" but plenty wet enough farther down. I have seen many a plant saved from drowning through the use of this simple probe.

can no longer draw moisture from it, leaving the foliage susceptible to desiccation.

Once trees and shrubs are established, they will likely need watering only during periods of excessive drought. To keep water use to a minimum, avoid watering in the heat of the day because much will be lost to evaporation. Work organic matter into the soil to help the soil absorb and retain water, and apply mulch to help prevent water loss. Collect and use rainwater whenever possible.

FERTILIZING

Most garden soils provide all the nutrients plants need, particularly if you use organic mulch and mix compost into the soil before planting. Simply allowing leaf litter to remain on the ground after the leaves drop in autumn promotes natural nutrient cycling of nitrogen and other elements in the soil.

Not all plants have the same nutritional requirements, however. Some plants are heavy feeders, while others thrive in poor soils. Pay attention to the leaf color of your plants as an indicator of nutritional status. Yellowing leaves, for example, may be a sign of a nitrogen, iron or manganese deficiency.

When you do fertilize, use only the recommended quantity because too much can be very harmful. Most fertilizers are salts, and roots are easily burned by these compounds applied in too high a concentration. Chemical fertilizers are more concentrated and therefore may cause more problems than organic fertilizers.

Granular fertilizers consist of small, dry particles that can be spread with a fertilizer spreader or by hand. In garden beds you can mix the fertilizer right into the soil. Consider using primarily slow-release granular fertilizers. They cost slightly more but save you time and reduce the risk of burn because the nutrients are released gradually. Two applications per year are normally sufficient, one in early spring and one in late fall. If you fertilize only once per year, fall is preferable because it helps plants build carbohydrate reserves for winter and gets them off to a strong start in spring. It is best to start around the beginning of October and continue up until December.

Tree spikes are slow-release fertilizers that are appropriate mainly for shrubs and young trees. They are quick and easy to use. Pound the spikes into the ground around the dripline of the tree or shrub (see diagram, p. 47) or just beyond the original planting hole. These spikes work very well for fertilizing trees and shrubs in lawns, because the grass tends to consume most of the nutrients released from surface applications.

For larger, more mature ornamental and shade trees, drill-hole fertilizing (vertical mulching) and deep-root liquid irrigation are commonly used. Call a certified arborist for advice.

If fertilizer is not applied correctly or not needed, your plant will not benefit. In fact, it will make a tree or shrub more susceptible to some pests and diseases and can accelerate a plant's decline.

Fertilize to correct a visible nutrient deficiency, to correct a deficiency identified by a soil and tissue test, to increase vegetative, flower or fruit growth or to increase the vigor of a plant that is flagging. New research will soon give us a better understanding of how to fertilize our plants properly and how exactly they use the nutrients we give them.

Do not fertilize trees or shrubs
• when there are sufficient nutrients in the soil as determined by a soil and tissue test
• if your plants are growing and appear healthy
• during times of drought. Roots will not absorb nutrients during drought, and excess partially wetted fertilizer can burn root hairs.

If you do not wish to encourage fast growth, fertilize only enough to maintain good health. Remember that most trees and shrubs do not need much fertilizer and that fast growth may make plants more susceptible to problems. In particular, heavy early-fall fertilizing with chemical fertilizers is not recommended because it may encourage new growth late in the season. This growth is easily damaged in winter. Organic fertilizers can be applied in fall because they are activated by soil organisms that are not as active in cooler weather.

Unnecessary or excessive fertilizer pollutes our local lakes, streams and groundwater. Use fertilizers wisely, and we all benefit. Misuse them, and we all pay the price.

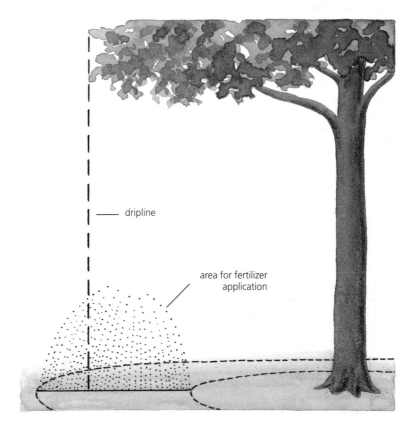

dripline

area for fertilizer application

Pruning

Pruning helps to maintain the health and attractive shape of a woody plant. It also increases the quality and yield of fruit, controls and directs growth, and creates interesting plant forms and shapes, such as espalier, topiary and bonsai. Pruning is perhaps the most important maintenance task when growing trees and shrubs—and the easiest to mess up. Fortunately for new gardeners, it is not difficult to learn and can even be enjoyable if done correctly from the beginning and continued on a regular basis.

Proper pruning combines knowledge and skill. General knowledge about how woody plants grow and specific knowledge about the growth habits of your particular plant can help you avoid pruning mistakes that ruin a plant's shape or make it prone to disease and insect damage.

If you are unsure about pruning, take a pruning course. Courses may be offered by a local garden center, botanical garden, community college or master gardener. Excellent books are also available on the subject.

Another option is to hire a professional, such as an arborist certified by the International Society of Arboriculture (ISA); see Resources (p. 350). Certified professionals understand the plants and have all the specialty pruning equipment to do a proper job. They might even be willing to show you some pruning basics. *Always* call a professional to prune trees—especially large trees or those growing near power lines and other hazardous areas—or to prune large branches that could fall and damage buildings, fences, cars or pedestrians. Many gardeners have injured themselves or others, or caused significant property damage, because they simply didn't have the equipment or the know-how to remove a large branch or tree. Follow this old adage: 'Go as high in a tree as necessary, as long as you keep one foot planted solidly on the ground.'

Genetically programmed to grow to a certain size, plants will always try to reach that potential. If you are doing a lot of pruning to keep a tree or shrub in check, the plant may be too large for that site. We cannot emphasize enough how important it is to consider the mature size of a plant before you put it into the ground.

WHEN & HOW MUCH TO PRUNE

Aside from removing damaged growth, do not prune for the first year after planting a tree or shrub. After that time, the first pruning should develop the plant's structure. For a strong framework, do not prune branches that have a wide angle at the crotch (where the branch meets another branch or the trunk), because these branch intersections are the strongest. Prune out branches with narrower crotches, while ensuring an even distribution of the main (scaffold) branches. These branches will support all future top growth.

Trees and shrubs vary greatly in their pruning needs. Some plants, such as boxwood, tolerate or even thrive on heavy pruning and shearing, while other plants, such as cherry, may be killed if given the same treatment. Pruning guidelines are given in each species entry in this book.

The amount of pruning also depends on your reasons for doing it. Much less work is involved in simply tidying the growth, for example, than in creating an intricate bonsai specimen. Inspect trees and shrubs annually for any dead, damaged, diseased or awkwardly growing branches that need to be

Proper hand pruner orientation

removed and to determine what other pruning, if any, is needed.

Many gardeners are unsure about what time of year they should prune. Knowing when a plant flowers is the easiest way to know when to prune. (See p. 54 for information on pruning conifers.)

Trees and shrubs that flower before about July, such as rhododendron and forsythia, should be pruned after they are finished flowering. These plants form flower buds for the following year over summer and fall. Pruning just after the current year's flowers fade allows plenty of time for the next year's flowers to develop and avoids taking away any of the current year's blooms.

Trees and shrubs that flower in about July or later, such as PeeGee hydrangea and rose-of-Sharon, can be pruned early in the year. These plants form flower buds on new growth as the season progresses, and pruning in spring just before or as the new growth begins to develop will encourage the best growth and flowering.

Some plants, such as maple, have a heavy spring flow of sap. As long as proper pruning cuts are made,

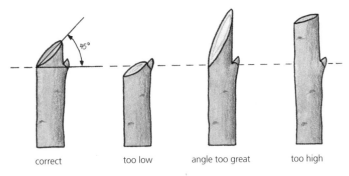

Heading back cuts

these trees can be pruned in spring. If the excessive bleeding is aesthetically unappealing or is dripping on something inappropriately, wait until these species are in full leaf before pruning.

Take care when pruning any trees in early spring, when many canker-causing organisms are active, or in fall, when many wood-rotting fungi release their spores. These are times when the weather is cool and plants are fairly inactive, making it difficult for them to fight off invasion.

Always remove dead, diseased and damaged branches as soon as you notice them, any time of year.

THE KINDEST CUT

Trees and shrubs have a remarkable ability to repair their wounds, but it is critical to make proper pruning cuts. A proper pruning cut, while still a wound, minimizes the area where insect and disease attack can occur and takes advantage of the areas on a plant where it can best deal with wounds. The tree or shrub can then heal as quickly as possible, preventing disease and insect damage.

Using the right tools makes pruning easier and more effective. The size of the branch being cut determines the type of tool to use.

Hand pruners, or secateurs, should be used for cutting branches up to $3/4$" in diameter. Using hand pruners for larger stems increases the risk of damage, and it can be physically strenuous.

Loppers are long-handled pruners used for branches up to $1^1/_2$" in diameter. Loppers are good for removing old stems. Hand pruners and loppers must be properly oriented when making a cut (see photo, p. 49). The blade should be to the plant side of the cut and the hook to the side being removed. If the cut is made with the hook toward the plant, the cut will be ragged and slow to heal.

Pruning saws have teeth specially designed to cut through green wood. They can be used to cut branches up to 6" in diameter and sometimes larger. Pruning saws are easier to use and much safer than chainsaws.

Hedge clippers, or shears, are intended only for shearing and shaping hedges.

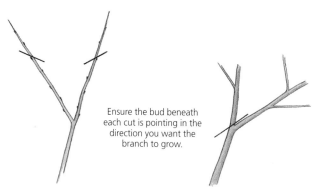

Ensure the bud beneath each cut is pointing in the direction you want the branch to grow.

Heading back cuts   Cutting to a lateral branch

Make sure your tools are sharp and clean before you begin any pruning task. If the branch you are cutting is diseased, sterilize the tool before using it again. A solution of 1 part bleach to 10 parts water is effective for cleaning and sterilizing.

TYPES OF PRUNING CUTS

You should be familiar with the following types of pruning cuts.

Heading back cuts are used for shortening branches, redirecting growth or maintaining the size of a tree or shrub. The cut should be made slightly less than 1/4" above a bud (see diagram, p. 50). If the cut is too far away from or too close to the bud, the wound will not heal properly. Cut back to buds that are pointing in the direction you want the new growth to grow in (see diagram, above).

Cutting to a lateral branch is used to shorten limbs and redirect growth. The diameter of the branch to which you are cutting back must be at least one-third of the diameter of the branch you are cutting. Cut slightly less than 1/4" above the lateral branch, and line up the cut with the angle of the branch that is to remain (see diagram, above). Make cuts at an angle whenever possible so that rain won't sit on the open wound.

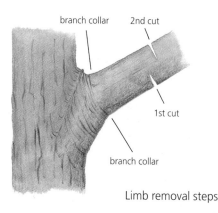

branch collar   2nd cut

1st cut

branch collar

3rd cut at branch collar

Limb removal steps

Removing limbs can be a complicated operation for large branches. Because of the large size of the wound, it is critical to cut in the correct place—at the branch collar (see diagram, p. 51, and sidebar, p. 53)—to ensure quick healing. The cut must be done in steps to avoid damaging the bark.

The first cut is on the bottom of the branch to be removed, a short distance from the trunk or branch intersection. This cut should be 12–18" up from the crotch and should extend one-third of the way through the branch. The purpose of the first cut is to prevent bark from peeling down the tree when the second cut causes the main part of the branch to fall. The second cut is made a bit farther along the branch from the first cut and is made from the top of the branch. This cut removes most of the branch. The final cut should be made just above the branch collar. The plant tissues at the branch collar quickly create a barrier against insects and diseases. Do not make flush cuts and do not leave stubs; both can be slow to heal.

The use of pruning paint or paste has been much debated. The current consensus is that these substances do more harm than good. Trees and shrubs have a natural ability to create a barrier between living wood and dead and decaying sections. An unpainted cut will eventually heal, but a treated cut may never heal properly.

Shearing is used to trim and shape hedges. Only plants that can handle heavy pruning should be sheared because some of the normal pruning rules (such as being careful where you cut in relation to buds) are disregarded here.

Informal hedges take advantage of the natural shape of the plant and require only minimal trimming. These hedges generally take up more room than formal hedges, which are trimmed more severely to assume a neat, even appearance. Formal hedges are generally sheared a minimum of twice per growing season.

For both informal and formal hedges, make sure all sides are trimmed to encourage even growth.

incorrect   correct

Hedge shape

The base of the hedge should *always* be wider than the top to allow light to reach the entire height of the hedge and to prevent it from thinning out at the base. A hedge will gradually increase in size despite shearing, so allow room for this expansion when planting.

Thinning is a rejuvenation process that maintains the shape, health and productivity of shrubs. It opens up space for air and light to penetrate and provides room for younger, healthier branches and selected suckers to grow. Thinning often combines the first three cuts discussed above, and it is the most frequently performed pruning practice. Plants that produce new growth from ground level (suckers) can be pruned this way.

A shrub that is thinned annually should have one-quarter to no more than one-third of the growth removed. Cutting the oldest stems encourages new growth without causing excess stress from loss of top growth. Although some plants can be cut completely to the ground and bounce back, it is generally better to remove only up to one-third of the growth.

Follow these four steps to thin most multi-stemmed shrubs:
1) Remove all dead, diseased, damaged, rubbing and crossing branches to branch junctions, buds or ground level.
2) Remove a maximum of one-third of the growth each year, leaving a mix of old and new growth, and cutting unwanted stems at or close to the base. Do not cut stems below ground level because many disease organisms are present in soil.

3) Thin the top of the shrub to allow air and light penetration and to balance the shape. This step is not always necessary because removing one-third of the stems generally thins out the top as well.

Thinning cuts

To learn to identify branch collars, look at the branch intersections of an apple or pear tree. There will be a slight swelling at the base of each branch. This swelling is actually trunk tissue and must be protected to ensure quick and complete wound closure. Once you see and feel this collar on an apple or pear, you'll have an easier time finding it on other trees. If you aren't sure where a collar ends, err on the side of caution and cut slightly farther out from the trunk.

Sheared arborvitae

4) Repeat the process each year on established, mature shrubs. Regular pruning of shrubs will keep them healthy and productive for many years.

PRUNING CONIFERS

Coniferous trees and shrubs, such as spruce, pine and juniper, generally require little or no pruning other than to fix damage or to correct wayward growth. Proper pruning procedures do differ, however, for different conifers.

Fully extended mugo pine candles

Spruce trees have buds all along their stems and can be pruned at almost any time of year. Branches can be pruned back into the last two or three years of growth.

Pines, on the other hand, must be shaped and directed in mid- to late spring, after the danger of frost has passed. At this time, the new growth, called candles, should have almost fully extended but should still be pliable. Pinch the candles by up to half their length before they are fully extended. Pines do not have side buds along their stems, but when pinched at the proper time new buds will set near the pinched end. For bushy, dense growth, pinch all candles by half. Pinching should be done by hand and not with shears or hand pruners. This technique can be time consuming and has a limited effect. It is better to choose a cultivar that is expected to reach a size appropriate for the space you have and that already has a dense and bushy habit.

Yews, junipers and arborvitae can be lightly sheared for hedging. It is a good idea to begin training hedge plants when they are very young. Yews can be pruned heavily during dormancy, but it is better to shear them on an ongoing basis. As specimens, yews can be heavily hand pruned at almost any time to keep their natural shape.

When removing a coniferous branch, cut it back to the branch collar at the trunk. Take a good look at a few branches before you start cutting because the collar can be difficult to find on a conifer. There is no point in cutting a branch back partway because most coniferous species, including pine and fir, will not regenerate from old wood.

Junipers can regenerate from old wood, but it is a lengthy process and may result in an oddly shaped plant. Make sure you really need to remove a branch before you do so, to avoid disfiguring the plant. Here is another reason to think about mature size before you plant any tree or shrub.

If the central leader on a young conifer is broken or damaged, cleanly remove it and train a new leader in its place. In doing so you reduce the chance of infection and prevent many opportunistic leaders from competing. Place a straight stake next to the main trunk. Do not insert the stake into the ground. Tie the stake to the main trunk, being careful not to girdle the tree by tying it too tightly. Bend the chosen new leader as upright as possible and tie it loosely to the stake. Remove the stake when the new leader is growing strongly upright. Remove any other leaders that attempt to form, or cut their tips.

Older, larger trees may be irreparably damaged by the loss of a leader.

Topping disfigures and stresses trees.

TREE TOPPING

One pruning practice that should never be used is tree topping. Topping is done in an attempt to control height or size, to prevent trees from growing into overhead power lines, to allow more light onto a property or to prevent a tall tree from potentially toppling onto a building.

Topped trees are ugly, weak and hazardous. A tree can be killed by the stress of losing so much of its photosynthetic growth, or by the gaping, slow-to-heal wounds that are vulnerable to attack by insects and wood-rotting fungi. The heartwood of a topped tree rots out quickly, resulting in a weak trunk. The crotches on new growth also tend to be weak. Topped trees, therefore, are susceptible to storm damage and blowdown. Hazards aside, topping trees spoils the aesthetic value of the tree and of the landscape it is growing in.

It is much better to completely remove a tree, and start again with one that will grow to a more appropriate size, than to attempt to reduce the size of a large, mature specimen. *To top a tree is to kill it, even if slowly.*

SPECIALTY PRUNING

Custom pruning methods are used to create interesting plant shapes.

Topiary is the shaping of plants into animal, abstract or geometric forms. True topiary uses sheared hedge plants, such as boxwood and yew, which can tolerate heavy pruning. A simpler form of topiary involves growing vines or other trailing

Boxwood true topiary (above)

Apple espalier
Spruce and juniper bonsai

plants over a wire frame to achieve the desired form. Small-leaved ivy and other flexible, climbing or trailing plants work well for this kind of topiary.

Those who live in or travel to Columbus should be sure to visit the corner of Town and Washington. An entire Georges Seurat painting, *A Sunday Afternoon on the Island of La Grande Jatte*, has been recreated there in three dimensions, with people, animals and boats portrayed in topiary.

Espalier involves training a tree or shrub to grow in two dimensions instead of three, with the aid of a solid wire or other framework. The plant is often trained against a wall or fence, but it can also be free-standing. This method is popularly applied to fruit trees, such as apples, when space is at a premium. Many gardeners consider the forms attractive and unusual, and you may wish to try your hand at it even if you have lots of garden space. It can be great fun and good practice for learning directional pruning.

Bonsai is the art of developing miniature versions of large trees and landscapes. A gardener severely prunes the top growth and roots and uses wire to train the plant to the desired dwarfed form. Many books are available on the subject, and courses may be offered at colleges or by horticultural or bonsai societies in many metro areas. Visit the Dawes Arboretum in Newark and the Franklin Park Conservatory in Columbus to see particularly notable bonsai collections.

Propagating Trees & Shrubs

Many gardeners enjoy the art and science of starting new plants. Although some gardeners are willing to try growing annuals from seeds and perennials from seeds, cuttings or divisions, they may be unsure how to go about propagating their own trees and shrubs. Yet many woody plants can be propagated with ease, allowing the gardener to buy a single specimen and then clone it, rather than buying additional plants.

Do-it-yourself propagating does more than just cut costs. It can become an enjoyable part of gardening and an interesting hobby in itself. It also allows us to add to our gardens species that may be hard to find at nurseries.

A number of methods can be used to propagate trees and shrubs. Many species can be started from seed; this can be a long, slow process, but some people enjoy the variable and sometimes unusual results. Generally quicker techniques include cuttings, ground layering, mound layering and grafting.

CUTTINGS

Cut segments of stems can be encouraged to develop their own roots and form new plants. Cuttings are treated differently depending on the maturity of the growth.

Cuttings taken in spring or early summer from new growth are called **greenwood** or **softwood** cuttings. They can actually be the most

Katsura-tree (above)

Potentilla (center), false cypress (below)

difficult cuttings to start because they require warm, humid conditions that are as likely to cause the cuttings to rot as to root.

Cuttings taken in fall from mature, woody growth are called **hardwood** or **ripe** cuttings. In order to root, these cuttings require a coarse, gritty, moist and preferably warm soil mix, and cold, but not freezing, air temperatures. They may take all winter to root. These special conditions make it difficult to start hardwood cuttings unless you have a cold frame, heated greenhouse or propagator.

The easiest cuttings to start are taken in late summer or early fall from new, but mature, growth that has not yet become completely woody. These are called **semi-ripe, semi-mature** or **semi-hardwood** cuttings.

Follow these steps to take and plant semi-ripe cuttings:

1) Take cuttings about 2–4" long from the tip of a stem, cutting just below a leaf node (the node is the place where a leaf meets the stem). There should be at least two nodes on the cutting. The tip of each cutting will be soft, but the base will be starting to harden.

2) Remove the leaves from the lower half of the cutting. Moisten the stripped end and dust it lightly with rooting hormone powder. Consult your local garden center to find an appropriate rooting hormone for your cutting.

3) Plant cuttings directly in the garden, or in a cold frame or pots. The soil mix should be well drained but moist. Firm the cuttings into the soil to ensure there are no air spaces that will dry out roots as they emerge.

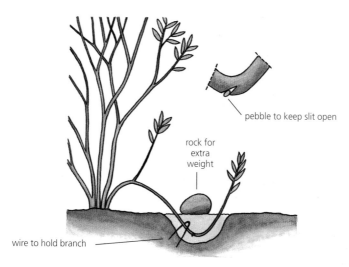

pebble to keep slit open

rock for
extra
weight

wire to hold branch

Ground layering

4) Keep the cuttings out of direct
   sunlight and keep the soil moist.
5) Make sure roots are well established before transplanting.
   Plants should root by the time
   winter begins.
6) Protect the new plants from
   extreme cold for the first winter.
   Plants in pots should be kept in a
   cold but frost-free location.

Plants for Semi-Ripe Cuttings
Butterfly bush
Cotoneaster
Dawn redwood
False cypress
Forsythia
Hydrangea
Katsura-tree
Potentilla
Willow

GROUND LAYERING

Layering, and ground layering in
particular, is the easiest method and
the one most likely to produce suc-
cessful results. Layering allows

future cuttings to form their own
roots before being detached from
the parent plant. In ground layering,
a section of a flexible branch is
buried until it produces roots. The
method is quite simple.

1) Choose a branch or shoot low
   enough on the plant to reach the
   ground. Remove the leaves from
   the section of at least four nodes
   that will be underground. At least
   another four nodes should pro-
   trude above ground at the new
   growth end.
2) Twist the leafless section of the
   branch, or make a small cut on
   the underside near a leaf node.
   This damage will stimulate root
   growth. A toothpick or small
   pebble can be used to hold the
   cut open.
3) Bend the branch down to see
   where it will touch the ground,
   and dig a shallow trench about 4"
   deep in this position. The end of
   the trench nearest the shrub can
   slope gradually upwards, but the

Dogwood (above)

Fothergilla (center), cotoneaster (below)

end where the branch tip will be should be vertical to force the tip upwards.

4) Use a peg or bent wire to hold the branch in place. Fill the soil back into the trench, and water well. A rock or brick on top of the soil will help keep the branch in place.

5) Keep the soil moist but not soggy. Roots may take a year or more to develop. Once roots are well established, the new plant can be severed from the parent and planted in a permanent location.

The best shrubs for layering have low, flexible branches. Spring and fall are the best times to start the layer, and many species respond better in one season or the other. Some, such as rhododendron, respond equally well in spring and fall.

Plants to Layer in Spring

Aronia
Beautyberry
Dogwood
Flowering quince
Lilac
Magnolia
Smokebush
Wisteria
Witchhazel

Plants to Layer in Fall

Arborvitae
Euonymus
Filbert
Forsythia
Fothergilla
Honeysuckle
Pieris
Serviceberry
Viburnum

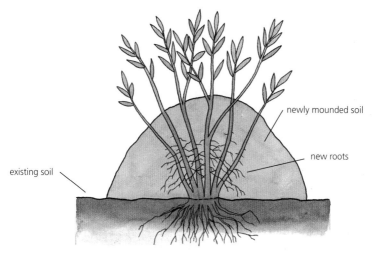

existing soil

newly mounded soil

new roots

Mound layering

MOUND LAYERING

Mound layering is a simple way to propagate low, shrubby plants. With this technique, the shrub is partially buried in a mound of well-drained soil mix. The buried stems will then sprout roots along their lengths. This method can provide many new plants with little effort.

Mound layering should be initiated in spring, once new shoots begin to grow. Make a mound from a mixture of sand, peat moss and soil over half or more of the plant. Leave the branch tips exposed. More soil can be mounded up over the course of the summer. Keep the mound moist, but not soggy.

At the end of the summer (or in the following season, for large plants), gently wash the mound away and detach the rooted branches. Plant them out either directly where you want them or in a protected, temporary spot if you want to shelter them for the first winter.

Plants to Mound Layer

Cotoneaster
Dogwood
Euonymus
Forsythia
Lilac
Potentilla
White forsythia
Winterhazel

GRAFTING

Grafting is another way to produce new plants and often very unique ones, such as rose or juniper tree standards. It involves joining a stem or bud from one plant to the rootstock of another plant of a closely related species. Even though the process is not complicated, this technique is best learned from someone familiar with it. Try taking a class at an arboretum or garden center, or from a master gardener. It can be great fun to create your own five-in-one apple or have two or three flower colors on one magnolia.

Problems & Pests

Tree and shrub plantings can be both assets and liabilities when it comes to pests and diseases. Many insects and diseases attack only one plant species. Mixed plantings can make it difficult for pests and diseases to find their preferred hosts and establish a population. At the same time, because woody plants are in the same spot for many years, any problems can become permanent. The advantage is that many beneficial birds, insects and other pest-devouring organisms can also develop permanent populations.

For many years pest control meant spraying or dusting, with the goal to eliminate every pest in the landscape. A more moderate approach advocated by most authorities today is known as IPM (Integrated Pest Management or Integrated Plant Management). The goal of IPM is to reduce pest problems to levels at which only negligible visual or monetary damage is done. Of course, you, the gardener, must determine what degree of damage is acceptable to you. Consider whether the pest's damage or that of a noninfectious disease is localized or covers the entire plant. Will the damage being done kill the plant or is it affecting only the outward appearance? Will it happen again next year, even with different weather conditions? Are there methods of controlling the pest without chemicals?

IPM is an interactive system in which observation and identification are the primary tools. Observing your plants on a regular basis will give you the chance to uncover problems when they are just beginning. Catching problems early makes them easier to control with minimal effort and by the least toxic method. Seeing an insect, however, does not mean you have a problem. Most insects do no harm at all, and many are beneficial to your garden as pollinators or predators. Take immediate action against the well-known pests you are already familiar with, but for all other insects, wait until you have positively identified them as harmful before attempting control. You may even find that an insect you are concerned about is actually eating the ones you don't want.

Chemicals should always be the last resort. They can endanger gardeners and their families and pets, and they kill as many good organisms as bad ones, leaving the whole garden vulnerable to even worse attacks.

A good IPM program begins with eternal vigilance and includes learning about the following aspects of your plants: the conditions they need for healthy growth; what pests might affect your particular plants; where and when to look for those pests; and how and when to best control them. Keep records of pest damage because your observations can reveal patterns useful in spotting recurring problems and in planning your maintenance regimen. Most problems strike at about the same time each year.

There are four steps in effective and responsible pest management. Cultural controls are far and away the most important. Physical controls should be attempted next, followed by biological controls. Resort to chemical controls only when the first three possibilities have been exhausted.

Sticky trap (above)

Leaf galls cause aesthetic damage.

Cultural controls are the gardening techniques you use in the day-to-day care of your garden. Perhaps the best defense against pests and diseases is to grow your woody plants in the conditions for which they are adapted. It is also very important to

Frogs eat many insect pests.

Ladybird beetles are garden friends.

keep your soil healthy, with plenty of organic matter added.

Other cultural controls are equally straightforward. Choose resistant varieties of trees and shrubs that are not prone to problems. Space your plants so that they have good air circulation in and around them and are not stressed from competing for light, nutrients and space. Remove plants that are decimated by the same pests every year. Dispose of diseased foliage and branches by burning the material or by taking it to a permitted dump site. Prevent the spread of disease by keeping your gardening tools clean and by tidying up dead

plant matter at the end of every growing season.

Physical controls are generally used to combat insect and mammal problems. An example of such a control is picking insects off shrubs by hand, which is not as daunting as it may seem if you catch the problem when it is just beginning. Simply drop the offenders into a bucket of soapy water kept around for that purpose (soap prevents them from floating and climbing out and may suffocate them).

Other physical controls include traps, barriers, scarecrows and natural repellants that make a plant taste or smell bad to pests. Physical control of diseases usually involves removing the infected plant or parts to keep the problem from spreading.

Biological controls make use of predators that like to eat pests. Animals such as birds, snakes, frogs, spiders, ladybird beetles and certain bacteria can play an important role in keeping pest populations manageable. Encourage these creatures to take up permanent residence in your garden. A birdbath and birdfeeder will encourage birds to enjoy your yard and feed on a wide variety of insect pests. Beneficial insects are probably already living in your landscape, and you can encourage them to stay by planting their favorite foods. Many beneficial insects eat nectar from plants such as yarrow and daisies. In many cases it is the young and not the adults that are predatory.

Another form of biological control is the naturally occurring soil bacterium *Bacillus thuringiensis* var. *kurstaki,* or B.t. for short, which breaks down the gut lining of some insect pests. It is commonly available in garden centers.

Chemical controls should rarely be necessary, but if you must use them, many low-toxicity and organic options are available. Organic sprays are no less dangerous than chemical ones, but they break down more readily into harmless compounds. The main drawback to using any chemical is that it may also kill the beneficial insects you have been trying to attract to your garden. Some products claim to control insects selectively.

Organic chemicals are available at most garden centers, and you should follow the manufacturer's instructions very carefully. Be sure to always keep the label intact. A larger amount or concentration of insecticide is not any more effective in controlling insect pests than the recommended dosage. Always practice target application; rarely does the whole area or even the whole plant need to be sprayed.

Note that if a particular pest is not listed on the package, it will probably not be controlled by that product. It is also important to find out at what stage in an insect's life cycle you will get the best control. Some can be controlled only at certain stages. Proper and early identification of pests is vital for finding a quick solution.

Consumers are demanding effective pest-control products that do not harm the environment, and less toxic, more precisely targeted pesticides are becoming available. Alternatives to commercial chemicals are also available or can be made easily at home. Horticultural oils and insecticidal soaps, for example (see p. 73), are effective and much safer to use for pest control. Always read and follow directions. Bear in mind that even 'natural' products derived from plants can be toxic to humans and animals; nicotine-based pest controls are an excellent example.

Cultural, physical, biological and chemical controls are all possible defenses against insect pests. Many diseases, however, can be dealt with only culturally. It is most often weakened plants that succumb to diseases, although some diseases can infect plants regardless of their level of health. Some diseases, such as powdery mildew, are largely a cosmetic concern, but they may weaken a plant and make it susceptible to other diseases and to pests. Prevention is often the only hope. Once a plant has been infected, ailing portions or occasionally the whole plant should be destroyed to prevent the disease from spreading.

Ladybird beetle larvae are voracious predators of garden pests.

GLOSSARY OF PESTS & DISEASES

Anthracnose

Fungus. Yellow or brown spots on leaves; sunken lesions and blisters on stems; can kill plant.

What to Do. Choose resistant varieties and cultivars; keep soil well drained; thin out stems to improve air circulation; avoid handling wet foliage. Remove and destroy infected plant parts; clean up and destroy debris from infected plants at end of growing season. Applying liquid copper can minimize damage.

Aphids

Tiny, pear-shaped insects, winged or wingless; green, black, brown, red or gray. Cluster along stems, on buds and on leaves. Example: woolly adelgids. Suck sap from plants; cause distorted or stunted growth.

Green aphids

Sticky honeydew forms on surfaces and encourages sooty mold.

What to Do. Squish small colonies by hand; dislodge with brisk water spray from hose. Predatory insects and birds feed on them. Spray serious infestations with insecticidal soap or neem oil according to directions.

Woolly adelgids

Beetles

Many types and sizes; usually rounded in shape with hard, shell-like outer wings covering membranous inner wings. Some types are garden helpers, e.g., ladybird beetles (ladybugs); others are not, e.g., bark beetles, elm-leaf beetles, Japanese beetles, leaf skeletonizers and weevils. Larvae: see Borers, Grubs. Leave wide range of chewing damage above

and below ground: make small or large holes in or around margins of leaves; consume entire leaves or areas between leaf veins ('skeletonize'); may also chew holes in flowers and eat through root bark. Some bark beetles carry deadly plant diseases.

What to Do. For shrubs, pick beetles off at night and drop them in an old coffee can half filled with soapy water; spread an old sheet under small trees and shrubs and shake off beetles to collect and dispose of them; use a broom to reach tall branches. Hot Pepper Wax insect repellent discourages beetles and may also repel rabbits and deer.

Japanese beetles

Blight
Fungal or bacterial diseases, many types; e.g., leaf blight, needle blight, petal blight, snow blight, twig blight. Leaves, stems and flowers blacken, rot and die. See also Fire Blight.

What to Do. Thin out stems to improve air circulation; keep mulch away from base of plant; remove debris from garden at end of growing season. Remove and destroy infected plant parts. Sterilize equipment after each cut to avoid reinfecting plant and spreading fungus to other plants.

Borers
Larvae of some moths, wasps and beetles; among the most damaging of plant pests. Young, small borers burrow under bark or into plant stems, leaves or roots, destroying conducting tissue and weakening structural strength. Worm-like; vary in size and get bigger as they eat under bark tissue and sometimes into heartwood. Tunnels left by borers create sites for infection and decomposition to begin; some borers carry infection.

What to Do. Site tree or shrub properly and keep as healthy as possible with proper fertilizing and watering. May be able to squish borers within leaves. Remove and destroy bored parts; may need to remove entire plant.

Bugs (True Bugs)
Small insects up to $1/2"$ long; green, brown, black or brightly colored and patterned. Many beneficial; a few pests, such as lace bugs, pierce plants to suck out sap. Toxins may be injected that deform plants; sunken areas left where tissue pierced; leaves rip as they grow; leaves, buds and new growth may be dwarfed and deformed.

What to Do. Remove debris and weeds from around plants in fall to destroy overwintering sites. Spray plants with insecticidal soap or neem oil according to directions.

Canker
Swollen or sunken lesions on stems or branches, surrounded by living tissue. Caused by many different bacterial and fungal diseases. Most canker-causing diseases enter through wounded wood. Woodpeckers may infect plants when they drill for insects.

What to Do. Maintain plant vigor; avoid wounding or injuring trees (e.g., string trimmer damage), especially in spring when canker-causing organisms most active; control borers and other bark-dwelling insects. Prune out and destroy infected material. Sterilize pruning tools before, during and after use on infected plants.

Case Bearers
see Caterpillars

Caterpillars
Larvae of butterflies, moths, sawflies. Include bagworms, budworms, case bearers, cutworms, leaf rollers, leaf tiers, loopers, webworms. Chew foliage and buds. Can completely defoliate a plant if infestation severe.

Caterpillar on conifer bud

What to Do.
Removal from plant is best control. Use high-pressure water and soap, or pick caterpillars off by hand if plant is small enough. Cut off and burn large tents or webs of larvae (don't have to remove branches themselves). Control biologically using B.t. (see p. 64). Apply horticultural oil in spring. Wrap or band tree trunks to prevent caterpillars from climbing tree to access leaves.

Dieback
Plants slowly wilt, brown and die, starting at branch tips. Can be caused by wide range of disease organisms, cultural problems and nutrient deficiencies.
What to Do. Keep plants healthy by providing optimal growing conditions. Cut off dead tips below dead sections.

Fire Blight
Highly destructive bacterial disease of the rose family, which includes apple, plum, pear, cotoneaster, cherry, hawthorn, serviceberry and firethorn. Infected areas appear to have been burned. Look for bent twig tips (resembling a shepherd's hook), branches that retain leaves over winter and cankers on lower parts of plant. Disease usually starts at young tips and kills its way down the stems.
What to Do. Choose resistant plant varieties. Remove and burn infected parts, making cuts at least 24" below infected areas. Sterilize tools after each cut on infected plant. Reinfection is possible because fire blight is often carried by pollinating birds and insects and enters plant through flowers. If whole plant is infected it must be removed and burned. Fish emulsion applied as foliar spray on infected trees may prevent reinfection.

Galls
Unusual swellings of plant tissues caused by insects or diseases. Can affect leaves, buds, stems, flowers, fruit or trunks. Often a specific gall affects a single genus or species.
What to Do. Cut galls out of plant and destroy them. Galls caused by insects usually contain the insect's eggs and juvenile forms. Prevent these galls by controlling insect before it lays eggs; otherwise, try to remove and destroy infected tissue before young insects emerge. Generally insect galls more unsightly than damaging to plant. Galls caused by diseases often require destruction of plant. Avoid placing other plants susceptible to same disease in that location.

Fuzzy oak galls

Gray Mold (Botrytis Blight)
Fungal disease. Gray fuzz coats affected surfaces. Leaves, flowers or fruits may blacken, rot and die. Common on dead plant matter and on damaged or stressed plants in cool, damp, poorly ventilated areas.

What to Do. Thin stems for better air circulation; keep mulch away from base of plant, particularly in spring when plant starts to sprout; remove debris from garden at end of growing season; do not overwater. Remove and destroy any infected plant parts.

Grubs

Larvae of different beetles, commonly found below soil level; usually curled in C shape. Body white or gray; head may be white, gray, brown or reddish. Problematic in lawns; may feed on roots of shallow-rooted trees and shrubs. Plant wilts despite regular watering; may pull easily out of ground in severe cases.

Leaf miner damage

What to Do. Toss any grubs found while digging onto a stone path or patio for birds to devour; apply parasitic nematodes or milky disease spore to infested soil (ask for information at your local garden center).

Leafhoppers & Treehoppers

Small, wedge-shaped insects; can be green, brown, gray or multicolored. Jump around frantically when disturbed. Suck juice from plant leaves, causing distorted growth. Carry diseases such as aster yellows. Treehoppers also damage bark when they slit it to lay eggs.

What to Do. Encourage predators by growing nectar-rich species such as yarrow. Wash insects off with strong spray of water; spray insecticidal soap or neem oil according to directions.

Leaf Miners

Tiny, stubby larvae of some butterflies and moths; may be yellow or green. Tunnel within foliage leaving winding trails; tunneled areas lighter in color than rest of leaf. Unsightly rather than health risk to plant.

What to Do. Remove debris from area in fall to destroy overwintering sites; attract parasitic wasps with nectar plants such as yarrow. Remove and destroy infected foliage.

Leaf Rollers

see Caterpillars

Leaf Scorch

Yellowing or browning of leaves beginning at tips or edges. Most often caused by drought or heat stress.

What to Do. Water susceptible plants during droughts, and avoid planting them where excessive heat reflects from pavement or buildings.

Leaf Skeletonizers

see Beetles

Leaf skeletonizer damage

Leaf Spot

Two common types. *Bacterial:* small brown or purple speckles grow to encompass entire leaves; leaves may drop. *Fungal:* black, brown or yellow spots; leaves wither; e.g., scab, tar spot.

What to Do. Bacterial infection more severe; must remove entire plant. For fungal infection, remove and destroy infected plant parts. Sterilize removal tools; avoid wetting foliage or touching it when wet; remove and destroy debris at end of growing season. Spray compost tea (see p. 73) on leaves.

Mealybugs

Tiny crawling insects related to aphids; appear covered with

Powdery mildew

white fuzz or flour. Sucking damage stunts and stresses plant. Mealybugs excrete honeydew that promotes sooty mold.

What to Do. Remove by hand on smaller plants; wash plants with soap and water; wipe surfaces with alcohol-soaked swabs; remove heavily infested leaves; encourage or introduce natural predators such as mealybug destroyer beetle and parasitic wasps; spray with insecticidal soap or horticultural oil. Keep in mind larvae of mealybug destroyer beetles look like very large mealybugs.

Mildew

Two types, both caused by fungus, but with slightly different symptoms. *Downy mildew:* yellow spots on upper sides of leaves and downy fuzz on undersides; fuzz may be yellow, white or gray. *Powdery mildew:* leaf surfaces have white or gray powdery coating that doesn't brush off.

What to Do. Choose resistant cultivars; space plants well; thin stems to encourage air circulation; tidy any debris in fall.

Remove and destroy infected leaves or other parts. For powdery mildew, spray foliage with compost tea or very dilute fish emulsion (1 tsp. per qt. of water). For downy mildew, spray foliage with mixture of 5 tbsp. horticultural oil, 2 tsp. baking soda and 1 gal. water. Apply once a week for three weeks.

Mites

Tiny, eight-legged relatives of spiders; do not eat insects, but may spin webs. Almost invisible to naked eye; red, yellow or green; usually found on undersides of plant leaves. Examples: bud mites, spider mites, spruce mites. Suck juice out of leaves. May see fine webbing on leaves and stems; may see mites moving on leaf undersides. Leaves become discolored, speckled; then turn brown and shrivel up.

What to Do. Wash off both sides of leaves with strong spray of water daily until all signs of infestation are gone; introduce predatory mites available through garden centers. Spray plants with insecticidal soap, or spray horticultural oil at a rate of 5 tbsp. to 1 gal.

of water. Repeat application may be needed after a month or so.

Mosaic
see Viruses

Needle Cast
Fungal disease causing premature needle drop. Spotty yellow areas turn brown; infected needles drop up to a year later. **What to Do.** Ensure good air circulation. Clean up and destroy fallen needles. Prune off damaged growth. To prevent recurrence the following year, treat plants with bordeaux mix twice, two weeks apart, as candles elongate the next spring.

Nematodes
Tiny, translucent worms, many types. Some, such as predatory and decomposer nematodes, are beneficial. Pest nematodes give plants disease symptoms. Different nematodes infect foliage, stems and roots. *Foliar and stem:* yellow spots that turn brown on leaves or stems; leaves shrivel and wither; lesions appear on stems; problem starts low on plant and works upwards. *Root-knot:* plant is stunted, may wilt; yellow spots on leaves; roots have tiny bumps or knots. **What to Do.** Mulch soil, add organic matter, clear garden debris in fall. Avoid wetting the leaves, and don't touch wet foliage of infected plants. Can add parasitic nematodes to soil. Remove infected plants in extreme cases.

Psyllids
Treat as for aphids (see Aphids).

Rot
Several different fungi and bacteria that cause decay and can kill plant. May affect wood, roots, stems, crowns, leaves, flowers and fruit. Rotted areas can be soft and moist or dry and crumbly. **What to Do.** Keep soil well drained; don't damage plant if you are digging around it; keep mulches away from plant base. Destroy infected plant if whole plant affected. Replant area with only rot-resistant species or cultivars and not the same species of plant that died.

Rust
Fungi. Pale spots on upper leaf surfaces; orange, fuzzy or dusty spots on leaf undersides. Examples: blister rust, cedar-apple rust, cone rust. **What to Do.** Choose varieties and cultivars resistant to rust; avoid handling wet leaves; provide plant with good air circulation; clear up garden debris at end of season. Remove and destroy infected plant parts. A late-winter application of lime-sulfur can delay infection the following year.

Sawflies
see Caterpillars

Scab
see Leaf Spot

Scale Insects (Scale)
Tiny, shelled insects that suck sap, weakening and possibly killing plant or making it vulnerable to other problems. Once female scale insect has pierced plant with mouthpart, it is there for life. Juvenile scale insects are called crawlers. **What to Do.** Wipe with alcohol-soaked swabs; spray with water to dislodge crawlers; prune out heavily infested branches; encourage natural predators and parasites; spray dormant oil in

spring before bud break.

Slugs & Snails

Both are mollusks; slugs lack shells whereas snails have spiral shells. Slimy, smooth skin; can be up to 8" long, though many are smaller; gray, green, black, beige, yellow or spotted. Leave large, ragged holes in leaves and silvery slime trails on and around plants.

What to Do. Attach strips of copper to wood around raised beds or to smaller boards inserted around susceptible plants; slugs and snails get shocked if they touch copper surfaces. Pick off by hand in the evening and squish with boot or drop in can of soapy water. Apply light dusting of wood ash or diatomaceous earth (available in garden centers) on the ground around plants; it will pierce and dehydrate mollusks' soft bodies. *Do not* use diatomaceous earth intended for swimming pool filters. Lay damp cardboard flat on the ground in the evening, then dispose of it and the resting slugs the following morning. Beer in a shallow dish may also be effective. Slug baits containing iron phosphate are not harmful to humans or animals and control slugs when used according to directions. If slugs damaged garden late in season, begin controls in spring as soon as green shoots appear.

Sooty Mold

Fungus. Thin black film forms on leaf surfaces and reduces amount of light getting to leaves.

What to Do. Wipe mold off leaf surfaces; control aphids, mealybugs, whiteflies (honeydew they deposit on leaves encourages sooty mold).

Tar Spot

see Leaf Spot

Thrips

Tiny, slender, yellow, black or brown insects with narrow, fringed wings. Difficult to see; may be visible if you disturb them by blowing gently on an infested flower. Thrips suck juice out of plant cells, particularly in flowers and buds, resulting in mottled petals and leaves, dying buds and distorted and stunted growth.

What to Do. Remove and destroy infected plant parts; encourage native predatory insects with nectar plants such as yarrow; spray severe infestations with insecticidal soap or neem oil according to directions. Use blue sticky cards to prevent recurrence. Horticultural oil controls adult thrips.

Viruses

Plant may be stunted and leaves and flowers distorted, streaked or discolored. Viral diseases in plants cannot be treated. Examples: mosaic virus, ringspot virus.

What to Do. Control disease-spreading insects such as aphids, leafhoppers and whiteflies. Destroy infected plants.

Weevils

see Beetles

Mosaic virus

Whiteflies

Tiny flying insects that flutter up into the air when plant is disturbed. Moth-like, white; live on undersides of plant leaves. Suck juice out of leaves, causing yellowed leaves and weakened plants; leave behind sticky honeydew on foliage, encouraging sooty mold.

What to Do. Destroy weeds that may be home to insects. Attract native predatory beetles and parasitic wasps with nectar plants such as yarrow and sweet alyssum; spray severe cases with insecticidal soap and repeat at regular intervals. Can make a sticky flypaper-like trap by mounting tin can on stake. Wrap can with yellow paper and cover with clear sandwich bag smeared with petroleum jelly; replace bag when full of flies. Apply horticultural oil.

Wilt

If watering hasn't helped a wilted plant, one of two wilt fungi may be the problem. *Fusarium wilt:* plant wilts, leaves turn yellow then die; symptoms generally appear first on one part of plant before spreading. *Verticillium wilt:* plant wilts; leaves curl up at edges, turn yellow then drop off or may remain on plant; plant may die.

What to Do. Both wilts difficult to control. Choose resistant varieties and cultivars; clean up debris at end of growing season. Destroy infected plants; solarize (sterilize) soil before replanting (this may help if you've lost an entire bed of plants to these fungi)—contact local garden center for assistance. Do not repeat the same crop.

Woolly Adelgids

see Aphids

Worms

see Caterpillars, Nematodes

Pest Control Recipes

Compost 'Tea'

Mix 1–2 lb. compost in 5 gal. of water. Let sit four to seven days, then strain off liquid and add remaining solids back to compost. Store liquid out of direct sunlight. For use, dilute until it resembles weak tea. Use during normal watering or apply as a foliar spray to prevent or treat fungal diseases.

Insecticidal Soap

Mix 1 tsp. mild dish detergent or pure soap (biodegradable options are available) with 1 qt. water in a clean spray bottle. Spray surfaces of insect-infested plants, and rinse well within an hour of spraying to avoid foliage discoloration.

Horticultural Oil

Mix 5 tbsp. horticultural oil per 1 gal. water and apply as a spray for a variety of insect and fungal problems. If purchased, follow package directions.

About This Guide

The trees and shrubs in this book are organized alphabetically by common name. Alternative common names and scientific names are given beneath the main headings and in the index. The illustrated **Trees & Shrubs at a Glance** allows you to become familiar with the different plants quickly, and it helps you find one if you aren't sure what it's called.

Clearly displayed at the beginning of each entry are the special features of the woody plant, height and spread ranges, preferred planting forms (bare-root, balled-and-burlapped or container), optimal planting seasons and plant hardiness zones (see map, p. 15).

Our favorite species, hybrids and cultivars are listed in each entry's Recommended section. Many more types are often available, so check with your local garden center. Some cultivated varieties are known by only the cultivar name proper, shown in single quotation marks (e.g., 'Little Giant'); others are known instead or also by a trade name registered by a particular company. Trade names are shown in small capitals (e.g., SPRING GROVE). For all plants, we present the most commonly used name first, with any alternative names following in parentheses.

Where height, spread and hardiness zones are not indicated in the Recommended section, refer to the information under the main heading. The ranges at the beginning of each entry always encompass the measurements for plants listed in the Recommended section.

Common pest and disease problems, if any, are also noted for each entry. Consult the Problems & Pests section of the introduction (pp. 62–73) for information on how to address these problems.

The **Quick Reference Chart** found at the back of the book (pp. 342–47) is a handy guide to planning a diversity of features, forms, foliage types and blooming times in your garden.

Because Ohio is climatically diverse, we can refer to seasons only in a general sense. Keep in mind the timing and duration of seasons in your area when planning your garden. Hardiness zones, too, can vary locally; consult your local cooperative extension agent, horticulturalist or garden center.

The Trees & Shrubs

Aralia

Aralia

Features: foliage, flowers, fruit, stems **Habit:** deciduous small tree or large shrub
Height: 10–30' **Spread:** 10–20' **Planting:** container, bare-root; early spring to
early winter **Zones:** 4–8

DEVIL'S WALKING STICK IS AN EXTREMELY APT COMMON NAME
for an aralia. The stem prickles are truly flesh eating if you carelessly wander
into the plant, as I made the mistake of doing only once. This apparent liabil-
ity can be an asset when the plant is properly sited. As guardians of remote
rear corners and unattended pathways, or as guides for pedestrian traffic in
commercial parking lots and other large areas, the armor is a definite
advantage. Aralias make for an appealing dichotomy in the landscape: the large leaves make the summer
appearance rather soft and graceful, while
the stout, prickly stems lend a coarse
visual interest in winter.

Growing

Aralias prefer **full sun** or **light shade**.
They grow best in **fertile, moist, well-drained** soil but tolerate
dry, clay or rocky soil. Provide **shelter** from strong winds, which can dry out
the foliage.

These shrubs rarely require pruning, which is fortunate considering their
plentiful prickles. You will, however, have to spend some time controlling the
suckers that sprout up around this shrub. Barriers such as buildings and driveways can help prevent spread, but you may still want to pull some or all of

the suckers. If you get the suckers while they are small, they are easier to remove and the prickles are a bit softer.

Tough gloves are an absolute requirement when handling aralias. I have found thick rubber gloves useful when pulling up suckers. They allow a good grip and will stretch rather than puncture when prickles are encountered on the young shoots.

A. elata 'Variegata'

Tips

These shrubs are best suited to an informal garden. They can be included in a border at the edge of a wooded area and should be used where their spread can be controlled and where you won't inadvertently brush against the thorny stems.

The berries should not be eaten; they are thought to be poisonous to humans. The berries rarely last long because they are quickly eaten by birds.

Recommended

A. elata (Japanese angelica tree) is the larger of the two recommended species, usually growing 20' tall, but potentially reaching 30'. It bears clusters of creamy flowers in late summer, followed by berries that ripen to dark purple. The foliage turns purple, orange or yellow in fall. This species doesn't sucker quite as vigorously as *A. spinosa* and is not quite as spiny. '**Variegata**' has leaves with creamy white margins. Suckers sometimes have solid green rather than variegated leaves and should be pulled up.

A. spinosa (Hercules' club, devil's walking stick) usually grows 10–15' tall. What this native species lacks in height, compared with *A. elata,* it makes up for by spreading vigorously. Unless you can provide this plant with lots of room to grow, be prepared to wade in with thick gloves at least once a year to pull up suckers. This species bears large clusters of white flowers in late summer, followed by black berries.

Problems & Pests

Problems are rare, limited to occasional trouble with fungal leaf spot, aphids or mealybugs.

A. elata

Arborvitae
Cedar
Thuja

Features: foliage, bark, form **Habit:** small to large evergreen shrub or tree
Height: 2–50' **Spread:** 2–20' **Planting:** B & B, container; spring or fall
Zones: 2–9

WHEN YOU NEED AN EVERGREEN IN A SUNNY SPOT, YOU MIGHT ASK which arborvitae you should consider. Once maligned, this genus has recently gained new respect. Unfortunately, many people's memories are clouded by winter scenes of straw brown, straggly, sparse plants or by an ugly, lonely sentry in an old cemetery. Many new varieties have been developed, and there is one for almost every need. Most welcome are those that stay shorter or narrower for screens, backgrounds or separation of spaces. Soft in appearance and to the touch, arborvitae are also welcome around young children. I have used them where soils are a little too dense and moist for other narrow, upright evergreens.

Growing

Arborvitae prefer **full sun**. The soil should be of **average fertility, moist** and **well drained**. These plants enjoy humidity and in the wild are often found growing near marshy areas. Arborvitae will perform best in a location with some **shelter** from wind, especially in winter, when the foliage can easily dry out and give the entire plant a rather brown, drab appearance.

These plants take very well to pruning and are often grown as hedges. Though they may be kept formally shaped, they are also attractive if just lightly clipped to maintain a loose but compact shape and size.

Tips

Large varieties of arborvitae make excellent specimen trees, and smaller cultivars can be used in foundation plantings, shrub borders and formal or informal hedges.

Deer enjoy eating the foliage of eastern arborvitae. If deer or other ungulates are a problem in your area, you may wish to avoid using this species. Alternatively, consider using western arborvitae, which is relatively resistant to deer browsing.

Recommended

T. occidentalis (eastern arborvitae, American arborvitae) is native to much of eastern and central North America. In the wild this tree can grow to about 60' tall and 10–15' wide. In cultivation it grows about half this size or smaller. '**Aurea**' has bright yellow foliage and grows about 36" tall, with an equal spread.

T. plicata SPRING GROVE

Crush some foliage between your fingers to enjoy the wonderful aroma. Be cautious, though, if you have sensitive skin; the pungent oils may irritate.

T. occidentalis 'Sunkist'

'DeGroot's Spire' is a narrow, upright cultivar about 9' tall and 24–36" in spread. 'Elegantissima' forms a narrow pyramid up to 15' tall, with a spread of 5'. It has yellow-tipped dark green foliage that turns a bronze color in winter. 'Emerald' ('Smaragd') can grow 10–15' tall, spreading about 4'. This cultivar is small and very cold hardy; the foliage does not lose color in winter. 'George Peabody' ('Lutea') is a pyramidal tree that grows 15–30' tall and spreads 10–20'. It has bright yellow foliage that turns orange in winter. 'Hetz Midget' is a dwarf, rounded cultivar. It grows to 2–4' tall and wide but can be kept smaller with pruning. 'Holmstrup' is a slow-growing, pyramidal tree that grows about 9' tall and 36" wide. The foliage keeps its bright green color all winter. 'Little Giant' is a bright green, rounded cultivar. It grows 24–36" tall, with an equal spread. 'Nigra' ('Nigra Dark Green') has a neat pyramidal habit and keeps its dark green foliage color in winter. It grows 20–30' tall and 8' wide. 'Rheingold' is an upright cultivar that grows 4–5' tall and spreads 3–4'. The golden yellow foliage becomes orangy brown in winter. 'Sunkist' is

T. occidentalis cultivar (above), 'Nigra' (below)

a low, slow-growing, pyramidal cultivar with bright yellow foliage. It grows 5–10' tall and 5–8' wide. 'Techny' is a very hardy cultivar with a broad pyramidal form. It grows 10–20' tall and 5–8' wide and keeps its bluish green color all winter. 'Woodwardii' is a globe form that grows 3–5' tall and wide. (Zones 2–7; cultivars may be less cold hardy)

T. plicata (western arborvitae, western redcedar) can grow up to 200' tall in its native Pacific Northwest but usually stays under 50' in Ohio. This narrowly pyramidal evergreen grows quickly, resists deer browsing and maintains good foliage color all winter. 'Atrovirens' is popular for its dark green, glossy foliage. It grows 15–20' tall and 5–10' wide. SPRING GROVE ('Grovepli') is a very narrow, very hardy cultivar with bright green foliage. It grows about 20' tall and up to 10' wide. 'Zebrina' has foliage variegated yellow and green. This pyramidal cultivar can grow more than 30' tall and 12' wide. (Zones 5–9)

Problems & Pests

Bagworm, leaf miners, red spider mites, scale insects, blight, canker and heart rot are possible, though not frequent, problems. The most likely problem is winter browning, which usually occurs in cold, windy areas where the foliage easily loses moisture. Leaf miner damage may resemble winter browning—hold branch tips up to the light and look for tiny caterpillars feeding inside. Trim and destroy infested foliage before June.

T. plicata 'Zebrina'

Many diverse arborvitae cultivars are available, from pyramidal forms that make excellent specimens, to yellow types that add color to the winter landscape, to dwarf, globe-shaped forms for the mixed border or rock garden.

T. occidentalis 'Emerald'

Aronia
Chokeberry
Aronia

Features: flowers, fruit, fall foliage **Habit:** suckering, deciduous shrub
Height: 3–10' **Spread:** 3–10' **Planting:** container, bare-root; spring or fall
Zones: 3–8

CHOKEBERRY IS AN UNFORTUNATE ALTERNATIVE NAME FOR AN
extremely versatile landscape shrub. The name arose because the fruit is so bitter. Even after a winter, it will still require much sweetening to make it palatable. Its bitterness has an aesthetic advantage, however; the birds avoid eating
it, so the red or black fruit persists from the time it appears in mid-fall right
through winter. Even in Ohio's 'finest' heavy clays, these plants can handle
excess moisture for a short time if planted slightly high in the ground. Once
established, they tend to spread in even really rugged circumstances. I have
often recommended an aronia as a plant of last resort in shady, moist areas.

Growing

Aronias grow well in **full sun** or **partial shade,** but the best flowering and
fruiting occur in full sun. Plants grow best in **well-drained** soil of **average
fertility,** but they adapt to most soils and tolerate wet, dry or poor soil.

Up to one-third of the stems, preferably the older ones, can be pruned out
annually once flowering is finished.

Tips

These plants are useful in a shrub or mixed border. They also make interesting, low-maintenance specimen plants. Left to their own devices, they will naturalize to cover a fairly large area.

Recommended

A. arbutifolia (*Photinia floribunda;* red chokeberry) is an upright shrub that grows 3–6' tall. White flowers are borne in late spring, followed by bright red waxy fruit in fall. 'Brilliantissima' has brilliant red fall foliage.

A. melanocarpa (top & bottom)

A. melanocarpa (*A. prunifolia, Photinia melanocarpa;* black chokeberry) is an upright, suckering shrub that is native to Ohio and the eastern U.S. It grows 3–6' tall and can spread to about 10'. It bears white flowers in late spring and early summer, followed by dark fruit that ripens in fall and persists through winter. The foliage turns bright red to purplish red in fall. 'Elata' (var. *elata*) is identical to the species except that it has larger leaves, flowers and fruit and grows 6–10' tall, with an equal spread. IROQUOIS BEAUTY ('Morton') is a compact cultivar that grows only 3–4' tall. 'Viking' has glossy dark green foliage that turns dark red in fall. It grows 3–5' tall. The persistent large, dark fruit is edible, but bitter.

IROQUOIS BEAUTY (center)

Aronia fruit is high in vitamins, especially vitamin C. It was used as an easily available alternative to citrus in eastern Europe during the Cold War.

Problems & Pests

Aronias rarely suffer from any major problems, though fungal leaf spot or rust is possible.

Barberry
Berberis

Features: foliage, flowers, fruit **Habit:** prickly deciduous shrub **Height:** 1–6'
Spread: 18"–6' **Planting:** container; spring or fall **Zones:** 4–8

THORNY, ORNERY, OBNOXIOUS, SPITEFUL—THESE ARE ADJECTIVES
gardeners have used to describe barberry. If you aren't wearing long pants
and good leather gloves when working with this plant, you may come up
with a few graphic descriptions of your own. Still, it has contributed greatly
to the beauty of our landscapes, and it will continue to do so long into the
future. The variation available in plant size, foliage color and fruit makes
barberry a real workhorse of the plant world. When we choose the right barberry for the job, give it full
sun in well-drained soil,
and equip ourselves with
good gloves, it is a wonderful landscape plant.

Extracts from the rhizomes of
Berberis have been used to treat
rheumatic and other inflammatory
disorders as well as the common
cold.

Growing

Barberry develops the best fall color when grown in **full sun,** but it tolerates partial shade. Any **well-drained** soil is suitable. This plant tolerates drought and urban conditions but suffers in poorly drained, wet soil.

Barberry is flexible when it comes to pruning. It can take heavy pruning well and is often grown as a hedge. A plant in an informal border can be left unpruned or can be lightly pruned. Remove old or dead wood and unwanted suckers.

Tips

Large barberry plants make great hedges with formidable prickles. Barberry can also be included in shrub and mixed borders. Small cultivars can be grown in rock gardens, in raised beds and along rock walls.

Var. *atropurpurea* (above), 'Rose Glow' (below)

B. thunbergii (above), var. *atropurpurea* cultivar (below)

Recommended

B. thunbergii (Japanese barberry) is a dense shrub with a broad, rounded habit. It grows 3–5' tall and spreads 4–6'. The foliage is bright green and turns variable shades of orange, red or purple in fall. Yellow spring flowers are followed by glossy red fruit later in summer. **Var. *atropurpurea*** is similar to the species but has purple foliage and purple-tinged flowers. This form has been used to develop many purple-leaved cultivars. **Var. *a.* 'Bagatelle'** is a small, very slow-growing cultivar with purple foliage. It eventually forms a dense mound about 18–24" tall, with an equal or slightly greater spread. **Var. *a.* 'Crimson Pygmy'** ('Nana') is a dwarf cultivar with reddish purple foliage. It grows 18–24" tall and spreads up to 36". **Var. *a.* 'Rose Glow'** (rosy glow barberry) has purple foliage variegated with white and pink splotches. It grows 5–6' tall, with an equal spread. **'Aurea'** (golden barberry) grows up to 5' tall,

with an equal spread. It has bright yellow new growth. **BONANZA GOLD** ('Bogozam') has golden yellow foliage that doesn't scorch in the sun. It grows 18" tall and spreads about 36". **GOLD NUGGET** ('Monlers') is a slow-growing, mounding plant with bright yellow foliage that turns orange in fall. It grows about 12" tall and spreads to about 18". 'Kobold' is a dense plant with bright green foliage. It forms a 24–36" mound of equal height and width.

Problems & Pests
Stress-free barberry rarely suffers from problems, but stressed plants can be affected by aphids, scale insects, spider mites, weevils, leaf spot, mosaic, root rot or wilt.

Var. *atropurpurea* 'Crimson Pygmy' (both photos)

Because some barberry species harbor the overwintering phase of the devastating wheat rust fungus, some regions have banned all Berberis. *Many of these regions are now lifting the ban on* B. thunbergii *and other species that have never been proven to harbor the fungus.*

Beautyberry

Callicarpa

Features: late-summer and fall fruit **Habit:** bushy deciduous shrub with arching stems
Height: 3–10' **Spread:** 3–6' **Planting:** container; spring or fall **Zones:** 5–10

IN LATE SEPTEMBER AND OCTOBER, VERY FEW PLANTS ELICIT MORE
reaction than beautyberries. When passersby discover the showy, shiny fruit
in someone's garden, comments along the line of 'What *is* this?' and 'Wow!'
are commonplace. These plants flower on new wood, so the occasional bout
of winter damage is no problem—unless you've taken the time to train two-
and three-year-old shoots onto a split-rail fence. The espalier-like form,
which can spread 8' to either side of the stem base, creates an 'I wish I had
my camera' effect your heart would break to lose.

To encourage vigorous new growth,
fertilize beautyberry plants that suffer
winter dieback.

Growing

Beautyberries grow well in **full sun** or **light shade**. The soil should be **well drained** and of **average fertility**.

These plants may die back completely each winter. This isn't a problem because the flowers and fruit form on the current year's growth. Cut the dead stems back completely in spring. New growth will sprout from ground level.

C. japonica 'Leucocarpa' (above)

Tips

Beautyberries can be used in naturalistic gardens and in shrub and mixed borders. The fruit-covered branches are cut for fresh and dried flower arrangements. The colorful fruit persists on the branches when they are cut and dried.

Recommended

C. dichotoma (purple beautyberry) grows about 3–4' tall, with an equal or slightly greater spread. The purple fruit is borne in dense clusters that surround the arching branches at the base of each leaf. '**Issai**' is a compact cultivar that bears plentiful fruit.

C. dichotoma 'Issai' (center), *C. japonica* (below)

C. japonica (Japanese beautyberry) is a large, open shrub with arching branches and decorative purple fruit. This shrub can grow to 10' tall and spread 4–6', but it is unlikely to grow more than 4' tall when it dies back each winter. '**Leucocarpa**' is an attractive white-fruited cultivar.

Problems & Pests

Scale insects, leaf spot and mildew are possible problems, but they are not serious and do not occur frequently.

Beauty Bush

Kolkwitzia

Features: late-spring flowers **Habit:** suckering, deciduous shrub with arching branches **Height:** 6–15' **Spread:** 5–11' **Planting:** B & B, container; spring or fall **Zones:** 4–8

OFTEN, WHEN A PLANT BECOMES LESS AND LESS USED, THE REASON is very obvious. A new disease may have begun to ravage it, or a better variety may have risen in popularity and supplanted it. Beauty bush doesn't fall into either of these categories. Still, it is rarely offered at garden centers these days, and customers don't know to ask for it—too bad, because it can be hard to find good rear corner fillers, border plants and background shrubs without disease or insect problems. The height and spread of beauty bush tend to exclude it from smaller gardens. In larger gardens, the legginess it develops with age can be easily disguised with foreground plantings. I find its rather bold winter outline appealing. The two weeks of gorgeous pink blooms alone make this old-time beauty well worth giving a new future.

Beauty bush is resistant to most pests and diseases.

Growing

Beauty bush flowers most profusely in **full sun**. The soil should be **fertile** and **well drained**. This shrub adapts to various pH levels.

Prune out one-third of the old wood each year after flowering is complete. Old, overgrown plants can be cut right back to the ground if they need rejuvenation. Start new plants by removing rooted suckers from the base of the plant in spring.

Tips

Beauty bush can be included in a shrub border. It can also be grown as a specimen shrub, but it isn't exceptionally attractive when not in flower.

Recommended

K. amabilis is a large shrub with arching canes. Clusters of bell-shaped flowers in many shades of pink are borne in late spring or early summer. **'Pink Cloud'** is a popular cultivar with deep pink flowers. It is not quite as cold hardy as the species.

The name Kolkwitzia *honors Richard Kolkwitz, a German professor of botany;* amabilis, *appropriately, is Latin for 'lovely.'*

K. amabilis (above)

'Pink Cloud' (center & below)

Beech

Fagus

Features: foliage, bark, habit, fall color **Habit:** large, oval, deciduous shade tree
Height: 30–80' **Spread:** 10–65' **Planting:** B & B, container; spring **Zones:** 4–9

AMERICAN BEECH HAS ALWAYS BEEN ONE OF MY FAVORITE TREES.
It is attractive at any age, from its big, bold, beautiful youth through to its
slow, craggy decline. Its temperamental root system restricts it to use as a
woodland tree. The European beech is a different story. It lost out as the chosen tree for my own front yard only because there is a beautiful 'Tricolor' just
a few homes away. The European forms are many, and they are good, reliable
trees; the only use I do not recommend is as a street tree because of the low
branching. As far as uniquely shaped trees are concerned, 'Pendula' is a real
winner. Even side by side, each tree of this cultivar will have its own distinct
character.

*Beeches retain their very smooth
and elastic bark long into
maturity.*

Growing

Beeches grow equally well in **full sun** or **partial shade.** The soil should be of **average fertility, loamy** and **well drained,** though almost all well-drained soils are tolerated.

American beech doesn't like having its roots disturbed and should be transplanted only when very young. European beech transplants easily and is more tolerant of varied soil conditions than American beech.

Very little pruning is required. Remove dead or damaged branches in spring or any time after the damage occurs. European beech is a popular hedging species and responds well to severe pruning if trained from an early age.

Tips

Beeches make excellent specimens. They are also used as shade trees and in woodland gardens. These

F. sylvatica

Beech nuts provide food for a wide variety of animals, including squirrels and birds. They were a favorite food of the now-extinct passenger pigeon.

Weeping form of *F. sylvatica* 'Purpurea'

trees need a lot of space, but the European beech's adaptability to pruning makes it a reasonable choice in a small garden.

The nuts are edible when roasted.

Recommended

F. grandifolia (American beech) is a broad-canopied tree that can grow 50–80' tall and often almost as wide. This species is native to most of eastern North America.

F. sylvatica (European beech) is a spectacular tree that can grow 60' tall and wide or even larger. Too massive for most settings, the species is best kept pruned and used as a hedge in smaller gardens. You can find a number of interesting cultivars of this tree, and several are small enough to use in the home garden. **'Fastigiata'** ('Dawyck') is a narrow, upright tree. It can grow to 80' tall but spreads only about 10'. Yellow- or purple-leaved forms are available. **'Pendula'** (weeping beech) is a dramatic cultivar whose pendulous branches reach down to the ground. It varies in form; some trees spread widely, resulting in a cascade effect, while other specimens may be rather upright with branches drooping from the central trunk. This cultivar can grow as tall as the species, but a specimen with the branches drooping from the central trunk

Young lovers' initials carved into a beech may, unfortunately, deface the tree for the remainder of its life—an effect that outlasts many young relationships.

F. sylvatica 'Pendula'

F. sylvatica 'Tricolor'

may be narrow enough for a home garden. '**Purpurea**' is a purple-leaved form with the same habit as the species. Purple-leaved weeping forms are also available. '**Tricolor**' ('Roseo-marginata') has striking foliage with pink and white variegation that develops best in partial shade. This slow-growing tree matures to about 30'. It can be grown as a smaller tree if constrained to a large planter.

Problems & Pests

Aphids, borers, scale insects, bark disease, canker, leaf spot and powdery mildew can afflict beech trees. None of these pests causes serious problems.

F. sylvatica 'Tricolor' (above)

Birch

Betula

Features: foliage, fall color, habit, bark, winter and early-spring catkins **Habit:** open, deciduous tree **Height:** 25–90' **Spread:** 10–60' **Planting:** B & B, container; spring or fall **Zones:** 3–9

BIRCHES ARE A LARGE GROUP OF plants, presenting rather daunting problems for the scientists who classify and name them. A more general problem for gardeners is the specific cultural needs of these trees. Birches must have a fertile soil with a good deal of organic matter. The soil must stay moist, but it can only rarely and temporarily be waterlogged. These trees also tend to prefer living as part of a community or grove in the understory of their own kind or other trees. Many are truly magnificent when seen as specimens, but this use rarely offers them appropriate conditions. Site them properly, water and mulch as needed, and you should be rewarded with a wonderful birch display.

The bark of B. papyrifera *(paper birch) has been used to make canoes, shelters, utensils and—as both the Latin and common names imply—paper.*

Growing

Birches can grow well in **full sun, partial shade** or **light shade**. The soil should be of **average to rich fertility, moist** and fairly **well drained**. Many birch species naturally grow in wet areas, such as along streams. They don't, however, like to grow in places that remain wet for prolonged periods. Provide supplemental water during periods of extended drought.

Minimal pruning is required. Remove any dead, damaged, diseased or awkward branches as needed. Any pruning of live wood should be done in late summer or fall to prevent the excessive bleeding of sap that generally occurs when branches are cut in spring.

Tips

Birch trees are usually grown for their attractive, often white and peeling bark. The bark contrasts nicely with the dark green leaves in summer and with the glossy red or chestnut-colored younger branches and twigs in winter. Often used as specimen trees, birches' small leaves and open canopy provide light shade that will allow perennials, annuals or lawns to flourish underneath. Birch trees are also attractive when grown in groups near natural or artificial water features. They do need quite a bit of room to grow and are not the best choice in gardens with limited space.

The common and popular European white birch *(B. pendula)* and its weeping cultivars are poor choices for gardens because of their susceptibility to pests and diseases,

B. lenta (above)

B. nigra (center), *B. platyphylla* (below)

B. nigra

Don't let worries about bronze birch borer discourage you from growing birch. If you choose the right species or variety and take care to water during droughts, you are likely to enjoy a beautiful tree for many years.

B. platyphylla var. japonica 'Whitespire'

particularly the fatal bronze birch borer. If you plan to grow or already have one of these trees, consult a local gardening center or tree specialist to begin a preventive program.

Recommended

B. lenta (cherry birch) has glossy, serrated leaves and brown-black bark. The fall color is a delicate gold. This birch is excellent for naturalizing. It will grow 25–50' tall and 20–45' wide. (Zones 3–7)

B. nigra (river birch, black birch, red birch) has shaggy, cinnamon brown bark that flakes off in sheets when it is young but thickens and becomes ridged as it matures. This fast grower attains a height of 60–90' and a spread of 40–60'. The bright green leaves are silvery white on the undersides. River birch is one of the most disease-resistant species. It also resists bronze birch borer. HERITAGE ('Cully') is an excellent cultivar. It is a vigorous grower and resistant to leaf spot and heat stress. The leaves are larger and glossier than those of the species. The bark begins peeling when the tree is quite young, to show off white or pink areas that mature to salmon brown as the tree ages. (Zones 3–9)

B. platyphylla (Asian white birch) is rarely grown, but several varieties and cultivars are quite common. 'Crimson Frost' is a purple-leaved cultivar that was developed from a cross between *B. platyphylla* var. *szechuanica* and *B. pendula* 'Purpurea.' It grows 25–30' tall and about 10' wide. Selected for its resistance to birch borer, **var. japonica** 'Whitespire' is similar in appearance to the European white birch. It has white bark that doesn't exfoliate and is resistant to borers. 'Whitespire' has an upright habit, growing about 40' tall, with a spread of 15–20'. Be certain the tree you purchase is a clone, meaning it was propagated asexually and not grown from seed. Only clones will resist borers. (Zones 4–8)

Problems & Pests
Aphids are fond of birch trees, and the sticky honeydew these insects secrete may drip off the leaves. Avoid planting birch where drips can fall onto parked cars, patios or decks. Other potential problems include birch skeletonizer, leaf miners and tent caterpillars. The bronze birch borer can be fatal; plant a resistant species or cultivar.

B. nigra HERITAGE

Some people make birch syrup from the sap of cherry birch. The heavy flow of sap in spring is tapped and the sap is boiled down, the same way maple syrup is made.

Black Jetbead
White Kerria
Rhodotypos

Features: habit, flowers, fruit **Habit:** arching, deciduous shrub **Height:** 3–6'
Spread: 3–8' **Planting:** container; any time **Zones:** 4–8

IF THERE IS AN UNSUNG LITTLE HORTICULTURAL WORKHORSE,
this is it. Black jetbead flourishes in light from full sun to nearly full shade.
It can tolerate abusive soil right up to the positively too wet, and it is unboth-
ered by pH to almost either extreme. It can easily be kept to 36" but will grow
to nearly 6', arching out to at least 5' in width. Without being considered
invasive, it is a real jungle fighter and will fill in spaces when other plants in
the area falter. The flowers are not notable, but the jet-black beads in autumn
are more striking. The light to medium green foliage provides a nice contrast
to brightly colored flowers in sun and stands out well in shade.

The genus name, from rhodo, *'rose,'
and* typos, *'type,' refers to the rather
rose-like flowers.*

Growing

Black jetbead prefers **full sun** but tolerates shade well. The soil should preferably be of **average fertility, moist** and **well drained,** but this plant adapts to most soil conditions and tolerates pollution.

Little pruning should be needed. To keep the shrub vigorous, one-third of the older growth can be removed each year in spring before growth begins or later in the season after flowering has finished.

Tips

This tough, adaptable plant is useful in difficult garden situations and poor soil locations. It makes an attractive addition to a natural woodland garden or to a shrub or mixed border, where the foliage creates a good backdrop for brightly colored flowers. The black berries persist and add winter interest.

The berries are poisonous.

Recommended

R. scandens is a mound-forming shrub with arching branches. It grows 3–6' tall, with an equal or greater spread. A flush of white flowers is produced in late spring, with sporadic blooms appearing over the summer. Hard, black, round fruits follow the flowers and often persist on the branches over the winter. The foliage emerges early in spring and persists long into fall.

Black jetbead rarely suffers from any pest or disease problems.

The berries bring to mind the ornamental stone called jet, which has often been worn as a symbol of mourning.

Boxwood
Box
Buxus

Features: foliage, habit **Habit:** dense, rounded, evergreen shrub **Height:** 2–20'
Spread: equal to height **Planting:** B & B, container; spring **Zones:** 4–9

WHEN USING THE BOXWOODS GENERALLY AVAILABLE ON THE
market today, we can expect plants that are hardy to 0° F, or even in some
cases down to –20° F. Buy from plant growers who are established in your
area, and depend on their past successes. Boxwoods are a blessing as hedge
plants in the heavy clay and highly alkaline soils of two-thirds of Ohio.
Although most are sheared as hedges, boxwoods can also be grown informally when pruned by alternating cuts. I use the latter approach in my border plantings to create a winter attraction without formality. At the same
time, I have two 'Vardar Valley' boxwoods at the front entrance that have
been cut very formally.

Growing

Boxwoods prefer **partial shade** but adapt to full shade or to full sun if kept well watered. The soil should be **fertile** and **well drained**. Once established, boxwoods are drought tolerant.

Many formal gardens include boxwoods because they can be pruned to form neat hedges, geometric shapes or fanciful creatures. The dense growth and small leaves form an even green surface, which, along with the slow rate of growth, makes these plants among the most popular for creating topiary.

For a neat but informally trimmed plant, use alternating cuts. As you prune around a bush, alternate trimming longer shoots with trimming shorter shoots. This technique keeps plants neat and bushy but maintains the natural shape and growth habit of the boxwood. Even when left unpruned, a boxwood shrub forms an attractive, rounded mound.

B. microphylla var. *koreana*

The wood of Buxus, *particularly the wood of the root, is very dense and fine-grained, making it valuable for carving. It has been used to make ornate boxes, hence the common name.*

B. microphylla with *Acer palmatum* cultivar

'Green Velvet'

Boxwoods will sprout new growth from old wood. A plant that has been neglected or is growing in a lopsided manner can be cut back hard in early spring, before any growth has started. By the end of summer the exposed areas will have filled in with new green growth.

A good mulch benefits these shrubs because their roots grow very close to the surface. For the same reason, it is best not to disturb the earth around a boxwood once it is established.

Tips

These shrubs make excellent background plants in a mixed border. Brightly colored flowers show up well against the even, dark green surface of the boxwood. Dwarf cultivars can be trimmed into small hedges for edging garden beds or walkways. An interesting topiary piece can create a formal or whimsical focal point in any garden. Larger species and cultivars are often used to form dense evergreen hedges.

Boxwood foliage contains toxic compounds that, when ingested, can cause severe digestive upset.

Recommended

B. microphylla (littleleaf boxwood) grows about 4' in height and spread. This species is quite pest resistant. It is hardy in Zones 6–9. The foliage tends to lose its green in winter, turning shades of bronze, yellow or brown. **Var.** *koreana* is far more cold resistant than the species, hardy to Zone 4. **Var.** *koreana* 'Wintergreen' has foliage that keeps its light green color through the winter. Like its parent variety it is hardy to Zone 4.

B. sempervirens (common boxwood) is a much larger species. If left unpruned it can grow up to 20' in height and width. It has a low

B. sempervirens

tolerance of extremes of heat and cold and should be grown in a sheltered spot. The foliage stays green in winter. Many cultivars are available with interesting features, such as compact or dwarf growth, variegated foliage and pendulous branches. **'Vardar Valley'** is a wide, mounding cultivar, with dark bluish green foliage. It grows up to 36" tall and spreads about 5'. It is prone to winter damage in Zone 5. (Zones 5–8)

Several cultivars have been developed from crosses between *B. m.* var. *koreana* and *B. sempervirens*. Some of these have inherited the best attributes of each parent—hardiness and pest resistance on the one hand and attractive foliage year-round on the other. CHICAGOLAND GREEN ('Glencoe') has a neat, rounded habit and grows quickly to a mature height of 24–36". **'Green Gem'** forms a rounded 24" mound. The deep green foliage stays green all winter. **'Green Mound'** is an attractive rounded cultivar that grows 36" tall, with an equal spread. **'Green Mountain'** forms a large upright shrub 5' tall, with dark green foliage. It has survived −25° F in Columbus. **'Green Velvet'** is a hardy cultivar developed in Canada. It has glossy foliage and a rounded habit, growing up to 36" in height and spread. (Zones 4–8)

Problems & Pests

Leaf miners, mites, psyllids, scale insects, leaf spot, powdery mildew and root rot are all possible problems affecting boxwoods.

B. sempervirens

Boxwoods are steeped in legend and lore. The foliage was a main ingredient in an old mad-dog bite remedy, and boxwood hedges were traditionally planted around graves to keep the spirits from wandering.

B. microphylla var. *koreana* 'Wintergreen' (center)

'Green Velvet'

Buckeye
Horsechestnut
Aesculus

Features: late-spring to mid-summer flowers, foliage, spiny fruit **Habit:** rounded or spreading, deciduous tree **Height:** 8–80' **Spread:** 8–70' **Planting:** B & B, container; spring or fall **Zones:** 3–9

AT OVER 6'3" TALL AND COMPLETELY BALD, A FORMER OHIO STATE alumni director used to introduce himself as a true buckeye, 'a worthless hairless nut.' I often wonder why the Ohio buckeye was chosen as our state tree, but for gardeners there are many choices in the genus. One of the best understory trees we have for shade is the bottlebrush buckeye. It grows 8–12' tall and spreads widely to consume space as provided. In good light, its white flowers look like Fourth of July rockets taking off. Red buckeye is a nice, refined small tree, and yellow buckeye is an admirable large tree to consider because of its interesting bark. All have spectacular flowers.

Growing

Buckeyes grow well in **full sun** or **partial shade**. *A. pavia* is an understory plant that tolerates partial and light shade. The soil should be **fertile, moist** and **well drained**.

These trees dislike excessive drought. Little pruning is required. Remove wayward branches in winter or early spring.

A. hippocastanum (above & below), *A. glabra* (center)

Tips

The tree-sized *Aesculus* species and hybrids are best suited to large gardens as specimen and shade trees. Their roots can break up sidewalks and patios if planted too close. These trees give heavy shade, excellent for cooling buildings but difficult to grow grass beneath. Use a shade-loving groundcover instead of grass.

All parts of buckeyes, especially the seeds, are toxic. People have been poisoned when they confused the nuts of Aesculus *species with edible sweet chestnuts (from* Castanea *species).*

The smaller, shrubbier buckeyes are useful in a space-restricted setting, where they can be used as specimens, in shrub or mixed borders or in mass plantings to fill unused corners or cover hard-to-mow banks.

Recommended

A. x *carnea* (red horsechestnut) is a dense, rounded to spreading tree. It grows 30–70' tall, with a spread of 30–50'. It is smaller than *A. hippocastanum* but needs more regular water in summer. Spikes of dark pink flowers are borne in late spring and early summer. (Zones 4–8)

A. flava (*A. octandra*; yellow buckeye) is an upright tree with a conical to oval or spreading habit. It grows 50–80' tall and spreads 30–50'. The mature bark forms large, plate-like

A. x carnea cultivar

Buckeye flowers attract hummingbirds to the garden. Though the nuts are poisonous to people, squirrels enjoy them with no apparent harm.

A. hippocastanum

scales in shades of gray and brown. Spikes of yellow flowers are borne in mid- to late spring, followed by smooth-skinned capsules. The leaves may turn orange in fall. (Zones 3–8)

A. glabra (Ohio buckeye) is the state tree of Ohio. This dense, rounded species grows 20–50' tall and spreads 20–40'. Spikes of greenish yellow flowers are borne in mid- to late spring but are often somewhat hidden by the foliage. The capsules are somewhat spiny. This species often suffers from leaf scorch in drought conditions and is, unfortunately, often defoliated early in fall by a leaf spot disease. (Zones 3–7)

A. hippocastanum (common horsechestnut) is a large, rounded tree that branches right to the ground if grown in an open setting. It grows 50–80' tall and spreads 40–70'. The flowers, borne in spikes up to 12" long, appear in late spring; they are white with yellow or pink marks. '**Baumannii**' bears spikes of white double flowers and produces no capsules. (Zones 3–7)

A. parviflora (bottlebrush buckeye) is a spreading, mound-forming, suckering shrub 8–12' tall and 8–15' wide. It becomes covered with spikes of creamy white flowers in mid-summer. This species is not prone to any of the pest and disease problems that plague its larger cousins. (Zones 4–9)

A. parviflora (above)

A. pavia (red buckeye, damask horsechestnut) forms a large shrub or small tree 10–20' tall, with an equal or greater spread. It bears spikes of red or pinkish red flowers in late spring or early summer. (Zones 4–8)

Problems & Pests

Buckeyes are most susceptible to disease when under stress. Scale insects, anthracnose, canker, leaf scorch, leaf spot, powdery mildew and rust can all cause problems.

A. x *carnea* (center), *A. hippocastanum* (below)

Butterfly Bush
Summer Lilac
Buddleia (Buddleja)

Features: flowers, habit, foliage **Habit:** large deciduous shrub or small tree with arching branches **Height:** 4–20' **Spread:** 4–20' **Planting:** container; spring or summer **Zones:** 5–9

EVERY SPRING I WAIT AND WAIT FOR MY orange-eye butterfly bush to emerge from its sleep through the winter doldrums. On the odd occasion, I have even offered a short prayer when it's exceptionally late. But by late April, I am usually rewarded by little shoots emerging from deep in the ground. Never fear that you won't get copious blooms, because this plant grows like the proverbial beanstalk and flowers on new growth. Unfortunately, butterfly bushes can be so cantankerous and late to sprout in Ohio that I am certain many have been dug up and disposed of alive. What a shame!

Growing
Butterfly bushes prefer to grow in **full sun**. Plants grown in shady conditions will produce few, if any, flowers. The soil should be **average to fertile** and **well drained**. These shrubs are quite drought tolerant once established.

Alternate-leaf butterfly bush forms flowers on the previous year's growth. Prune once flowering is finished in mid-summer. This species may require a sheltered location to prevent winter dieback.

Orange-eye butterfly bush forms flowers on the current year's growth. Early each spring cut the shrub back to within 6–12" of the ground to encourage new growth and plenty of flowers. Deadheading will encourage new shoots, extend the blooming period and prevent self-seeding.

B. davidii (both photos)

Tips

These plants make beautiful additions to shrub and mixed borders. The graceful, arching branches make them excellent specimen plants as well. Dwarf forms that stay under 5' are suitable for small gardens.

Recommended

B. alternifolia (alternate-leaf butterfly bush) is a large shrub or small tree with long, slender, arching branches and narrow gray-green leaves. It grows 10–20' tall, with an equal spread. Clusters of small, light purple flowers appear in early summer. (Zones 5–7)

B. davidii (orange-eye butterfly bush, summer lilac) is the most commonly grown species. It grows 4–10' tall, with an equal spread. This plant has a long bloom, bearing flowers in bright and pastel shades of purple, white, pink or blue from mid-summer to fall. A few popular cultivars are '**Black Knight**,' with dark purple flowers; '**Ellen's Blue**,' with dark blue flowers; '**Pink Delight**,'

with pink flowers; and '**White Profusion**,' with fragrant white flowers. (Zones 5–9)

Problems & Pests

Many insects are attracted to butterfly bushes, but most come just for the pollen. Spider mites can cause trouble occasionally. Good air circulation helps keep spider mites at bay and helps prevent the fungal problems that might otherwise afflict these plants.

Caryopteris
Bluebeard, Blue Spirea
Caryopteris

Features: flowers, foliage, scent **Habit:** rounded, spreading deciduous shrub
Height: 2–4' **Spread:** 2–5' **Planting:** container; spring or fall **Zones:** 5–9

CARYOPTERIS IS A VARIABLE GROWER IN OHIO. IT CAN THRIVE FOR several years in well-drained soil, only to suffer winterkill in an extra cold winter or fall prey to another, more mysterious malady. Still, one long, hedge-like planting in central Ohio has been doing well for several years in a completely open, windswept area, providing a screen between an active roadway and a series of ball fields. In the southern 60% of the state, following the hardiness zones map, I consider caryopteris a shrub. In the north, it behaves as more of a herbaceous perennial. Either way, this fall bloomer flowers on new wood and is spectacular.

Growing
Caryopteris prefers **full sun** but tolerates light shade. It does best in soil of **average fertility** that is **light** and **well drained**. Wet and poorly drained soils can kill this plant. Caryopteris is very drought tolerant once it is established.

Caryopteris is cultivated for its aromatic stems, foliage and flowers. A few cut stems in a vase will delicately scent a room.

Pruning this shrub is easy. It flowers in late summer, so each spring cut the plant back to within 2–6" of the ground. Flowers will form on the new growth that emerges. Deadheading or lightly shearing once the flowers begin to fade may encourage more flowering. This plant can be treated as a herbaceous perennial if it is killed back each winter.

Tips

Include caryopteris in your shrub or mixed border. The bright blue, late-season flowers are welcome when many other plants are past their flowering best.

Recommended

C. x *clandonensis* forms a dense mound up to 36" tall and 3–5' in spread. It bears clusters of blue or purple flowers in late summer and early fall. The cultivars are grown more often than *C.* x *clandonensis*. To find cultivars other than 'Blue Mist' and 'Longwood Blue,' you may have to contact a specialty grower. **'Blue Mist'** has fragrant, light blue flowers. It is a low-growing, mounding plant, rarely exceeding 24" in height and spread. **'First Choice'** is

'Blue Mist' (above), 'Worcester Gold' (below)

a compact, early-flowering cultivar with dark blue flowers. **GRAND BLEU** ('Inoveris') is a compact cultivar that matures to about 30" tall and wide. It has glossy green foliage and dark violet blue flowers. **'Longwood Blue'** is a large, mound-forming cultivar that grows to about 4' in height and spread. It has light purple-blue flowers and gray-green foliage. **'Worcester Gold'** has bright yellow-green foliage that contrasts vividly with the violet blue flowers. It grows about 36" tall, with an equal spread. This cultivar is often treated as a herbaceous perennial because the growth may be killed back in winter. New growth will sprout from the base in spring.

Cherry
Plum, Almond
Prunus

Features: spring to early-summer flowers, fruit, bark, fall foliage **Habit:** upright, rounded, spreading or weeping, deciduous tree or shrub **Height:** 4–75'
Spread: 4–50' **Planting:** bare-root, B & B, container; spring **Zones:** 2–9

THE GENUS *PRUNUS* IS RICH IN BEAUTIFUL SHRUBS AND TREES. Some are susceptible to various pest and disease problems, which can decrease the tree's life span significantly. I don't feel, however, that a plant has to last forever. After 40-plus years, I have become a little hardened. I recommend such plants not be used as focal points, so that with their loss, the entire landscape doesn't lose balance or form. I also suggest starting a tree fund, to be built up over time, so you can afford to put in the largest reasonable replacement upon the anticipated loss. Alternatively, choose species and cultivars that are less prone to problems, saving your admiration of *Prunus* for those with the best odds of survival.

Growing

These flowering fruit trees prefer **full sun**. The soil should be of **average fertility, moist** and **well drained**. Plant on mounds when possible to encourage drainage. Shallow roots will emerge from the ground if the tree is not getting sufficient water.

Most cherries and their relatives require little or no pruning if grown as individual shrubs or trees. Remove dead or damaged growth as needed and awkward growth in spring, after flowering is finished. Hedges can be trimmed back after flowering is complete. Dwarf flowering almond can be pruned to 3–4" above the ground each year, after flowering is complete.

Tips

Prunus species are beautiful as specimen plants, and many are small enough to be included in almost any garden. Small species and cultivars can also be included in borders or grouped to form informal hedges or barriers. Pissard plum and purple-leaf sand cherry can be trained as formal hedges.

Because of the pest problems that afflict many cherries, they can be rather short-lived. Choose resistant species, such as Sargent cherry or Higan cherry. If you plant a more susceptible species, such as Japanese flowering cherry, enjoy it while it thrives but be prepared to replace it once the problems surface.

The fruits, but not the pits, of *Prunus* species are edible. Too much of the often sour fruit can cause stomachaches.

Pissard plum was one of the first purple-leaved cultivars, introduced into cultivation in 1880.

P. sargentii

Recommended

P. cerasifera 'Atropurpurea' (Pissard plum) is a shrubby, often multi-stemmed tree that grows 20–30' tall, with an equal spread. Light pink flowers emerge before the deep purple foliage and fade to white. The leaves turn dark green as they mature. MT. ST. HELENS ('Frank-threes') originated as a branch sport of 'Newport.' It is fast growing, with large, deep purple leaves that emerge early and hold their color well through summer. Light pink flowers are produced in mid-spring. This cultivar has a rounded habit and grows about 20' tall, with an equal spread. 'Newport' was bred by cross-ing 'Atropurpurea' with *P.* 'Omaha.' 'Newport' is commonly available in Ohio because it is cold hardy and flowers early. (Zones 4–8)

P. x *cistena* (purpleleaf sand cherry, purpleleaf dwarf plum) is a dainty, upright shrub that grows 5–10' high, with an equal or lesser spread. It can be trained to form a small tree in space-restricted gardens. The deep purple leaves keep their color all sea-son. The fragrant white or slightly pink flowers open in mid- to late spring after the leaves have devel-oped. The fruits ripen to purple-black in July. BIG CIS ('Schmidtcis') is a fast-growing cultivar that matures to about 14' tall, with a spread of 12'. It has reddish purple flowers and bears pink flowers in mid- to late spring. (Zones 3–8)

P. glandulosa (dwarf flowering almond) is a scruffy-looking shrub that grows 4–6' in height and width. The beautiful pink or white, single or double flowers completely cover the stems in early spring, before the leaves emerge. Though very attrac-tive when in flower, this species loses much of its appeal once flowering is done. Companion planting with other trees and shrubs will allow it

P. subhirtella 'Pendula'

to fade gracefully into the background as the season wears on. This shrub may spread by suckers; keep an eye open for plants turning up in unexpected and unwanted places. 'Rosea Plena' bears pink double flowers. (Zones 4–8)

P. 'Hally Jolivette' forms a small, bushy tree 15–20' tall, with an equal spread. The light pink double flowers do not open all at once, so the blooming period may last up to three weeks in mid-spring. (Zones 5–7)

P. maackii (Amur chokecherry) is a rounded tree that grows 30–45' tall and spreads 25–45'. It tolerates cold winter weather and does especially well in the northern regions of Ohio. Fragrant, white mid-spring flowers are followed by red fruits that ripen to black. The glossy, peeling bark is a reddish or golden brown and provides interest in the garden all year. (Zones 2–6)

P. sargentii (Sargent cherry) is a rounded or spreading tree that grows 20–70' tall, with a spread of 20–50'. Fragrant light pink or white flowers appear in mid- to late spring, and the fruits ripen to a deep red by mid-summer. The orange fall color and glossy, red-brown bark are very attractive. 'Columnaris' is a narrow, upright cultivar that is suitable for tight spots and small gardens. (Zones 4–9)

P. serrulata (Japanese flowering cherry) is a large tree that grows up to 75' tall, with a spread of up to 50'. It bears white or pink flowers in mid- to late spring. The species is rarely grown in favor of the cultivars.

P. glandulosa 'Rosea Plena'

P. serrulata 'Kwanzan'

planted in such large numbers, it has become susceptible to many problems. These problems may shorten the life of the tree, but for 20 to 25 years it can be a beautiful addition to the garden. (Zones 5–8)

P. x SNOW FOUNTAINS ('Snofozam,' 'Snow Fountain,' 'White Fountain'; snow fountains weeping cherry) is hardier than most flowering cherries. Graceful cascading branches are covered in white double flowers in mid-spring. It grows about 12' tall, with an equal spread. (Zones 3–8)

'Kwanzan' (Kwanzan cherry) is a popular cultivar with drooping clusters of pink double flowers. It is sometimes grafted onto a single trunk, creating a small, vase-shaped tree. Grown on its own roots it becomes a large, spreading tree 30–40' tall, with an equal spread. Because this cultivar has been

P. subhirtella (Higan cherry) is a rounded or spreading tree that grows 20–40' tall and spreads 15–25'. The light pink or white flowers appear in early to mid-spring. The trees are often grafted onto a standard trunk, creating a small weeping tree about 15' tall, with an equal spread. The cultivars are grown more frequently than the species.

P. subhirtella 'Pendula'

'**Autumnalis**' (autumn flowering cherry) bears light pink flowers sporadically in fall and prolifically in mid-spring. It grows up to 25' tall, with an equal spread. '**Pendula**' (weeping Higan cherry) has flowers in many shades of pink, appearing before the leaves in mid-spring. The weeping branches make this tree a cascade of pink when in flower. (Zones 4–8)

P. virginiana (common choke-cherry) is an upright, rounded to columnar tree that grows 20–30' tall and 15–25' in spread. It bears clusters of small white flowers in mid- to late spring. The fruit ripens from red to dark purple. Despite the rather astringent taste, it has been used to make jellies, wine and other fruity concoctions. '**Schubert Select**' ('Canada Red Select') has green foliage that matures to purple over the summer. (Zones 2–8)

P. x yedoensis (Yoshino cherry) is a spreading tree with arching branches. It grows 25–50' tall, with an equal spread. It is covered with clusters of white flowers in early to mid-spring, usually before the leaves emerge. (Zones 5–8)

Problems & Pests
The many possible problems include aphids, borers, caterpillars, leafhoppers, mites, nematodes, scale insects, canker, crown gall, fire blight, powdery mildew and viruses. Root rot can occur in poorly drained soils. Plants grown in stress-free locations often escape problems.

P. x cistena

Many important fruit and nut crops belong to the genus Prunus, *including apricot* (P. armeniaca), *garden plum* (P. domestica), *almond* (P. amygdalus) *and peach and nectarine (both* P. persica).

P. sargentii in fall color

Cotoneaster

Cotoneaster

Features: foliage, early-summer flowers, persistent fruit, variety of forms
Habit: evergreen or deciduous groundcover, shrub or small tree **Height:** 4"–15'
Spread: 4–12' **Planting:** container; spring or fall **Zones:** 4–9

WITH THEIR DIVERSE SIZES, SHAPES, FLOWERS, FRUIT AND FOLIAGE, cotoneasters are so versatile that they border on being overused. There will be one suitable for your particular design needs, whether you desire a 4" high spreader or a 14' small tree. The spread is naturally variable and manageable by pruning. These plants almost beg for occasional renewal and respond well to it, especially when cut back in late winter. Individuals easily stand alone, even as specimens when espaliered or top-grafted. Cotoneasters also work well when grown in masses or blended with other shrubs or evergreens.

The name is pronounced cuh-TONE-ee-aster *rather than* cotton-easter.

Growing

Cotoneasters grow well in **full sun** or **partial shade**. The soil should be of **average fertility** and **well drained**.

Though pruning is rarely required, these plants tolerate even hard pruning. Pruning cotoneaster hedges in mid- to late summer will let you see how much you can trim off while still leaving some of the ornamental fruit in place. Hard pruning will encourage new growth and can rejuvenate plants that are looking worn out.

Tips

Cotoneasters can be included in shrub or mixed borders. Low spreaders make good groundcovers, and shrubby species can be used to form hedges. Larger species are grown as small specimen trees, and some low growers are grafted onto standards and grown as small, weeping trees. All cotoneasters have somewhat shiny to very shiny foliage, an attribute that is useful for highlighting areas in the landscape.

C. horizontalis (above), *C. dammeri* (below)

Although cotoneaster berries are not poisonous, they can cause stomach upset if eaten in large quantities. The foliage may be toxic.

Recommended

C. adpressus (creeping cotoneaster) is a low-growing deciduous species that is used as a groundcover. It grows about 12" high and spreads 4–6'. Red-tinged white flowers are produced in summer, followed by fruit that ripens to red in fall. The foliage turns reddish purple in fall. **Var.** *praecox* is larger than the species, growing to about 36" in height and about 6' in spread. The leaves and fruit are also a bit larger that those of the species. (Zones 4–6)

C. apiculatus (cranberry cotoneaster) is a deciduous species that forms a mound of arching, tangled branches. It grows about 36" high and spreads up to 7'. White flowers are borne in summer. The bright red fruit persists into winter. This species is sometimes available in a tree form. (Zones 4–7)

C. dammeri (bearberry cotoneaster) is evergreen. Its low-growing, arching stems gradually stack up on top of one another as the plant matures. This species grows to 18" in height and spreads to 7'. Small white flowers blanket the stems in early summer, followed by bright red fruit in fall. **'Coral Beauty'** is a groundcover that grows up to 36" tall and spreads 7'. The abundant fruit is bright orange to red. **'Mooncreeper'** ('Moon Creeper') is a low-growing cultivar with large white flowers. (Zones 4–8)

C. divaricatus (spreading cotoneaster) is a bushy, deciduous shrub that grows 5–7' tall and spreads 6–8'. It has slightly pendulous stem tips, and

C. horizontalis

its small leaves give the plant a fine texture. Small pink flowers are produced in late spring. The leaves turn red in fall, and the fruit is dark red. (Zones 4–7)

C. x 'Hessei' is a tidy, low-growing deciduous cultivar with an irregular branching habit. It grows about 18" tall and spreads about 6'. The dark pink, late-spring flowers are followed by fruit that ripens to bright red. The leaves turn burgundy in fall. This cultivar is resistant to spider mites and fire blight. (Zones 4–7)

C. horizontalis (rockspray cotoneaster) is a low-growing deciduous species with a distinctive, attractive herringbone branching pattern. It grows 24–36" tall and spreads 5–8'. Light pink flowers in early summer are followed by red fruit in fall. The leaves turn bright red in fall. (Zones 5–9)

C. salicifolius (willowleaf cotoneaster) is an upright evergreen shrub. It can grow up to about 15' tall and spreads about 12'. The clusters of small, white, late-spring flowers are often hidden by the leaves. The bright red fruit often persists through the winter. 'Scarlet Leader' is a low, mounding groundcover. It grows 4–24" tall and spreads 6–8'. This cultivar grows quickly and produces plentiful red fruit. (Zones 5–8)

Problems & Pests
These plants are generally problem free, but occasional attacks of lace bugs, scale insects, slugs, snails, spider mites, canker, fire blight, powdery mildew and rust are possible.

C. apiculatus (above)

C. salicifolius 'Scarlet Leader'
C. x 'Hessei'

Try a mix of low-growing cotoneasters as a bank planting, or use a shrubby type for foundation plantings.

Crabapple
Malus

Features: spring flowers, late-season and winter fruit, fall foliage, habit, bark
Habit: rounded, mounded or spreading, small to medium deciduous tree
Height: 5–30' **Spread:** 6–30' **Planting:** B & B, container; spring or fall **Zones:** 4–8

I HAVE HEARD WORLD-RENOWNED HORTICULTURAL AUTHORITY
Dr. L.C. Chadwick say that flowering crabapples are, without a doubt, the
very best ornamental trees for the Midwest. The more I have observed them,
the more I agree, especially with current breeding efforts developing scab-
resistant cultivars. Pure white through deep pink flowers; heights between
5' and 30' with similar spreads; tolerance of winter's extreme cold
and summer's baking heat; and yellow through candy
apple red fruit often persisting through the winter—
what more could anyone ask from a tree? Be sure to
properly prune crabapples while they are young to
help them become the unique mature specimens
that are so universally admired.

*Some gardeners use crabapple
fruit to make preserves, cider or
even wine.*

Growing

Crabapples prefer **full sun** but tolerate partial shade. The soil should be of **average to rich fertility, moist** and **well drained**. These trees tolerate damp soil.

One of the best ways to prevent the spread of crabapple pests and diseases is to clean up all the leaves and fruit that fall off the tree. Many pests overwinter in the fruit, leaves or soil at the base of the tree. Clearing away their winter shelter helps keep populations under control.

Crabapples require very little pruning but adapt to aggressive pruning. Remove damaged or wayward branches and suckers when necessary. Branches that shoot straight up should be removed because they won't flower as much as horizontal branches. The next year's flower buds form in early summer, so any pruning done to form the shape of the tree should be done by late spring, or as soon as the current year's flowering is finished.

Tips

Crabapples make excellent specimen plants. Many varieties are quite small, so there is one to suit almost any size of garden. Some forms are even small enough to grow in large containers. Crabapples' flexible young branches make them good choices for creating espalier specimens along a wall or fence.

Recommended

The following are just a few suggestions from among the hundreds of crabapples available. When choosing a species, variety or cultivar, one

of the most important attributes to look for is disease resistance. Even the most beautiful flowers, fruit or habit will never look good if the plant is ravaged by pests or diseases. Ask for information about new, resistant cultivars at your local nursery or garden center.

Five of the following crabapples are marked with an asterisk (*). These are recommended by the Ohio Nursery and Landscape Association for their disease resistance and excellent performance in Ohio. All of the following crabapples flower in mid- to late spring, unless otherwise noted.

*M. 'Adirondack' resists all diseases. It is an upright oval tree that grows about 10' tall and spreads about 6'. Red buds open to red-tinged white flowers. The fruit is red or orange. (Zones 4–8)

M. 'Bob White' is resistant to scab and fairly resistant to fire blight. It is a dense, rounded tree that grows about 20' tall, with an equal spread. Red buds open to white petals. The persistent yellow fruit turns red after a heavy frost and attracts birds to the garden for as long as the fruit lasts. (Zones 4–8)

M. CENTURION ('Centzam') is highly resistant to all diseases. This upright tree becomes rounded as it matures. It grows to 25' in height, with a spread of 20'. Dark pink flowers appear in late spring. The bright red fruit persists for a long time. (Zones 5–8)

M. CORALBURST ('Coralcole') is disease resistant. This crabapple has a rounded habit and can be grown as a small tree or large shrub 8–15' tall, with an equal spread. Red buds open to coral pink semi-double flowers.

This cultivar produces some, but not a lot, of orange fruit. (Zones 4–8)

M. floribunda (Japanese flowering crabapple, showy crabapple) is a medium-sized, densely crowned, spreading tree. It grows up to 30' in both height and width. This species is fairly resistant to crabapple problems. Pink buds open to pale pink flowers. The apples are small and yellow. (Zones 4–8)

M. **HARVEST GOLD** ('Hargozam') is highly disease resistant. It has an upright spreading to rounded habit, grows 20–25' tall and spreads 15–25'. The pink buds open to white flowers, followed by yellow fruit that persists into early winter. (Zones 4–8)

M.* **HOLIDAY GOLD ('Hozam') is disease resistant. This rounded tree grows 15–18' tall, with an equal spread. It bears white flowers followed by golden yellow fruit that matures in September and persists through to March for an exciting and long-lasting show. (Zones 4–8)

An espalier specimen

M. **'Indian Magic'** is somewhat susceptible to scab. This rounded tree grows 15–20' tall, with an equal spread. The red buds open to pink flowers and are followed by red fruit that turns orange. (Zones 4–8)

M.* **'Louisa' is generally disease resistant but may be afflicted by scab. This tree has a weeping habit, growing 12–15' tall, with an equal spread. Both buds and flowers are pink. The yellow fruit persists. (Zones 4–8)

Though crabapples are usually grown as trees, their excellent response to training makes them good candidates for bonsai and espalier.

M. MADONNA ('Mazam') is fairly resistant to disease. This tree has an upright form, growing about 20' tall and spreading 10'. The pink buds open to long-lasting white double flowers. The yellow fruit is flushed with red. (Zones 4–8)

**M.* 'Prairifire' ('Prairie Fire') is very disease resistant. This rounded tree grows about 20' tall, with an equal spread. The new leaves have a reddish tinge but mature to dark green. The red buds and flowers are followed by persistent dark red fruit. (Zones 4–8)

M. 'Red Jade' is somewhat disease resistant. This small, weeping cultivar grows 10–15' tall, with an equal spread. The pink buds open to white flowers and are followed by glossy red fruit. This cultivar tends to flower best in alternate years. (Zones 4–8)

M. sargentii (Sargent crabapple) is a small, mounding tree that is fairly

resistant to disease. It grows 6–10' tall and spreads 8–15'. In late spring, red buds open to white flowers. The dark red fruit is long lasting. The cultivar '**Candymint**' has a horizontal spreading to somewhat weeping form, growing 8–10' tall and spreading 10–15'. Deep pink or red buds open to red-edged pink flowers. The fruit is purple. The foliage has a purple tinge and turns purple in fall. The bark is an attractive reddish brown. '**Tina**' is almost identical to the species, except that it grows only 5' tall and spreads up to 10'. With a bit of pruning to control the spread, this cultivar makes an interesting specimen for a large container on a balcony or patio. (Zones 4–8)

M. '**Sentinel**' is somewhat resistant to disease. It has an upright, fairly columnar habit, growing 15–20' tall and about 10' wide. Both buds and flowers are pink, and the fruit is red and persistent. (Zones 4–8)

M. '**Snowdrift**' is a dense, quick-growing, rounded tree that is somewhat susceptible to disease. It grows 15–20' tall, with an equal spread. Red buds open to white flowers in late spring or early summer. The foliage is dark green and the fruit is bright orange. (Zones 5–8)

M. '**Spring Snow**' is susceptible to scab but is somewhat resistant to other diseases. This upright, rounded tree grows 20–25' tall and spreads 15–20'. It bears white double flowers and has the advantage, for those who resent cleaning up after their trees, of bearing very little to no fruit. (Zones 4–8)

*M. SUGAR TYME ('Sutyzam') is very disease resistant. This upright tree grows about 18' tall and spreads about 15'. The buds are pale pink and the flowers are white. The bright red fruit persists through winter. (Zones 4–8)

M. SUGAR TYME (center)

M. 'White Angel' is not as disease resistant as some of the other selections but is admired for its masses of white flowers and red fruit. The habit is rounded, but the branches often bend down with the weight of the fruit. This cultivar grows about 20' tall, with an equal spread. (Zones 4–8)

M. 'Winter Gold' is somewhat susceptible to disease. This rounded tree grows 20–25' tall, with an equal spread. Reddish pink buds open to white flowers. The yellow fruit persists into winter. (Zones 4–8)

M. 'Snowdrift' (below)

M. zumi 'Calocarpa' (M. sieboldii var. zumi 'Calocarpa') is fairly disease resistant. This dense, rounded tree grows 20–25' tall, with an equal spread. Red buds open to fragrant white or pink flowers. The red fruit persists into early winter. (Zones 4–8)

Problems & Pests
Aphids, leaf rollers, leaf skeletonizers, scale insects and tent caterpillars are insect pests to watch for, though the damage they cause is largely cosmetic. Leaf drop caused by apple scab is the most common problem with susceptible cultivars. Cedar-apple rust, fire blight, leaf spot and powdery mildew can also be problematic, depending on the weather.

Dawn Redwood

Metasequoia

Features: foliage, bark, cones, buttressed trunk **Habit:** narrow, conical, deciduous conifer **Height:** 70–125' **Spread:** 15–25' **Planting:** bare-root, B & B, container; spring or fall **Zones:** 4–8

WHAT A LONG HISTORY THIS TREE HAS IN NORTH AMERICA! FOSSIL dating shows that millions of years ago it was native to our continent as well as to Asia. It was thought to be extinct until the 1940s, when it was rediscovered in China and reintroduced to us. In the ensuing 60-plus years, it has proven itself most worthy of our use. Based on the sizes I have seen this species attain in fairly short periods, I reserve it for large sites, or for areas where smaller temporary plants can be removed once this forest giant needs more space. Dawn redwood's beauty is enhanced when the bottom branches are left in place to encourage the interesting buttress flares to develop.

Growing

Dawn redwood grows well in **full
sun** or **light shade.** The soil should
be **humus rich,** slightly **acidic, moist**
and **well drained.** Wet or dry soils
are generally tolerated, though the
rate of growth will be reduced in
dry conditions. This tree likes
humid conditions and should be
mulched and watered regularly until
it is established.

Pruning is not necessary. The lower
branches must be left in place in
order for the buttressing to develop.
Buttressed trunks are flared and
grooved, and the branches appear to
grow from deep inside the grooves.

M. glyptostroboides (above), cultivar (below)

Tips

This large tree needs plenty of room
to grow. Larger gardens and parks
can best accommodate it. As a single
specimen or in a group planting,
dawn redwood looks attractive and
impressive.

Recommended

M. glyptostroboides has a pyramidal,
sometimes spire-like form. The tree's
needles turn gold or orange in fall
before dropping. Cultivars do not
differ significantly from the species.

Problems & Pests

Dawn redwood is not generally
prone to pest problems, although it
can be killed by canker infections.

*This tree looks like a large
evergreen—until fall. Then the
leaves turn color and drop, proving
that dawn redwood is actually a
deciduous conifer.*

Deutzia
Deutzia

Features: early-summer flowers **Habit:** bushy, deciduous shrub **Height:** 2–8'
Spread: 3–8' or more **Planting:** container; spring to fall **Zones:** 4–9

DEUTZIAS ARE PLANTS THAT I HAVE PUT TO SOME RUGGED USES.
They definitely bloom best in full sun, but I have had them growing under
Austrian pines for the last dozen or so years with a very adequate flower display in mid-May. *D. gracilis* is a lovely small shrub for a mid-border to background planting or as a small, easily managed, informal hedge. The fine texture
makes a beautiful contrast to many larger shrubs. Even if the larger plants are
left unchecked, they won't intimidate this tenacious little beauty. I have also
become fond of the shorter cultivar 'Nikko' because of its compact growth.

Growing
Deutzias grow best in **full sun**. They tolerate light shade but may not bear
as many flowers. The soil should be of **average to high fertility, moist** and
well drained.

These shrubs bloom on the previous year's growth. After the bloom, cut flowering stems back to strong buds, main stems or basal growth as needed to shape the plant. Remove one-third of the old growth on established plants at ground level to encourage new growth.

Tips

Include deutzias in shrub or mixed borders or in rock gardens. You can also use them as specimen plants.

D. x *elegantissima* 'Rosealind'

Recommended

D. x *elegantissima* (elegant deutzia) is an upright shrub with a rounded habit. It grows 4–6' tall, spreads about 5' and bears clusters of pinkish white flowers in early summer. **'Rosealind'** ('Rosalind') bears darker pink flowers. (Zones 5–8)

D. gracilis (slender deutzia) is a low-growing, mounding species hardy in Zones 5–8. It grows 2–4' high, with a spread of 3–7'. In late spring the plant is completely covered with white flowers. **'Nikko'** has white double flowers, and its foliage turns purple in fall. This compact cultivar grows about 24" tall and spreads about 5'. It is hardier than the species, to Zone 4.

D. x *hybrida* **'Magician'** ('Magicien') is a large, arching shrub hardy to Zone 5. It grows 6–8' tall, with an equal or greater spread. The pink-and-white-streaked flowers are borne in loose clusters in early to mid-summer.

D. x *lemoinei* is a dense, rounded, upright hybrid 5–7' tall, with an equal spread. The early-summer

blooms are white. **'Avalanche'** is a dense, compact plant that grows about 4' tall, with an equal spread. The flowers are borne in clusters on the arching branches. **'Compacta'** ('Boule de Neige') also has denser, more compact growth than *D.* x *lemoinei*. It bears large clusters of white flowers. (Zones 5–9)

Problems & Pests

Problems are rare, though these plants can have trouble with aphids, leaf miners and fungal leaf spot.

D. x *lemoinei* 'Compacta'

Dogwood
Cornus

Features: late-spring to early-summer flowers, fall foliage, fruit, stem color, habit
Habit: deciduous large shrub or small tree **Height:** 5–30' **Spread:** 5–30'
Planting: B & B, container; spring to summer **Zones:** 2–9

IT HAS ALWAYS AMAZED AND DISAPPOINTED ME THAT SO OFTEN
people think of only the common flowering dogwood *(C. florida)* when dogwoods are mentioned. This is an amazingly versatile group of plants. Flowering dogwood is the only fickle one in the bunch; the two-thirds of Ohioans
on alkaline clay soil have to fuss, cuss or even pray to cajole it into growth.
All the rest of these plants are easy to live with and almost beg for more frequent use. Stem color, leaf variegation, fall color, growth habit, soil adaptability and hardiness are all positive attributes to be found in the dogwoods.

*Ornamental dogwoods fall
into two main categories: the
tree dogwoods (including*
C. florida *and* C. kousa),
*with large, showy blooms;
and the shrubby dogwoods
(including* C. alba *and*
C. sericea), *grown mainly
for their colorful stems.*

Growing

The tree-sized dogwoods grow well in **light shade** or **partial shade**. Shrub dogwoods prefer **full sun** or **partial shade**, with the best stem colors developing in full sun. For most dogwoods of both types, the soil should be of **average to high fertility,** rich in **organic matter, neutral to slightly acidic** and **well drained**. *C. mas* grows well in slightly alkaline soils. Shrub dogwoods adapt to most soils but prefer moist soil. *C. sericea* tolerates wet soil.

C. sericea (above)

Tree dogwoods and *C. drummondii* require very little pruning. Simply removing damaged, dead or awkward branches in early spring is sufficient.

The shrubby *C. alba* and *C. sericea,* which are grown for the colorful stems that are so striking in winter, require ongoing rejuvenation pruning because the color is best on young growth. There are two ways to encourage new growth. A drastic, but effective, method is to cut back all stems to within a couple of buds of the ground, in early spring. To make up for the loss of top growth, feed the plant once it starts growing. The second, less drastic, method is to cut back about one-third of the old growth to within a couple of buds of the ground, in early spring. This procedure leaves most of the growth in place, and branches can be removed as they age and lose their color.

C. florida 'Cherokee Chief'

C. kousa var. *chinensis*

Tips

The tree species make wonderful specimen plants and are small enough to include in most gardens. Use them along the edge of a woodland garden, in a shrub or mixed border, alongside a house, or near a pond, water feature or patio. Shrub dogwoods can be included in any shrub or mixed border. They look best in groups rather than as single specimens.

Recommended

C. alba (Tatarian dogwood, red-twig dogwood) is a shrub dogwood grown for the bright red stems that provide winter interest. The stems are green all summer, turning red as winter approaches. This species can grow 5–10' tall, with an equal spread. It prefers cool climates and can develop leaf scorch and canker problems if the weather gets very hot. **'Argenteo-marginata'** ('Elegantissima') has gray-green leaves with cream margins. **'Sibirica'** (Siberian dogwood) has pinkish red to bright red winter stems. (Zones 2–7)

C. x **CONSTELLATION** ('Rutcan') is an upright to somewhat spreading tree dogwood that grows 15–25' tall and spreads 15–20'. This hybrid was developed through crosses between *C. kousa* and *C. florida*. It is fast growing and resistant to anthracnose and borers. The white blossoms are borne in late spring and early summer, and the leaves become reddish in fall. (Zones 5–9)

C. drummondii (*C. asperifolia* var. *drummondii*; giant gray dogwood, roughleaf dogwood, swamp dogwood) forms a tall shrub or small tree 15–20' tall, with a similar spread. It suckers minimally. Small white flowers appear in late spring, followed in fall by white fruit that persists into winter. This native species is good for natural plantings as well as massed and border plantings. (Zones 4–8)

C. florida (flowering dogwood) is native to the eastern and south-central U.S. It is usually grown as a small tree 20–30' tall, with an equal or greater spread. It features horizontally layered branches and late-spring flowers with showy pink or white bracts. **'Apple Blossom'** has light pink bracts with white at the bases. **'Cherokee Chief'** has dark pink bracts. **Var.** *rubra* has light pink bracts. **'Spring Song'** has rose pink bracts. This species and its cultivars are susceptible to blight. (Zones 5–9)

C. kousa (Kousa dogwood) is grown for its flowers, fruit, fall color and interesting bark. This tree dogwood grows 20–30' tall and spreads 15–30'. It is more resistant to leaf blight and other problems than *C. florida*. The white-bracted, early-summer flowers are followed by bright red fruit. The foliage turns red and purple in fall. **Var.** *chinensis* (Chinese dogwood) grows more vigorously and has larger flowers. (Zones 5–9)

C. mas (Cornelian cherry dogwood) makes an excellent understory tree or stand-alone specimen. It grows to about 20' in height, with an equal spread, and bears yellow blooms even before forsythias begin flowering. The bright cherry red, edible fruit forms in early fall and attracts birds. (Zones 4–8)

C. sericea (*C. stolonifera;* red-twig dogwood, red-osier dogwood) is a widespread, vigorous native shrub with bright red stems. It grows about 6' tall, spreads up to 12' and bears clusters of small white flowers in early summer. The fall color is red or orange. '**Cardinal**' has pinkish red stems that become bright red in winter. '**Flaviramea**' (yellow-twig dogwood) has bright yellow-green stems. '**Silver and Gold**' has yellow-green stems and excellent green and white variegation on the leaves. (Zones 2–8)

C. sericea 'Cardinal'

C. x **STELLAR PINK** ('Rutgan') is a tree dogwood with an attractive rounded habit. It grows 15–25' tall, with an equal spread. The late-spring or early-summer flowers have pale pink bracts with darker pink veins. The leaves become pinkish to red in fall. This cultivar resists borers and anthracnose. (Zones 5–8)

The showy parts of tree dogwood blooms are actually bracts, not petals; the true flowers are small and clustered in the center of the four bracts.

Problems & Pests

The many possible problems for dogwoods include aphids, borers, leafhoppers, nematodes, scale insects, thrips, weevils, anthracnose, blight, canker, leaf spot, powdery mildew and root rot.

C. kousa (below), *C. florida* cultivar (center)

Elder
Elderberry
Sambucus

Features: early-summer flowers, fruit, foliage **Habit:** large, bushy, deciduous shrub
Height: 5–15' **Spread:** 5–15' **Planting:** bare-root, container; spring or fall
Zones: 3–9

ANY PLANT ROBUST ENOUGH TO SPROUT FROM SEED IN GRAVEL BY railroad tracks and then grow to a full-sized flowering shrub, as I have seen elders do, should be given significant notice. Elders should be grown more often in Ohio as large, tough shrubs for some of our hard-to-handle landscape spots. They are especially good in damp patches and naturalized areas where care and maintenance will be minimal. Cultivars are available that will provide light texture in a dark area, dark foliage in a bright area, or variegated yellow foliage and bright stems in brilliant sunshine.

Growing

Elders do well in **full sun** or **partial shade**. Cultivars grown for burgundy or black leaf color develop the best color in full sun; cultivars with yellow leaf color develop the best color in light or partial shade. The soil should be of **average fertility, moist** and **well drained**. These plants tolerate dry soil once established.

S. racemosa (both photos)

Elder fruit attracts birds to the garden and can be used to make wine or jelly.

Though elders do not require pruning, they can become scraggly and untidy if ignored. These shrubs will tolerate even severe pruning. Plants can be cut back to within a couple of buds of the ground in early spring. This treatment controls the spread of these vigorous growers and encourages the best foliage color on specimens grown for this purpose.

Plants cut right back to the ground will not flower or produce fruit that season. If you desire flowers and fruit as well as good foliage color, remove only one-third to one-half of the growth in early spring. Fertilize or apply a layer of compost after pruning to encourage strong new growth.

Tips

Elders can be used in a shrub or mixed border, in a natural woodland garden or next to a pond or other water feature. Plants with interesting or colorful foliage can be used as specimen plants or to create focal points in the garden.

Both the flowers and the fruit can be used to make wine. The berries are popular for pies and jelly. The raw berries are marginally edible but not palatable and can cause stomach

S. nigra 'Madonna'
S. nigra 'Pulverulenta'

upset, particularly in children. Cooking the berries before eating them is recommended. Try them in place of blueberries in pies, scones or muffins.

All other parts of elders are toxic.

Recommended

S. canadensis (*S. nigra* subsp. *canadensis;* American elderberry) is a shrub about 12' tall, with an equal spread. White flowers in mid-summer are followed by dark purple berries. Native to much of the U.S., this species is generally found growing in damp ditches and alongside rivers and streams. '**Laciniata**' has lacy foliage that gives the plant a fern-like appearance. This cultivar grows 8–10' tall, with an equal spread. (Zones 4–9)

S. nigra (*S. nigra* subsp. *nigra;* European elderberry, black elderberry) is a large shrub that can grow 15' tall, with an equal spread. The early-summer flowers are followed by purple-black fruit. **BLACK BEAUTY** ('Gerda') has dark foliage that gets blacker as the season progresses. It grows 8–12' tall, with an equal spread. '**Laciniata**' has deeply dissected leaflets that give the shrub a feathery appearance. It grows up to 10' tall. '**Madonna**' has dark green foliage with wide, irregular, yellow margins. '**Marginata**' has creamy white margins around the leaves. '**Pulverulenta**' has unusually dark green and white mottled foliage. It grows slower than other cultivars but reaches 10'. (Zones 4–8)

S. pubens (scarlet elder) is a large shrub or small tree that grows 10–25' tall, with an equal spread. It bears clusters of small, creamy white flowers in mid- to late spring. The fruit ripens to red in summer. (Zones 4–6)

S. racemosa (red elderberry, European red elderberry) grows 8–12' tall, with an equal spread. This shrub bears pyramidal clusters of white flowers in spring, followed by bright red fruit. **'Sutherland Gold'** ('Sutherland Golden') has deeply cut, yellow-green foliage. It grows 5–10' tall. (Zones 3–7)

Problems & Pests
Borers, canker, dieback, leaf spot and powdery mildew may occasionally affect elders.

S. nigra BLACK BEAUTY

These versatile shrubs can be cut back hard each year or trained into a small tree form.

S. nigra cultivar

Euonymus
Euonymus

Features: foliage, habit, corky stems *(E. alatus)* **Habit:** deciduous or evergreen shrub, small tree, groundcover or climber **Height:** 18"–20' **Spread:** 18"–20'
Planting: B & B, container; spring or fall **Zones:** 3–9

EUONYMUS IS A LARGE GENUS THAT INCLUDES SEVERAL SPECIES of unusually good character. So dependable are the dwarf burning bush types that they are almost overused. The species *(E. alatus)* works well as a background or border plant for stunning fall color and interesting bark, and it also makes a fine specimen as a small tree. The evergreen types (*E. fortunei* and cultivars), with their interesting leaf colorings and plant habits, also have many uses. I have planted several variegated forms at the base of small trees. They meander up the trunks and out along the branches to create four-season interest. I have also grown an espaliered 'Vegetus' on the back of my house to break up the plain stucco walls.

Growing

Euonymus prefer **full sun** but tolerate light or partial shade. Soil that is of **average to rich fertility** is preferable, but any **moist, well-drained** soil will suit these plants.

Burning bush and its cultivars require very little pruning except to remove dead, damaged or awkward growth as needed. They tolerate severe pruning and can be used to form hedges.

Wintercreeper euonymus is a vigorous, spreading evergreen that can be trimmed as required to keep it in the desired growing area; it too tolerates severe pruning. It is also easy to propagate. Bend a branch to the ground, bury the middle section under a bit of soil and hold it down with a rock. Cut this branch off once roots have formed and plant it where you wish.

E. alatus (both photos)

E. alatus *achieves the best fall color when grown in full sun.*

Tips

Burning bush adds season-long color in a shrub or mixed border, as a specimen, in a naturalistic garden or as a hedge. Dwarf cultivars can be used to create informal hedges.

Wintercreeper euonymus can be grown as a low shrub in borders or as a hedge. It is a reasonable substitute for boxwood. Its trailing habit also makes it suitable as a groundcover or climber.

The name Euonymus *translates as 'of good name'—rather ironically, given that all parts of these plants are poisonous and can cause severe stomach upset.*

E. alatus FIRE BALL
E. fortunei BLONDY

Recommended

E. alatus (burning bush, winged euonymus) is an attractive, open, mounding, deciduous shrub. It grows 15–20' tall, with an equal or greater spread. When this shrub is planted in the sun, the foliage turns a vivid red in fall. The small, red fall berries are somewhat obscured by the bright foliage. Winter interest is provided by the corky ridges, or wings, that grow on the stems and branches. This plant is often pruned to form a neat, rounded shrub, but if left to grow naturally it becomes an attractive, wide-spreading, open shrub. **'Compactus'** (dwarf burning bush) is a popular cultivar. It has more dense, compact growth— reaching up to 10' tall and wide— and has less prominently corky ridges on the branches. It may suffer winter damage during unusually cold winters. **FIRE BALL** ('Select') is a hardier selection of 'Compactus' that grows up to 7' tall. It has brilliant red fall color and suffers no winter damage. **'Rudy Haag'** is a dwarf plant with consistent bright red fall color. It grows 3–5' tall. (Zones 3–8)

E. fortunei (wintercreeper euonymus) as a species is rarely grown in favor of the wide and attractive variety of cultivars. These can be prostrate, climbing or mounding broad-leaved evergreens, often with attractive, variegated foliage. **BLONDY** ('Interbolwji') has bright yellow foliage with narrow, irregular dark green margins. It grows 18–24" tall. **Var.** *coloratus* ('Coloratus'; purple leaf wintercreeper) is a popular variety, usually grown as a groundcover. The foliage turns red or purple over the winter. **'Emerald Gaiety'** is a vigorous, shrubby cultivar that grows about 5' tall without support, with an equal or greater spread. It will grow taller with support, sending out long shoots that will attempt to scale any nearby wall. This rambling habit can be encouraged, or the long shoots can be trimmed back to maintain the plant as a shrub. The foliage is bright green with irregular, creamy margins that turn pink in winter. **'Emerald 'n' Gold'** has bright green leaves with yellow margins. It grows 18–24" tall or taller, with an equal spread. **'Gold Tip'** has green leaves with narrow gold margins that mature to creamy white. It grows about 24" tall, with an equal spread. **'Sun Spot'** ('Sunspot') has yellow-centered green leaves. This mound-forming cultivar grows about 36" tall and spreads about 6'. **'Vegetus'** grows up to 5' in height and width. It has large, dark green leaves, and it can be trained up a trellis as a climber or trimmed back to form a shrub. (Zones 5–9)

Problems & Pests
The two worst problems for euonymus are scale insects and crown gall, both of which can prove fatal to the infected plant. Other possible problems include aphids, leaf miners, tent caterpillars, leaf spot and powdery mildew.

E. alatus has become a serious invasive species that is escaping into the wild in the Midwest.

E. alatus

E. fortunei 'Emerald 'n' Gold'

False Cypress
Chamaecyparis

Features: foliage, habit, cones
Habit: narrow, pyramidal evergreen tree or shrub **Height:**
10"–100' **Spread:** 1–55'
Planting: B & B, container;
spring or fall **Zones:** 4–8

FORTY YEARS AGO,
interest in using false
cypresses waned, for reasons
I don't understand. As a
group, they offer color, size,
shape and growth habits
not available in most
other evergreens.
Fortunately, in the
last 10 years, these
plants have been redis-
covered by the public—
to the point of near
overuse in some places. And,
unfortunately, the buyer and/or
seller may not always be aware of the
mature size of what starts out as a cute,
colorful little plant. Gardeners also need
to know that false cypresses demand hand
pruning, if any at all, because shearing
destroys the natural beauty of almost all
species in this genus. I have found that they
thrive with decent drainage, and the more
sun, the better!

*There is room in every garden for at least one
selection from this highly diverse group.*

Growing

False cypresses prefer **full sun**. The soil should be **fertile, moist, neutral to acidic** and **well drained**. Alkaline soils are tolerated. In shaded areas, growth may be sparse or thin.

No pruning is required on tree specimens. Plants grown as hedges can be trimmed any time during the growing season. Avoid severe pruning because new growth will not sprout from old wood. To tidy shrubs, pull dry, brown leaves from the base by hand.

Tips

Tree varieties are used as specimen plants and for hedging. The dwarf and slow-growing cultivars are used in shrub or mixed borders, in rock gardens and as bonsai. False cypress shrubs can be grown near the house.

As with the related arborvitae, oils in the foliage of false cypresses may be irritating to sensitive skin. Wear gloves when handling or pruning.

C. nootkatensis 'Pendula'

In the wild, C. nootkatensis *can grow as tall as 165' and as old as 1800 years.*

C. pisifera 'Vintage Gold'

C. obtusa 'Nana Gracilis'
C. pisifera cultivar

Recommended

C. nootkatensis (yellow-cedar, Nootka false cypress) grows 30–100' tall, with a spread of about 25'. The species is rarely grown in favor of the cultivars. '**Pendula**' has a very open habit and even more pendulous foliage than the species. (Zones 4–8)

C. obtusa (Hinoki false cypress), a native of Japan, has foliage arranged in fan-like sprays. It grows about 70' tall, with a spread of 20'. '**Minima**' is a very dwarf, mounding cultivar. It grows about 10" tall and spreads 16". '**Nana Aurea**' grows 3–6' in height and spread. The foliage is gold-tipped, becoming greener in the shade and bronzy in winter. '**Nana Gracilis**' (dwarf Hinoki false cypress) is a slow-growing cultivar that reaches 24–36" in height, with a slightly greater spread. (Zones 4–7)

C. pisifera (Japanese false cypress, Sawara cypress) is another Japanese native. It grows 70–100' tall and spreads 15–25'. The cultivars are more commonly grown than the species. '**Boulevard**' is a fairly narrow dwarf cultivar with silvery blue foliage. It grows 10–12' tall and spreads 3–5'. '**Filifera Aurea**' (var. *filifera* 'Aurea') (golden thread-leaf false cypress) is a slow-growing cultivar with golden yellow, thread-like foliage. It generally grows about 15–25' tall and spreads 12–20', but it can eventually become larger. '**Nana**' (var. *filifera* 'Nana') (dwarf false cypress) is a dwarf cultivar with feathery foliage similar to that of the species. It grows into a mound about 12" in height and width. '**Plumosa**' (plume false cypress) has very feathery foliage. It grows to about

20–25' tall, with an equal or greater spread. '**Squarrosa**' (moss false cypress) has less pendulous foliage than the other cultivars. Young plants grow very densely, looking like fuzzy stuffed animals. The growth becomes more relaxed and open with maturity. This cultivar grows about 65' tall, with a spread of about 55'. '**Vintage Gold**' is a dwarf cultivar with bright yellow, feathery foliage that resists fading in summer and winter. It grows 18–30" tall. (Zones 4–8)

Problems & Pests
False cypresses are not prone to problems but can occasionally be affected by spruce mites, blight, gall and root rot.

C. *nootkatensis*

Chamaecyparis *comes from the Greek and means 'low cypress,' even though many species are very tall trees.*

C. *obtusa* 'Nana Aurea'

False Spirea
Ural False Spirea
Sorbaria

Features: summer flowers, foliage **Habit:** large, suckering, deciduous shrub
Height: 5–10' **Spread:** 10' or more **Planting:** container; any time **Zones:** 2–8

FOR YEARS I IGNORED THIS PLANT, WITH A COMPLETE LACK OF
respect for its good qualities. I had seen only old, bedraggled plants that had
escaped into unwanted areas and continued to degenerate. But once I saw
false spirea properly used at a large estate under some high-headed old trees
on a 45° slope, I completely changed my tune. The roadways above and
below retained the plants, which had been pruned hard a year and a
half earlier. When I saw it in early July, it was in full fleecy white
bloom and not much else was flowering. What a revelation!
I have been suggesting false spirea for similar sites
ever since.

*False spirea can be useful in
preventing soil erosion on the
steep banks of a ditch.*

Growing

False spirea grows equally well in **full sun, partial shade** or **light shade**. The soil should be of **average fertility, moist, well drained** and high in **organic matter**. This plant tolerates hot, dry conditions.

Pruning false spirea is both easy and important. This suckering shrub can spread almost indefinitely. Use a barrier in the soil to help prevent excessive spread, and remove the suckering shoots whenever they appear in undesirable places. As well, yearly after flowering, remove about one-third of the oldest growth. When needed, rejuvenation pruning can be done in spring as the buds begin to swell. To rejuvenate, cut the entire plant back to within a few buds of the ground.

Tips

Use false spirea in large shrub borders, as barrier plants, in naturalized gardens and in lightly shaded woodland gardens. This plant can be aggressive, but its spread will be most troublesome in smaller gardens. It is ideal for steep roadway cuts.

Remove the faded brown seedheads if you find them unattractive.

Recommended

S. sorbifolia is a large, many-stemmed, suckering shrub. Clusters of many tiny, fluffy, white or cream flowers are produced in mid- or late summer. This shrub is native to Asia and is very cold hardy.

Sorbaria is in the rose family, along with Sorbus *(mountain-ash) and* Spiraea.

Problems & Pests

False spirea has no serious problems but can fall victim to fire blight in stressful conditions.

Filbert
Hazel
Corylus

Features: early-spring catkins, nuts, foliage, habit **Habit:** large, dense, deciduous shrub or small tree **Height:** 8–50' **Spread:** 10–35' **Planting:** B & B, container; spring or fall **Zones:** 4–8

FILBERTS, ALSO KNOWN AS HAZELS, ARE TREES OR LARGE SHRUBS that are rarely overused and usually ignored. These plants' attributes should earn them much greater respect and consideration. The purple giant filbert *(C. maxima* var. *purpurea)* is far more dependable than some other plants in the same size range, and its purple spring foliage is eye-catching. For unique, contorted growth, there is no other plant quite like Harry Lauder's walking stick (*C. avellana* 'Contorta'). I saved one in a relandscaping project with some judicious pruning and shaping, and it later became a prized photographers' background. The drought-tolerant Turkish filbert *(C. colurna)* should be sought out—even demanded—by the new generation of water-conscious buyers.

Though all filberts bear edible nuts, C. avellana *and* C. maxima *are two of the most common commercial species. They are grown for the delicious nuts themselves and for the extracted oil.*

Growing

Filberts grow equally well in **full sun** or **partial shade**. The soil should be **fertile** and **well drained**.

In general, filberts require very little pruning but tolerate it well. Dead, damaged and diseased growth can be removed as needed. Formative pruning and removal of awkward growth should be done in spring before the buds break. On grafted specimens of Harry Lauder's walking stick, suckers that come up from the roots should be cut out at their bases. They will be easy to spot because they won't have the twisted habit. Purple giant filbert can be cut back to within 6" of the ground in late winter to encourage new growth in spring or to control size.

C. avellana 'Contorta' (both photos)

Tips

Use filberts as specimens or in shrub or mixed borders.

Forked filbert branches have been used as divining rods to find underground water or precious metals.

C. maxima var. purpurea

C. avellana 'Contorta'

Recommended

C. avellana (European filbert, European hazel) grows as a large shrub or small tree. It reaches 12–20' in height and spreads up to 15'. Male flowers are borne in long, dangling catkins in late winter and early spring, and female flowers (on the same plant) develop edible nuts. Cultivars are more commonly grown than the species. 'Aurea' (golden European filbert, yellow-leaved European filbert) has bright yellow foliage that matures to light green over the summer. 'Contorta' (Harry Lauder's walking stick, corkscrew filbert, contorted filbert) is perhaps the best known cultivar. It grows 8–10' tall, with an equal or greater spread. The stems and branches are twisted and contorted. This is a particularly interesting feature in winter, when the bare stems are most visible. This cultivar makes an excellent specimen plant. (Zones 4–8)

C. colurna (Turkish filbert, Turkish hazel) is a rounded, pyramidal tree. It grows 40–50' tall, or sometimes

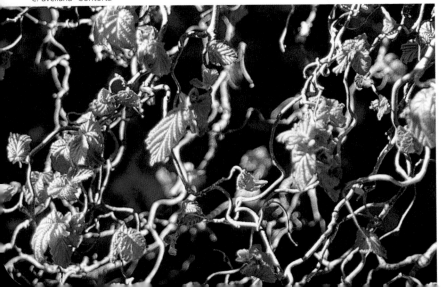

taller, and spreads 15–35'. This tree tolerates heat, cold and drought as long as it is provided with well-drained soil and is watered regularly for the first three years after planting. (Zones 4–7)

C. maxima (giant filbert) is a large shrub or small tree that is rarely seen in cultivation. More common is **var.** *purpurea* ('Purpurea'), the purple giant filbert. It grows 10–20' tall, with an equal spread. This variety adds deep purple leaf color and adapts to many soils. It makes a fine addition to the spring garden. The best leaf color develops in full sun, though the rich color usually fades in the heat of summer to dark green with subtle reddish overtones. (Zones 4–8)

Problems & Pests
Bud mites, Japanese beetle, tent caterpillars, webworm, blight, canker, fungal leaf spot, powdery mildew and rust may cause occasional problems.

C. avellana 'Contorta'

The common name for C. avellana *'Contorta,' Harry Lauder's walking stick, comes from the gnarled, twisted cane the famous vaudeville comedian used.*

C. maxima var. purpurea

Firethorn

Pyracantha

Features: foliage, early-summer flowers, fruit, thorns **Habit:** dense, thorny, evergreen or semi-evergreen shrub **Height:** 6–18' **Spread:** equal to or greater than height **Planting:** container; spring through summer **Zones:** 5–9

MY ENTHUSIASM FOR *PYRACANTHA* HAS ALWAYS BEEN POINTED (pun intended). These plants are beasts to manage, requiring good thick leather gloves and unceasing vigilance. I have always had them on my property because I believe their four-season interest justifies the battle. They offer an informal but trainable growth habit, good flowers in mid-spring to mid-summer, excellent berry color in late fall through mid-winter, and broad-leaved evergreen foliage all winter long. I have espaliered firethorn against weathered wood fences and walls. A client once staked 7' tall iron letters in the ground in front of a white barn. He trained one firethorn plant against each letter to spell his name in white flowers and orange berries—spectacular!

Growing

Firethorns prefer **full sun.** They tolerate partial shade but don't fruit as heavily. The soil should preferably be **rich, moist** and **well drained,** but these shrubs are fairly adaptable to any well-drained soil, and well-established plants tolerate dry soil. **Shelter** plants from strong winds. Firethorns resent being moved once established, and you will resent having to move these very prickly plants.

Some pruning is required to keep these shrubs looking neat. In a naturalized setting, they can be left much to their own devices. Remove any damaged growth or wayward branches, and trim back new growth to better show off the fruit. If using a firethorn in a shrub or mixed border, you will have to prune more severely to prevent it from overgrowing its neighbors. Trim hedges in early summer to mid-summer. Trim espalier and other wall-trained specimens in mid-summer. To extend the framework of the specimen, tie growth in place as needed.

P. coccinea (above), *P. coccinea* cultivar (below)

Firethorn obeys the version of Murphy's Law that states that the more prickly a plant is, the more pruning it will need.

P. coccinea (both photos)

Tips

Despite their potential for rampant growth, firethorns have a wide variety of uses. Their prickles make them useful for formal or informal hedges and barriers. They can be grown as large informal shrubs in naturalized gardens and borders. They can also be used as climbers if tied to a trellis or other support. Firethorns' responsiveness to pruning and dense growth make them ideal espalier specimens.

Recommended

P. angustifolia is a dense, bushy evergreen shrub with narrow leaves. It bears clusters of white flowers in mid-summer, followed by orange or yellow fruit in fall. The fruit often persists into winter. This species grows about 10' tall, with an equal spread. **YUKON BELLE** ('Monon') is a semi-evergreen cultivar that grows 6–10' tall, with an equal spread. The orange fruit persists into winter. (Zones 6–9)

P. coccinea is a large, spiny ever-green shrub 6–18' tall and wide. White flowers cover the plant in early summer, followed by bright orange to scarlet fruit in fall and winter. **'Gnome'** is a hardy, dense, spreading cultivar with orange fruit. It grows about 6' tall and spreads about 8'. **'Kasan'** ('Kazan') is a culti-var from Russia that is hardy to Zone 5. It has a spreading habit, growing up to 10' wide, and bears orange-red fruit. **'Red Column'** is an upright plant that bears bright red fruit. **'Thornless,'** as the name implies, lacks thorns; it is easier to handle but can be more susceptible to fire blight. This cultivar bears red fruit. (Zones 6–9)

Problems & Pests

The worst problems are fire blight and scab. Fire blight can kill the plant, and scab disfigures the fruit, turning it a sooty brown. Choose cultivars that are resistant to blight. A few less serious or less frequent problems are aphids, lace bugs, scale insects, spider mites and root rot.

P. coccinea cultivar (above), *P. coccinea* (below)

The showy fruits of firethorn resemble tiny apples and attract birds to the garden.

Flowering Quince
Chaenomeles

Features: spring flowers, fruit, spines **Habit:** spreading, deciduous shrub with spiny branches **Height:** 2–10' **Spread:** 2–15' **Planting:** B & B, container; spring or fall **Zones:** 5–9

FLOWERING QUINCES HAD FALLEN INTO DISUSE BUT ARE NOW returning to popularity with the introduction of smaller varieties. All of these plants seem able to grow anywhere except very wet and very shady sites. They do require respect and close attention when pruning, but at least the spines don't break off and fester in your flesh. Even so, I would recommend wearing long sleeves and leather gloves. Luckily, pruning is needed only infrequently. Flowering quinces are good plants to cut and force into bloom indoors in late winter. They are sometimes more enjoyable this way because many of the flowers are borne and hidden inside the outer branches.

Growing

Flowering quinces grow equally well in **full sun** or **partial shade** but bear fewer flowers and fruit in shaded locations. The soil should be of **average fertility**, **moist** and **well drained**. Slightly **acidic** soil is preferred. These shrubs tolerate pollution.

On established plants, prune back about one-third of the old growth right to the ground every year or so. Tidy plants by cutting back flowering shoots to a strong branch after flowering is finished.

Tips
Flowering quinces can be included in shrub or mixed borders. They look attractive grown against walls. The spiny habit also makes them useful for barriers. Use them along the edge of a woodland or in naturalistic gardens. The dark bark stands out well in winter.

Leaf drop in mid- to late summer may be caused by leaf spot. Draw attention away from the plant with later-flowering perennials or shrubs.

Recommended
C. japonica (Japanese flowering quince) is a spreading shrub that grows 24–36" tall and spreads up to 6'. Orange or red flowers appear in early to mid-spring, followed by small, fragrant, greenish yellow fruit. This species is not as commonly grown as *C. speciosa* and its cultivars. (Zones 5–9)

C. speciosa (common flowering quince) is a large, tangled, spreading shrub. It grows 6–10' tall and spreads 6–15'. Red flowers emerge in spring and are followed by fragrant, greenish yellow fruit. Many cultivars are available. '**Cameo**' has large, peach pink double flowers. '**Crimson and Gold**' has a low, spreading habit and bears crimson flowers. It grows 24–36" tall, with an equal or slightly greater spread.

C. speciosa 'Toyo-Nishiki'

'**Texas Scarlet**' bears many red flowers over a fairly long period on plants about half the size of the species. '**Toyo-Nishiki**' is more upright than the species, with white, pink and red flowers that all appear on the same plant. (Zones 5–8)

Problems & Pests
In addition to leaf spot (see above), possible but not often serious problems include aphids, mites, canker, fire blight, rust and viruses.

C. speciosa 'Texas Scarlet'

Forsythia
Forsythia

Features: early- to mid-spring flowers **Habit:** spreading, deciduous shrub with upright or arching branches **Height:** 2–10' **Spread:** 3–15' or more
Planting: B & B or container in spring or fall; bare-root in spring **Zones:** 4–9

I HAVE TENDED TO USE FORSYTHIAS MAINLY AS SHORT-TERM SPACE fillers. These plants generally grow quickly and cost little, so I place them between or around immature plants of greater visual interest and character. Later, when space is needed by the more desirable plants, I simply remove the forsythias. Still, forsythias always gain my respect with their ephemeral beauty and vigorous growth. These beacons of early-spring sunshine boast outstandingly beautiful 7–8' long stems covered end to end in golden flowers. I have seen weeping forsythia draped 25' down from the top of a wall: a wonder to behold, especially when in flower. Proper siting and pruning can solve most objections to forsythias, and some of the new lower growers are really exciting.

Growing

Most forsythias grow best in **full sun** but will tolerate light shade. *F. viridissima* var. *koreana* 'Suwan Gold' prefers **partial shade**. The soil should be of **average fertility, moist** and **well drained**.

Correct pruning is essential to keep forsythias attractive. Flowers are produced on growth that is usually at least two years old. Prune after flowering is finished. On mature plants, one-third of the oldest growth can be cut right back to the ground each year.

Some gardeners trim these shrubs into formal hedges, but this practice often results in uneven flowering. An informal hedge allows the plants to grow more naturally. Size can be restricted by cutting shoots back to strong junctions.

Tips

These shrubs are gorgeous while in flower, but they aren't very exciting the rest of the year. Include one in a shrub or mixed border where other flowering plants will take over once the forsythia's early-season glory has passed.

The cold-hardiness designation for forsythias can be somewhat misleading. The plants themselves are very cold hardy, surviving in Zone 3 quite happily. The flowers, however, are not as tolerant because the buds form in summer and are then vulnerable to winter cold. Hardiness zones listed here apply to bud and flower hardiness.

F. x *intermedia* 'Fiesta'

Forsythias can be used as hedging plants, but they look most attractive when grown informally.

F. x *intermedia* GOLD TIDE

F. viridissima var. koreana 'Kumson' (above)

F. x intermedia GOLDILOCKS

In the coldest areas, snow cover is often the deciding factor in flower bud survival. A tall shrub may flower only on the lower half—the part that was buried in and protected by snow. Don't despair, therefore, if your garden is outside the recommended zonal region. If you have a good snowfall every year and choose a hardy cultivar, pile some salt-free snow over the plant and you should be able to enjoy forsythia flowers each spring.

Recommended

F. 'Arnold Dwarf' is a fairly low, mounding hybrid with arching, trailing branches. It grows 3–6' tall and spreads about 7'. The yellow flowers appear in early to mid-spring. They are more profuse on older plants than on younger ones. (Zones 5–8)

F. x *intermedia* (border forsythia) is a large shrub with upright stems that arch as they mature. It grows 5–10' tall and spreads 5–12'. Yellow flowers emerge in early to mid-spring before the leaves. Many cultivars have been developed from this hybrid. 'Fiesta' has red young stems, and its foliage is variegated bright yellow and green. GOLDEN PEEP ('Courdijau') is a dwarf cultivar that grows up to 36" tall, with an equal spread. The bright yellow flowers are borne on wood that is only one year old. GOLDILOCKS ('Courtacour') is a dwarf cultivar that grows to 4' tall, with an equal spread. The flowers are densely clustered along the stems. GOLD TIDE ('Courtasol') is a unique low, spreading cultivar that grows only 24–30" tall but can spread up to 4'. 'Lynwood' ('Lynwood Gold') grows to 10' in both height and width. The light yellow flowers open widely and are distributed evenly along the branches. (Zones 6–9)

F. ovata (early forsythia) is an upright, spreading shrub that grows up to 6' tall, with an equal spread. This species has the hardiest buds, and its flowers open in early spring. It has been crossed with other species to create floriferous, hardy hybrids. 'New Hampshire Gold' is an attractive compact cultivar with very hardy buds. This reliable bloomer grows 4–5' tall, with an equal spread, and has the added attraction of developing red-purple fall color. 'Northern Gold' is a hardy, upright shrub that develops a more arching habit as it matures. It grows 5–8' tall and spreads up to 10'. The bright yellow flowers are very cold hardy. 'Ottawa' bears light yellow flowers in early spring. This compact, cold-hardy cultivar grows about 4' tall and spreads about 5'. (Zones 4–7)

F. suspensa var. *sieboldii* (weeping forsythia) is a large shrub with long, arching branches that trail to the ground. It grows 6–10' tall and spreads 10–15', but it can spread farther if trained up or down a wall. The arching growth makes this an excellent shrub to cover large banked areas. This variety produces golden yellow flowers in mid-spring. (Zones 5–8)

F. viridissima (greenstem forsythia) is an upright plant with shoots that stay green for several years. It grows 6–10' tall, with an equal spread. Bright yellow flowers adorn the stems in early and mid-spring. **Var.** *koreana* **'Kumson'** has silvery veins on the green leaves. It grows 4–8' tall, with an equal spread. **Var.** *koreana* **'Suwan Gold'** has bright yellow foliage and grows 3–4' tall, with an equal spread (Zones 5–8)

Problems & Pests
Most problems are not serious but may include root-knot nematodes, leaf spot and stem gall.

F. x intermedia (both photos)

For an early touch of spring indoors, cut forsythia for forcing. Simply cut the dormant stems, smash the ends with a hammer and place in warm water. Change the water daily and you should have blooms in about a week.

Fothergilla
Fothergilla

Features: spring flowers, scent, fall foliage **Habit:** dense, rounded or bushy, decid-uous shrub **Height:** 2–10' **Spread:** 2–10' **Planting:** B & B, container; spring or fall **Zones:** 4–9

FOTHERGILLAS HAVE LONG BEEN AMONG MY FAVORITE SHRUBS. Flowers, fragrance, fall color and interesting soft tan to brownish stems give these plants year-round appeal. The fall foliage is especially exciting because of its progression from light to solid yellow and eventually to a flaming orange-red. The plant almost looks like a small bonfire for a short time. Fothergillas will grow, when properly planted, even in alkaline soils, but be sure to use sulfur and an acid-type fertilizer annually in early spring for best results. When space allows, use *F. major* for even more of a good thing.

The bottlebrush-shaped flowers of fothergillas have a delicate honey scent. Use these generally problem-free plants with rhododendrons and azaleas.

Growing

Fothergillas grow well in **full sun** or **partial shade**. In full sun they will bear the most flowers and have the best fall color. The soil should be of **average fertility, acidic, humus rich, moist** and **well drained**.

These plants require little pruning. Remove wayward and dead branches as needed.

F. gardenii 'Blue Mist' (above & center)

Tips

Fothergillas are attractive and useful in shrub or mixed borders, in woodland gardens and in combination with evergreen groundcovers.

Recommended

F. gardenii (dwarf fothergilla) is a bushy shrub that grows 24–36" tall, with an equal spread. In mid- to late spring it bears fragrant white flowers. The foliage turns yellow, orange and red in fall. **'Blue Mist'** is similar to the species, but the summer foliage is blue-green rather than dark green. This cultivar has delicate growth that suffers in drought and other stressful conditions. It will require rich soil, even moisture and a bit of good luck to grow well.

F. major (below)

F. major (large fothergilla) is a rounded shrub that grows 6–10' tall, with an equal spread. The white, honey-scented flowers are borne in mid-spring and last for several weeks. The fall colors are yellow, orange and scarlet. **'Mount Airy'** is a more compact cultivar, growing 5–6' in height and width. It bears lots of flowers and has more consistent fall color than the species.

Fringe Tree
Chionanthus

Features: early-summer flowers, fall and winter fruit, bark, habit **Habit:** rounded or spreading, deciduous large shrub or small tree **Height:** 10–25' **Spread:** 10–25'
Planting: B & B, container; spring **Zones:** 4–9

WHAT WONDERFUL SMALL TREES OR LARGE SHRUBS FOR OHIO! The white fringe tree is native here and durable in all Ohio weather, yet it has been less frequently used in recent years. Both white fringe tree and Chinese fringe tree deserve wider consideration. They have so many appealing attributes, especially their adaptability to different soil conditions. These plants border on spectacular when their crowns are highlighted by the fringe-like white flowers. They are attractive up close, and the creamy white will draw your attention from afar. The dark blue fruit, borne in clusters on female plants, adds wonderful fall ornamentation to the garden. Your choice of pruning technique will encourage your fringe tree to grow into a large, full shrub or a wonderful small, multi-stemmed specimen tree.

Growing
Fringe trees prefer **full sun.** They do best in **fertile, acidic, moist** and **well-drained** soil but will adapt to most soil conditions. In the wild they are often found growing alongside streams.

Little pruning is required on mature fringe trees. Thin out the stems when the plant is young to encourage an attractive habit. Prune after flowering, or in spring for young plants that aren't yet flowering. To create a single- or multi-stemmed specimen, remove all stems from a young plant except the trunk or trunks you wish to encourage. Some of the lower branches can also be removed to show off the trunk or trunks and to encourage growth at the top of the plant. Never remove more than a quarter of the total growth at one time.

Tips

These small, pollution-tolerant trees work well as specimens, in borders or beside water features. Plants begin flowering at an early age.

A given tree may not produce fruit because not all trees of a species bear both female and male flowers. A male and a female tree must be growing near each other for the female to bear fruit. When fruit is produced it attracts birds.

Fringe trees can be difficult to find in nurseries, so you may want to propagate them at home. Seeds planted outdoors in early or mid-summer will germinate after about two years. Semi-ripe cuttings or layerings can be started from Chinese fringe tree in mid- or late summer. White fringe tree does not root well from cuttings.

Recommended

C. retusus (Chinese fringe tree) is a rounded, spreading shrub or small tree. It grows 15–25' tall, with an

C. virginicus

equal spread. In early summer it bears erect, fragrant white flowers followed in late summer by dark blue fruit. The bark is deeply furrowed and peeling. (Zones 5–9)

C. virginicus (white fringe tree) is a spreading small tree or large shrub that is native to the eastern U.S., including parts of southern Ohio. It grows 10–20' tall, with an equal or greater spread. In early summer it bears drooping, fragrant white flowers, followed by dark blue fruit. (Zones 4–9)

Problems & Pests

Problems are rarely serious but can include borers, canker, leaf spot and powdery mildew.

C. retusus

Ginkgo
Ginko, Maidenhair Tree
Ginkgo

Features: summer and fall foliage, habit, bark **Habit:** deciduous tree; conical in youth, variable with age **Height:** 40–100' **Spread:** 10–100' or more
Planting: B & B, bare-root, container; spring or fall **Zones:** 3–9

REMEMBER THE STORY ABOUT THE UGLY DUCKLING THAT TURNED into a beautiful swan? Be patient with ginkgo. Its gawky, irregularly angular youth will eventually pass to reveal a spectacular mature specimen. The unique fan-shaped leaves make frequent additions to children's pressed-leaf collections. The foliage is sensitive to freezing temperatures, and if there is a late-spring frost the young leaves may drop off. Don't panic, though; in about three weeks, the tree will leaf out again and return to its seasonal splendor. Ginkgo is a greatly underused tree and is well worth trying, especially if you're looking for something a little different.

Ginkgo appears to have been saved from extinction by its long-time use in Asian temple gardens. Today this 'living fossil' grows almost entirely in horticultural settings.

Growing

Ginkgo prefers **full sun**. The soil should ideally be **fertile, sandy** and **well drained,** but this tree adapts to most soils. It also tolerates urban conditions and cold weather. Little or no pruning is necessary.

Tips

Though its growth is very slow, ginkgo eventually becomes a large tree that is best suited as a specimen in parks and large gardens. It can also be used as a street tree. If you buy an unnamed plant, be sure it has been propagated from cuttings. Seed-grown trees may prove to be female, and the stinky fruit is not something you want dropping all over your lawn, driveway or sidewalk.

Recommended

G. biloba is variable in habit. It grows 50–100' tall, with an equal or greater spread. The leaves can turn an attractive shade of yellow in fall, after a few cool nights. Female plants are generally avoided because the fruit has an unpleasant odor. Several cultivars are available. AUTUMN GOLD is a broadly conical male cultivar. It grows 50' tall and spreads 30'. Fall color is bright golden yellow. 'Lakeview' is a com-pact, conical male cultivar with deep gold fall color. It grows about 45' tall and 26' wide. PRINCETON SENTRY is a narrow, upright male cultivar 40–80' tall and 10–25' in spread.

Problems & Pests

This species seems to have outlived most of the pests that might have afflicted it. A leaf spot may affect ginkgo, but it doesn't cause any real trouble.

G. biloba (both photos)

This tree sheds nearly all of its golden fall leaves within a single day, making raking a snap.

Golden Rain Tree

Koelreuteria

Features: habit, foliage, flowers **Habit:** rounded, spreading, deciduous tree
Height: 30' **Spread:** 30' **Planting:** B & B; spring **Zones:** 5–8

GOLDEN RAIN TREE IS ONE OF MY FAVORITE ORNAMENTAL TREES.
I strive to have something in flower in my garden right from February
through October, so golden rain tree's mid-July flowers make a good fit in
my bloom schedule. I even enjoy the clusters of fruit, which take more than
a month to mature into parchment-colored, papery, lantern-like capsules.
(Not all will concur with my positive view of this characteristic, as I have
heard the fruit described as a brown, seedy mess.) Based on my growing
experience, you should avoid dense
soils and poorly drained or low-lying
sites. I have seen several otherwise
healthy trees succumb when grown
in these conditions.

*Golden rain tree is one of the few
trees with yellow flowers and one of
the only trees to bloom in mid- or
late summer.*

Growing

Golden rain tree grows best in **full sun**. The soil should be **average to fertile, moist** and **well drained**. This tree tolerates heat, drought, wind and polluted air. It is also pH adaptable and fast growing.

Little pruning is required. Dead or broken branches can be removed as needed and awkward growth can be removed in late winter.

Tips

Golden rain tree makes an excellent shade or specimen tree for small properties. Its ability to adapt to a wide range of soils makes it useful in many situations. The fruit can be messy but will not stain a patio or deck if planted to shade these areas.

K. paniculata (both photos)

Recommended

K. paniculata is an attractive, rounded, spreading tree. Long, upright clusters of small yellow flowers appear in mid-summer, followed by red-tinged, green, capsular fruit that eventually turns papery.

The leaves are attractive and rather lacy in appearance. In some years, fall color may be bright yellow.

Problems & Pests

Rare problems with canker, leaf spot, root rot and wilt can occur.

Hawthorn

Crataegus

Features: late-spring or early-summer flowers, fruit, foliage, thorny branches
Habit: rounded, deciduous tree, often with a zigzagged, layered branch pattern
Height: 15–40' **Spread:** 12–40' **Planting:** B & B, container; early spring
Zones: 3–8

SEVERAL OF THE MANY HAWTHORNS HAVE BEEN ON MY PLANT palette for years. As the name suggests, many have thorns and you should be careful where you put them. This thorny trait can be an asset when perimeter security is needed for a large area. Washington hawthorn *(C. phaenopyrum)*, in its multi-stemmed form, makes a beautiful vase-shaped specimen tree. Almost daily I pass by and enjoy three that I planted at a bank 35 years ago. Each season brings different attributes to the forefront, but I especially admire the naked winter structure. Another one of my favorites is *C. viridis* 'Winter King,' with its good shape, size, foliage, flowers and, especially, the persistent winter fruit that lasts into early spring in nearly full red color. The fruit is excellent for attracting birds, especially cardinals.

Hawthorn fruits are edible but dry and seedy. Some people make jelly from them, or ferment them and mix them with brandy.

Growing

Hawthorns grow equally well in **full sun** or **partial shade**. They adapt to any **well-drained** soil and tolerate urban conditions.

When grown as trees, hawthorns need little pruning, though removing lower branches near walkways is a good idea to avoid harming unsuspecting pedestrians. When grown as hedges, hawthorns can be pruned after flowering or in fall.

Remove any dead or diseased growth immediately, to prevent the spread of diseases such as fire blight and rust. It is prudent to wear leather gloves and safety goggles when pruning hawthorns.

Hawthorns can become weedy, with seedlings and suckers popping up unexpectedly. Remove any that you find while they are young, because they can become quite tenacious once they get bigger.

Tips

Hawthorns can be grown as specimen plants or as hedges in larger urban sites and exposed locations. They are popular in areas where vandalism is a problem because very few people wish to grapple with plants bearing stiff 2" thorns. As a hedge, hawthorns create an almost impenetrable barrier.

These trees are small enough to include in most gardens. With the long, sharp thorns, however, a hawthorn might not be a good selection if there are children about.

C. laevigata 'Paul's Scarlet' (above)

C. laevigata (center & below)

C. laevigata (above), 'Paul's Scarlet' (below)

Recommended

C. crus-galli (corkspur hawthorn) is a wide-spreading tree that grows about 25' tall and about 30' wide. This tree is dense and very thorny and is sometimes used to control cattle. Clusters of white flowers appear in spring, followed by fruit that ripens to dark red in mid-fall and persists into early winter. The dark green foliage turns red and purple in fall. 'Hooks' is a smaller, more rounded cultivar with very shiny green foliage. It grows 15–20' tall, with an equal spread. **Var.** *inermis* (CRUSADER, 'Cruzam') is like the species, but without thorns. (Zones 3–7)

C. laevigata (*C. oxyacantha*; English hawthorn) is a low-branching, rounded tree with zigzagged layers of thorny branches. It grows 15–25' tall and spreads 12–25'. White or pink late-spring flowers are followed by bright red fruit in late summer. Many cultivars are available. **'Paul's Scarlet'** ('Paulii') has many showy, deep pink double flowers. This cultivar is popular but susceptible to blight. It should be used only in open breezy or windy sites so any moisture will dry quickly, reducing the spread of disease. (Zones 4–8)

C. phaenopyrum (*C. cordata*; Washington hawthorn) is an oval to rounded, or vase-shaped if multi-stemmed, thorny tree 25–30' tall, with a spread of 20–30'. It bears white flowers from early to mid-summer and has persistent shiny red fruit in fall. The glossy green foliage turns an appealing combination of red and orange in fall. This species is the least susceptible to fire blight. (Zones 3–8)

C. punctata (thicket hawthorn, dotted hawthorn) forms a spreading tree 20–25' tall and up to 35' in spread. It bears white flowers in spring. The fruit ripens to red in fall and drops soon after ripening. **Var.** *inermis* ('Ohio Pioneer') is a nearly thornless variety. It was selected at the Ohio State University Secrest Arboretum in Wooster, Ohio. This variety grows about 20' tall, with an equal or greater spread. It bears abundant white flowers in spring, followed by red fruit that ripens in mid-fall. (Zones 4–7)

C. viridis (green hawthorn) is a small, rounded tree with a dense habit. It grows 20–40' tall, with an equal or slightly lesser spread. Dense clusters of white flowers appear in late spring, followed by bright red fruit in fall. The glossy green leaves turn red or purple in fall. **'Winter King'** has an attractive rounded to vase-shaped habit. The red fruit is larger and persists longer than that of the species. The foliage is rust resistant though the fruit is somewhat susceptible. (Zones 4–7)

Problems & Pests

Borers, caterpillars, leaf miners, leaf skeletonizers, scale insects, canker, fire blight, fungal leaf spot, powdery mildew, rust and scab are possible problems. Stress-free hawthorns will be less susceptible.

C. laevigata (above), 'Paul's Scarlet' (below)

The genus name Crataegus *comes from the Greek* kratos, *'strength,' a reference to the hard, fine-grained wood.*

Hemlock
Eastern Hemlock, Canadian Hemlock
Tsuga

Features: foliage, habit, cones **Habit:** pyramidal or columnar, evergreen tree
Height: 1–80' **Spread:** 1–35' **Planting:** B & B, container; spring or fall
Zones: 3–8

THE HEMLOCK TREE, I AM TOLD, IS ONE OF ONLY A FEW NATIVE
Ohio evergreen trees. Its natural distribution in our state is limited to well-
drained areas of the Lake Erie coast and a few equally well-drained sites
in the Hocking Hills area. I have stood on a cliff 35' above the shaded
and cool rootzone and looked up 35' to the sunny top of a
hemlock tree 24" in diameter. It is important that we
situate these trees properly. I have been growing
a 'Sargentii' for more than 35 years. It is now
an unusual specimen 10' wide and 4' tall. As
well, I have bonsai dishes that house two of the
many dwarf cultivars, namely 'Jervis' and
'Cole's Prostrate,' so I can just
enjoy their uniqueness.

Growing

Hemlock generally grows well in any light from **full sun to full shade.** The
soil should be **humus rich, moist** and **well drained. Acidic** soil is preferred.
This tree is drought sensitive and the root system grows best in cool, moist
conditions. It is also sensitive to air pollution and suffers salt damage, so keep
it away from roadways.

Hemlock trees need little pruning though they respond well to it. The cultivars can be pruned to control their growth as required. Trim hemlock hedges in summer.

Tips

With its delicate needles, hemlock is among the most beautiful evergreens to use as a specimen tree. It can also be shaped to form a hedge. The smaller cultivars may be included in shrub or mixed borders. The many dwarf forms are useful in small gardens and rock gardens.

Recommended

T. canadensis is a graceful, narrowly pyramidal tree that grows 40–80' tall and spreads 25–35'. It is native to the eastern U.S. Many cultivars are available, including groundcovers and dwarf forms. **'Cole's Prostrate'** is a low, spreading cultivar that grows about 12" tall and spreads about 36". **'Gentsch White'** is a small, shrubby cultivar that grows 4' tall and wide. The new growth becomes creamy white its first fall and winter, contrasting with the older growth. **'Jeddeloh'** is a rounded, mound-forming, slow-growing cultivar 5' tall and 6' in spread. **'Jervis'** is a slow-growing, irregularly shaped dwarf cultivar. It grows 12–24" tall, with an equal spread. **'Pendula'** is a small, upright, weeping form that grows about 5' tall, with an equal spread. **'Sargentii'** is a graceful weeping and spreading tree that grows 5–15' tall and spreads 10–30'. The names 'Pendula' and 'Sargentii' are often used interchangeably, and, because both cultivars are somewhat variable in size and habit, they may well be the same plant.

'Jeddeloh'

Problems & Pests

Stress-free trees have few problems. Possible problems may be caused by aphids, mites, scale insects, weevils, woolly adelgids, gray mold, needle blight, rust and snow blight.

'Sargentii' (center), 'Jeddeloh' (below)

Holly
Inkberry, Winterberry
Ilex

Features: glossy, sometimes spiny foliage; fruit, habit **Habit:** erect or spreading, evergreen or deciduous shrub or tree **Height:** 3–50' **Spread:** 3–40'
Planting: B & B, container; spring or fall **Zones:** 3–9

HOLLIES VARY GREATLY IN SHAPE AND SIZE AND CAN BE SUCH delights when placed with full consideration of their soil needs. American holly trees should be used primarily in the acidic areas of eastern Ohio, or by gardeners who are willing to carefully amend less appropriate soils. Inkberry makes a good small hedge and is a little more adaptable, as long as it is planted in well-drained soil. The meserve group of holly hybrids has been a blessing to those of us in alkaline soils. All you have to do is amend the soil with plenty of organic matter, and keep the plants out of the most severe weather. The deciduous hollies grow in most soils amended with organic matter. They provide an excellent display of color all winter and a good source of food for birds in early spring.

The showy, scarlet berries look tempting, especially to children, but are not edible.

Growing

These plants prefer **full sun** but tolerate partial shade. The soil should be of **average to rich fertility, humus rich** and **moist**. Hollies perform best in an **acidic** soil with a pH of 6.5 to 6.0 or lower. **Shelter** from winter wind to help prevent the leaves from drying out. Apply a summer mulch to keep the roots cool and moist.

Hollies grown as shrubs require very little pruning. Simply remove any damaged growth in spring. Hollies grown as hedges can be trimmed in summer. Dispose of all trimmings carefully to prevent the spiny leaves from puncturing bare feet or paws.

Tips

Hollies can be used in groups, in woodland gardens and in shrub and mixed borders. They can also be shaped into hedges. Winterberry is good for naturalizing in moist sites in the garden.

I. glabra cultivar

A vase of cut winterberry branches is a perfect way to brighten a room during the long, gray winter months.

I. verticillata cultivar

Inkberry looks much like boxwood and has similar uses in the landscape. Use it as a low hedge or in a mass planting. It adapts to regular shearing and forms a fuller, more appealing plant when cut back hard on a regular basis.

All hollies have male and female flowers on separate plants, and both must be present for the females to set fruit. One male plant will adequately pollinate two to three females. The flowering times of different hollies vary somewhat, and purchasing hollies with matching flowering times can be important in encouraging good fruit set. Staff at most garden centers will be able to tell you which two to buy in order to have a good display of fruit.

Recommended

I. glabra (inkberry) is a rounded shrub with glossy, deep green, evergreen foliage and dark purple fruit. It grows 6–10' tall and spreads 8–10'.

'**Compacta**' is a female cultivar with a dense branching habit. It grows 3–6' tall and 6–8' wide. '**Densa**' is an upright cultivar that holds its foliage well right to the plant base. It grows up to 6' tall and wide. NORDIC ('Chamzin') is a compact, rounded male cultivar that grows to about 4' in height, with an equal spread. '**Shamrock**' has bright green foliage and an upright habit. It grows 3–4' tall and wide. (Zones 4–9)

I. x meserveae (meserve holly, blue holly) is a group of hybrids that originated from crosses between the tender English holly *(I. aquifolium)* and the hardy prostrate holly *(I. rugosa)*. The initial crosses created the blue hollies; additional crosses with other hardy hollies have expanded the group to what is called the meserve hollies. These dense, evergreen shrubs may be erect, mounding or spreading. They grow 5–15' tall, with a lesser to equal spread, and feature glossy red or

I. verticillata 'Red Sprite'

sometimes yellow fruit that persists into winter. Tolerant of pruning, they make formidable hedges or barriers. Many cultivars have been developed, often available in male and female pairs. The males and females can be mixed and matched with any of the other plants that share the same flowering period. **'Blue Boy'** and **'Blue Girl'** are bushy plants that hold their lower leaves well as they age. 'Blue Boy' grows 10–15' tall and 10–12' wide; 'Blue Girl' grows 8–10' tall and 6–8' wide. 'Blue Girl' bears bright red fruit. **'Blue Prince'** and **'Blue Princess'** have large leaves, and 'Blue Princess' bears red fruit prolifically. These cultivars grow 10–12' tall and wide. **BLUE STALLION** ('Mesan') has a long flowering period, making it useful for pollinating a variety of female hollies. **CENTENNIAL GIRL** (*I. centrochinensis* x *I. aquifolium*) is a fast-growing, winter-hardy, large, pyramidal bush that has persistent

I. x *meserveae* GOLDEN GIRL

Even with the most hardy selections of meserve holly, a sheltered, well-drained site is critical for success.

I. glabra 'Densa'

I. x *meserveae* cultivar

I. opaca

red fruit. This cultivar resists mites. CHINA BOY ('Mesdob') and CHINA GIRL ('Mesog') are cold and heat tolerant. Both are mound-forming plants with the male growing up to about 10' tall and the female 3–10' tall. Spread is a bit less than the height. The female bears red fruit. GOLDEN GIRL ('Mesgolg') is a broad, upright, pyramidal cultivar that produces yellow fruit. (Zones 5–8)

I. opaca (American holly) is an excellent evergreen tree holly that grows 40–50' tall and spreads 20–40'. This species is native to Ohio and grows best in the eastern parts of the state in well-drained, acidic soil. The form is often neatly pyramidal when young, becoming more open at maturity. Leaves and fruits vary among the many cultivars; ask at your local garden center for the types that grow best in your area. (Zones 5–9)

I. serrata x *I. verticillata* hybrids are deciduous hollies grown for their red fruit, which is larger than that of *I. serrata* and more plentiful than that of *I. verticillata*. 'Apollo' is an upright male plant that blooms at the same time as 'Sparkleberry.' It grows 8–12' tall and spreads 6–10'. 'Christmas Cheer' is a compact plant that bears deep red fruit. It grows about 6' tall, with an equal spread. 'Raritan Chief' is a dense, spreading male plant. It grows 6–8' tall and spreads 12–15'. 'Sparkleberry' is an upright female plant. It grows to 12–15' tall and spreads about 12'. It bears plentiful red fruit that persists well into winter. (Zones 3–9)

I. verticillata (winterberry, winterberry holly) is a deciduous native species grown for its explosion of red fruit that persists into winter. It grows 6–10' tall, sometimes taller, with an equal spread. 'Afterglow' is a slow-growing, compact plant that bears reddish orange fruit. The rounded plants grow about 10' tall, with an equal spread. 'Aurantiaca' (f. *aurantiaca*) bears reddish orange fruit that doesn't persist as long as that of some other winterberries. 'Cacapon' bears dark red fruit and grows 3–8' tall, with a lesser to equal spread. 'Earlibright' ('Early Bright') bears reddish orange fruit. 'Jim Dandy' is a compact male cultivar, useful for pollinating. It grows up to 6' tall and 7' wide. 'Red Sprite' is a dwarf cultivar that grows 3–4' tall and wide and bears bright red fruit. 'Southern Gentleman' is a popular male pollinator but is not as compact as 'Jim Dandy,' growing up to 9' tall and 7' wide. 'Sunset' bears plentiful red fruit. This rounded plant grows about 8' tall, with a slightly larger spread. 'Winter Gold' bears gold fruit. This multi-stemmed shrub grows 6–8' tall, with an equal spread. 'Winter Red' bears lots of attractive, persistent red fruit. This cultivar grows 8–10' tall and spreads 6–8'. (Zones 3–9)

Problems & Pests

Aphids may attack young shoots. Leaf miners and scale insects can present problems, as can root rot. Problems are more common in poorly drained and alkaline soils.

I. x *meserveae* cultivar (below)

Honeysuckle
Lonicera

Features: flowers, habit, fruit **Habit:** rounded, upright shrub or twining climber; deciduous, semi-evergreen or evergreen **Height:** 3–30' **Spread:** 3–10' **Planting:** container, bare-root; spring **Zones:** 3–9

INVASIVE BEAST, WONDERFUL SHRUB OR HEAVENLY FRAGRANT vine? Choosing the right plant, placing it in the proper situation and doing regular maintenance make all the difference in enjoying the positive aspects of honeysuckles. I used to walk to school down an alley that had a hedge of winter honeysuckle along part of it. Because the leaves held nearly all winter, I could hardly see the owner's house. When the snow melted, I enjoyed the soothing fragrance that let me know winter was finally over. Summer, too, was enhanced by the fragrance of the vine that climbed up the legs of my grandparents' old, retired farm windmill. With care, you too can find both beauty and utility among this group of plants.

Growing

Honeysuckles grow well in **full sun** or **partial shade**. The soil should be **average to fertile** and **well drained**. Climbing honeysuckles prefer a **moist, humus-rich** soil.

Remove one-third of the old growth from shrubby honeysuckles each year after they bloom. Trim back climbing honeysuckles in spring to keep them where you want them. Trim hedges twice a year to keep them neat, usually once in early summer and then again in mid- to late summer.

L. x heckrottii

Tips

Shrubby honeysuckles can be used in mixed borders, in naturalized gardens and as hedges. Most are large and take up a lot of space when mature, but smaller shrubby honeysuckles can be mass planted as slope stabilizers or to fill large areas. Climbing honeysuckles can be trained to grow up a trellis, fence, arbor or other structure.

Honeysuckle flowers are often scented and attract hummingbirds as well as bees and other pollinating insects.

L. x brownii 'Dropmore Scarlet'

Recommended

L. x *brownii* (scarlet trumpet honeysuckle, Brown's honeysuckle) is a twining deciduous climber with red or orange flowers that appear in summer. It can grow 15–25' tall or taller and is hardy in Zones 5–8. **'Dropmore Scarlet'** is a cultivar of this hybrid. It is one of the most cold-hardy climbing honeysuckles, to Zone 4. It bears bright red flowers for most of the summer.

L. canadensis (American fly honeysuckle, Canadian fly honeysuckle) is an upright or mound-forming, deciduous shrub that grows 3–5' tall,

L. sempervirens

L. fragrantissima (winter honey-suckle) is a large, bushy, deciduous or semi-evergreen shrub. It grows 6–10' high, with an equal spread. Over a long period in early or mid-spring it bears small, fragrant, creamy flowers. (Zones 4–8)

L. x *heckrottii* (goldflame honey-suckle) is a twining, deciduous to semi-evergreen vine with attractive blue-green foliage. It grows 10–20' tall and bears fragrant pink and yel-low flowers profusely in spring and sporadically into fall. (Zones 4–8)

L. japonica (Japanese honeysuckle) forms a twining, evergreen to semi-evergreen vine up to 30' tall. The fra-grant white flowers are often flushed with purple or pink and are pro-duced for most of the summer. The species can be invasive, so the less aggressive cultivar 'Aureoreticulata,' which has yellow-veined foliage, is preferable. (Zones 4–9)

L. periclymenum (common honey-suckle, woodbine) is a twining deciduous vine that grows 10–20' tall. It bears fragrant, red- or purple-flushed, white or yellow flowers over a long period in summer and fall. 'Belgica' (early Dutch honeysuckle) has red-streaked creamy white flow-ers. 'Graham Thomas' bears white blossoms that mature to yellow. 'Harlequin' has reddish purple stems, with leaves that are variegated green, pink and cream. The flowers are white or yellow with pale mauve outer petals. Var. *serotina* ('Serotina'; late Dutch honeysuckle) bears white or yellow flowers with reddish purple streaks. Var. *s.* 'Florida' is a noninvasive twining

with an equal spread. This Ohio native bears pendulous, creamy white flowers in spring. It will thrive and naturalize in the understory of a woodland garden. (Zones 3–6)

L. caprifolium (Italian honeysuckle, Italian woodbine) is a twining decid-uous vine that grows up to 20' tall. It bears creamy white or yellow, fra-grant flowers in late spring and early summer. This species is one of the longest cultivated of all the honey-suckles. (Zones 5–8)

L. dioica (limber honeysuckle) is a spreading or twining deciduous plant, native to the eastern and cen-tral U.S. It grows up to 5' tall or wide. The pairs of silvery blue leaves are joined at the bases so that the leaves appear to encircle the stems, like eucalyptus leaves. The yellow flowers, tinged purple, are produced in late spring and summer and are followed by berries that ripen to bright red. (Zones 5–8)

vine or groundcover. It bears flowers that are red on the outside and yellow and white inside. This cultivar is hardy only to Zone 5. (Zones 4–8)

L. sempervirens (trumpet honeysuckle, coral honeysuckle) is a twining, deciduous climber. It grows 10–20' tall and can spread equally to fill the space provided. It bears orange or red flowers in late spring and early summer. Many cultivars are available, with flowers in yellow, red or scarlet. **'Blanche Sandman'** (coral honeysuckle) bears orange-red flowers over a long period from early or mid-summer to frost. It is resistant to aphids and leaf diseases. This cultivar attracts hummingbirds. **'John Clayton'** bears golden yellow flowers in flushes from June until frost. (Zones 5–8)

L. x tellmanniana (Tellman honeysuckle) is a twining deciduous climber. This hybrid was developed in Hungary and bears large, showy, bright yellow-orange flowers. It climbs about 15'. (Zones 5–7)

L. xylosteum (European fly honeysuckle) is a mound-forming deciduous plant that grows 8–10' tall, with an equal or greater spread. The foliage is grayish green. White or yellow flowers are produced in late spring. **'Emerald Mound'** ('Nana') forms an attractive low mound of blue-green foliage. It grows to about 36" tall and can spread up to 6'. (Zones 4–6)

Problems & Pests

Occasional bouts with aphids, leaf miners, leaf rollers, scale insects, blight and powdery mildew can occur.

L. x heckrottii

Plant a honeysuckle in a pot and let it climb up a front stair railing.

L. periclymenum 'Harlequin'
L. x brownii 'Dropmore Scarlet'

Hornbeam
Carpinus

Features: habit, fall color **Habit:** pyramidal deciduous tree **Height:** 10–70'
Spread: 10–50' **Planting:** B & B; spring **Zones:** 3–9

OVER MANY YEARS AND DOZENS OF TREE EVALUATIONS AT THE
Ohio State University Wooster campus, the pyramidal European hornbeam
(*C. betulus* 'Fastigiata') came in seventh among all trees considered. Its
upright, broad-based, oval outline was consistent year after year. It makes a
great specimen tree and a superior large hedge or windbreak. Its American
cousin is great in the shade as an informally growing naturalizer. Give it
well-drained, rich soil and it will grow well even in alkaline areas of Ohio.
Its trunk is strong and unique. I still have a walking
stick I made from American hornbeam
wood on a Boy Scout campout
years ago.

Growing
Hornbeams prefer **full sun** but tolerate partial shade. The soil should be
average to fertile and **well drained**. American hornbeam prefers moist soil
conditions and grows well near ponds and streams.

Pruning is rarely required, though it is tolerated. Remove damaged, diseased and awkward branches as needed. Hedges can be trimmed in late summer.

Tips

These small- to medium-sized trees can be used as specimens or shade trees in smaller gardens or can be pruned to form hedges. The narrow, upright cultivars are often used to create barriers and windbreaks.

Recommended

C. betulus (European hornbeam) is a pyramidal to rounded tree that tolerates heavy pruning and urban conditions. It grows 40–70' tall and spreads 30–50'. The foliage turns bright yellow or orange in fall. **'Columnaris'** is a narrow, slow-growing cultivar. It grows 30' tall and spreads 20'. **'Fastigiata'** (pyramidal European hornbeam) is an upright cultivar that is narrow when young but broadens into an upright egg shape as it matures. It grows 30–50' tall, with a spread of 20–40'. **'Pendula'** is a mound-forming, prostrate cultivar that is usually grafted to a standard to create a weeping tree. (Zones 4–8)

C. caroliniana (American hornbeam, ironwood, musclewood, bluebeech) is a small, slow-growing tree that tolerates shade. This Ohio native grows 10–30' tall, with an equal spread. Its gray trunks and branches have a unique fluted, rather muscle-like appearance. The foliage turns yellow, red or purple in fall. (Zones 3–9)

C. caroliniana (both photos)

Problems & Pests

Rare problems with canker, dieback, powdery mildew and rot can occur.

Hydrangea

Hydrangea

Features: flowers, habit; also fall foliage of some species **Habit:** deciduous mounding shrub, woody climber or spreading shrub or tree **Height:** 2–80'
Spread: 2–20' **Planting:** container; spring or fall **Zones:** 3–9

HYDRANGEAS ARE A SOURCE OF CONSTANT WONDER FOR ME.
I often wonder exactly which named plant I'm looking at and, more importantly, how to get it to flower reliably each year. Many of the highly desirable lacecap types are completely hardy except for the flower buds, which may be killed deep in the tissue. But even if you get flowers only every several years, it is worth the wait. A climbing hydrangea has graced the north stucco wall of my garage for more than 25 years, flowering when it chooses. Yet it is a wonderful vine on the off years, too. Oakleaf hydrangea is manageable in size, flowers well, has excellent foliage character and displays its exfoliating, cinnamon-colored bark all winter. It is high on my list of favorite plants.

Growing

Hydrangeas grow well in **full sun or partial shade**. Smooth hydrangea tolerates full shade. Shade or partial shade will reduce leaf and flower scorch in the hotter regions. The soil should be of **average to high fertility, humus rich, moist** and **well drained**. These plants perform best in cool, moist conditions, although established oakleaf hydrangea tolerates some drought if the roots are kept well mulched.

Bigleaf hydrangea responds to the level of aluminum ions in the soil, and this level in turn depends on pH. In acidic soil, a plant will tend to have blue flowers, while the same plant grown in an alkaline soil will tend to have pink flowers. Most cultivars develop their best color in one or the other soil type.

Pruning requirements vary from species to species. See the Recommended section of this entry for specific suggestions.

Tips

Hydrangeas come in many forms and have many uses in the landscape. Include them in shrub or mixed borders, use them as specimens and informal barriers, or plant them in groups or containers. Train climbing varieties up trees, walls, fences, pergolas and arbors. They will also grow over rocks and can be used as groundcovers.

A hydrangea inflorescence (flower cluster) consists of inconspicuous fertile flowers and showy sterile flowers. *Mophead* (or *hortensia*) inflorescences consist almost

H. macrophylla cultivar (above)

H. macrophylla (center), *H. paniculata* (below)

H. paniculata 'Grandiflora'

entirely of showy sterile flowers clustered in a globular, snowball-like shape. *Lacecap* inflorescences consist of a combination of sterile and fertile flowers. The showy sterile flowers are borne in a loose ring around the smaller fertile ones, giving this flatter inflorescence a delicate, lacy look. Both types are well worth growing.

Traces of cyanide are found in the leaves and buds of some hydrangeas. Wash your hands well after handling these plants, and avoid burning clippings because the smoke can be toxic.

Recommended

H. anomala subsp. *petiolaris* (*H. petiolaris;* climbing hydrangea) is considered by some gardeners to be the most elegant climbing plant available. It grows 50–80' tall, clinging to any rough surface by means of little rootlets that sprout from the stems. Though this plant is shade tolerant, it will produce the best flowers when exposed to some direct sun each day. The leaves are a dark, glossy green and sometimes show yellow fall color. For more than a month in mid-summer, the vine is covered with white lacecap flowers, and the entire plant appears to be veiled in a lacy mist. This hydrangea can be pruned after flowering, if required, to restrict its growth. With careful pruning and some support when young, it can be trained to form a small tree or shrub. (Zones 4–9)

H. arborescens (smooth hydrangea) is native to the eastern U.S., including Ohio. It forms a rounded shrub 3–5' tall and wide. It is often grown as a perennial. The plants flower on new growth each year and will look best if cut right back to the ground in fall or very early spring, before any growth starts. The flowers of the species are not very showy, but the cultivars have large, showy blossoms for most of the summer and early fall. 'Annabelle' bears large, ball-like mophead clusters of white flowers. A single inflorescence may be up to 12" in diameter. This cultivar is more compact than the species and is useful for brightening up a shady wall or corner. This plant often collapses under its own weight, especially after a rain. **Subsp.** *radiata* ('Radiata') bears white lacecap flower clusters and has silvery white leaf undersides. **Subsp.** *r.* 'Samantha' bears large, snowy white mophead flower clusters. This excellent selection has silvery leaf undersides that make a showy contrast with the dark green leaf tops, especially on a breezy day. (Zones 3–9)

H. macrophylla (bigleaf hydrangea) is a rounded or mounding shrub that flowers from mid- to late summer. It grows 3–5' tall and spreads up to 6'. Flower buds form on the previous season's growth, and a severe winter or late-spring frost can kill this species back to the point where no flowering occurs. Prune flowering shoots back to the first strong buds once flowering is finished or early the following spring. On mature, established plants, you can remove one-third of the oldest growth yearly or as needed to encourage vigorous new growth. The many cultivars can have mophead or lacecap flower clusters in shades of pink, red, blue or purple. '**All Summer Beauty**' bears dark blue mophead clusters on the previous and sometimes the current season's growth, making this cultivar useful where other bigleaf hydrangeas are frequently killed back in winter. '**Alpenglow**' bears dark red mophead clusters. '**Dooley**' bears blue or pink mophead clusters. Flowers are produced all along the shoots, so if the buds at or close to the stem ends are killed by frost, the buds farther along the stems will still produce flowers. '**Forever Pink**' is a compact plant with pink to reddish pink mophead clusters. Plants grow to about 36" tall, with an equal spread. '**Glowing Embers**' bears dark pink or red mopheads. '**Mariesii Variegata**' has cream-margined leaves and features pink or mauve lacecap flower clusters that are light blue in acidic soils. '**Masja**' bears striking red mophead clusters that show well against the dark green foliage. This compact cultivar grows to about 36" tall, with

H. paniculata 'Tardiva' (above)

H. macrophylla 'Nikko Blue'

H. paniculata LIMELIGHT

H. quercifolia 'Snow Queen' in fall color

an equal spread. 'Nigra' bears dusty pink mophead clusters. The black stems provide contrast. 'Nikko Blue' bears many large blue to deep lavender mophead clusters. 'Parzifal' has large mophead clusters that vary from shades of blue to shades of pink depending on soil pH. PINK ELF ('Pia') bears reddish pink, white-centered mophead clusters. This dwarf cultivar grows about 24" tall and spreads about 36". 'Royal Purple' bears dark purple mophead clusters. 'Tokyo Delight' bears white lacecap clusters that mature to pink. (Zones 5–9)

H. paniculata (panicled hydrangea) is a spreading to upright large shrub or small tree. It grows 10–22' tall, spreads to 8' and bears white flowers from late summer to early fall. This species requires little pruning. When young it can be pruned to encourage

a shrub-like or tree-like habit. The entire shrub can be cut to within 12" of the ground each fall to encourage vigorous new growth the following summer. 'Brussels Lace' bears small, creamy white blossoms in lacecap clusters. 'Grandiflora' (PeeGee hydrangea) is a spreading large shrub or small tree 15–25' tall and 10–20' in spread. The mostly sterile flowers are borne in mophead clusters up to 18" long. 'Kyushu' bears white lacecap clusters from July to frost. LIMELIGHT ('Zwijnenburg') bears upright mophead clusters of bright lime green flowers that mature to pink and burgundy in fall. 'Pink Diamond' bears large lacecap clusters of white flowers that turn a deep pink in fall. THE SWAN ('Barbara') features large mophead clusters of huge white flowers. 'Tardiva' bears large white lacecap clusters in fall. 'Unique' bears large, upright mophead clusters of white flowers that turn pink in fall. 'White Moth' bears large mophead clusters of large sterile flowers in fall. (Zones 4–8)

H. quercifolia (oakleaf hydrangea) is a mound-forming shrub that is native to the southeastern U.S. It grows 4–8' tall, with an equal spread, and features attractive, cinnamon brown, exfoliating bark. The large leaves are lobed like an oak's and often turn bronze or bright red in fall. Conical clusters of sterile and fertile flowers persist from midsummer to fall. Prune after the bloom. Remove spent flowers and cut out some of the older growth to encourage young replacement growth. 'Alice' bears 12" clusters of white flowers. The dark green foliage turns burgundy in fall. 'Pee Wee' and 'Sikes Dwarf' are compact dwarf cultivars that grow half the size of the species. 'Snowflake' bears clusters of double flowers 12–15" long that open white and fade to pink as they age. The flowers are so heavy that they cause the stems to arch towards the ground. This cultivar prefers partial shade. 'Snow Queen' bears large, upright flower clusters. The foliage turns a deep, blood red color in fall. (Zones 4–8)

H. serrata (sawtooth hydrangea) has a compact, upright habit. It grows 4–5' tall, with an equal spread. The pink or blue flowers, usually in lacecap clusters, are produced in summer and fall. Prune flowering shoots back to the first strong buds once flowering is finished or early the following spring. On mature, established plants, remove one-third of the oldest growth yearly or as needed to encourage vigorous new growth. 'Blue Billow' bears lacecap clusters of blue flowers that mature to dark pink. 'Blue Bird' ('Bluebird') bears blue or light pink lacecap clusters. The leaves turn coppery red in fall. 'Preziosa' bears small, pink mophead clusters. (Zones 5–7)

Problems & Pests
Occasional problems for hydrangeas include slugs, gray mold, leaf spot, powdery mildew, ringspot virus and rust. Hot sun and excessive wind will dry out the petals and turn them brown.

Few plants are as bold and colorful as bigleaf hydrangea.

H. anomala subsp. *petiolaris* (above)

H. serrata 'Blue Bird' (center)
H. arborescens cultivar (below)

Japanese Hydrangea Vine

Schizophragma

Features: habit, foliage, flowers **Habit:** woody, deciduous climbing vine
Height: up to 40' **Spread:** up to 40' **Planting:** container; spring or fall
Zones: 5–8

RECENTLY I SAW A PLANTING I JUST DIDN'T UNDERSTAND AT ALL.
The plant in question looked like the climbing hydrangea on my garage
wall—but there were pink flowers on it in late June, rather than the white
flowers in late May I'd expect from the hydrangea. Closer inspection of this
anomaly revealed that a 'Roseum' Japanese hydrangea vine had been planted
5' away from a climbing hydrangea. The two had become intertwined, peace-
fully coexisting on the same stucco wall. I will soon swallow my pride, get
over the fact that I didn't think of this combination first, and duplicate the
seasonal color extension on my own garage wall.

Growing

Japanese hydrangea vine grows well in **full sun** or **partial shade**. The soil should be **average to fertile, humus rich, moist** and **well drained**.

Little pruning is required. Trim the vine's branches back to keep the plant within the desired space and to keep it looking neat and attractive.

Although this plant develops clinging rootlets, it's best to secure it in place until it is established. A rough surface is easiest for it to cling to. Over time, if the surface is too smooth, you may have to continue to secure the vine to the wall or other structure.

Tips

This vine will cling to any rough surface and looks attractive climbing a wall, fence, tree or arbor. It can also be used as a groundcover on a bank or allowed to grow up or over a rock wall.

Recommended

S. hydrangeoides is an attractive climbing vine similar in appearance to climbing hydrangea. It can grow up to 40' tall, clinging to the climbing surface with aerial rootlets. Lacy clusters of white flowers appear in mid-summer. **'Moonlight'** has silvery blue foliage. **'Roseum'** bears clusters of pink flowers. **'Strawberry Leaf'** has small leaves that resemble those of strawberry plants.

The lacy flower clusters consist of small, inconspicuous fertile flowers and showy sterile bracts.

S. hydrangeoides (both photos)

This vine rarely suffers from pest or disease problems.

Juniper

Juniperus

Features: foliage; variety of colors, sizes and habits **Habit:** conical or columnar tree, rounded or spreading shrub, or prostrate groundcover; evergreen **Height:** 4"–80'
Spread: 1–25' **Planting:** B & B, container; spring or fall **Zones:** 2–9

WHEN I FIRST ENTERED THE LANDSCAPING FIELD, JUNIPERS JUST consisted of a couple of green Pfitzer types, the larger gray-green 'Hetzii' and a few uprights of different foliage colors. Now we have so many different junipers to choose from, we can be selective. There is a juniper for almost every sunny area, and yet we have to be careful of too much of a good thing. There are plenty of different heights, widths and colors, but the texture of them all remains very much the same. Good design does require repetition and simplicity, but balance and especially dominance also have to be considered. Choose those junipers that will do a specific job, and then move on to the rest of the plant palette we have available.

Junipers come in all shapes and sizes and can suit almost any garden. Grow them in the sun to avoid open, straggly growth.

Growing

Junipers prefer **full sun** but tolerate light shade. Ideally the soil should be of **average fertility** and **well drained,** but these plants tolerate most soil conditions except excessively wet soil.

Though these evergreens rarely need pruning, they tolerate it well. They can be used for topiary and can be trimmed in summer as required to maintain their shape or limit their size.

Tips

With the wide variety of junipers available, there are endless uses for them in the garden. They make prickly barriers and hedges, and they can be used in borders, as specimens or in groups. The larger species can be used to form windbreaks, while the low-growing species can be used in rock gardens and as groundcovers.

The prickly foliage gives some gardeners a rash. It is a good idea to wear long sleeves and gloves when handling junipers. Juniper 'berries' are poisonous if eaten in large quantities.

Recommended

J. chinensis (Chinese juniper) is a conical tree or spreading shrub. It grows 50–70' tall and spreads 15–20'. Many cultivars have been developed from this species. 'Fairview' forms a narrow pyramid growing 15–20' tall and about 6' in width. 'Fruitlandii' is a vigorous spreader with bright green, dense foliage. It grows about 36" tall and 6' in spread. 'Hetzii' is an upright,

J. chinensis

J. scopulorum 'Skyrocket'

J. sabina 'Buffalo'

J. horizontalis with Thuja

spreading cultivar that grows 5–10' tall, with an equal spread. It has attractive gray-green needles. **'Hetzii Columnaris'** forms an attractive, narrow pyramid about 20' tall. **'Hooks'** grows 12–15' tall and spreads 24–36". **'Kallay's Compact'** is a low, compact spreader with dark green foliage. It grows 24–36" tall and spreads about 6'. **'Keteleeri'** forms a broad pyramidal tree 15–20' tall and 6–10' wide. **Var. *sargentii*** (Sargent juniper) is a low-growing, spreading variety. It grows only 12–24" tall but can spread to 10'. **Var. *s.* 'Viridis'** is similar in size and habit to var. *sargentii* but holds its light green color well all year. **'Saybrook Gold'** is a low, spreading cultivar with bright gold needles that take on a bronze hue in winter. It grows 24–36" tall, with a spread of about 6'. **'Sea Green'** is a compact, spreading cultivar with arching branches and bright green foliage. It grows 4–6' tall and spreads up to 8'. **'Spartan'** is a fast-growing, columnar or pyramidal cultivar with dense, rich green foliage. It grows about 15' tall and spreads 3–4'. (Zones 3–9)

J. conferta (shore juniper) is a stellar groundcover for dry, sandy soils. It grows 12–18" tall and spreads 6–9'. Shore juniper and its cultivars are reasonably salt tolerant. Most are hardy in Zones 6–9. **'Blue Pacific'** has excellent blue-green foliage and compact growth, rarely growing taller than 12". **'Emerald Sea'** is the hardiest cultivar, to Zone 5. It is similar to 'Blue Pacific' but has a looser habit and grows taller.

J. horizontalis (creeping juniper) is a prostrate, creeping groundcover that is native to Ohio and boreal regions across North America. It grows 12–24" tall and spreads up to 8'. This juniper looks attractive cascading down rock walls. The foliage is blue-green, with a purple hue in winter. '**Bar Harbor**' grows 12" tall and spreads 6–10'. The foliage turns a distinct purple in winter. '**Hughes**' grows about 12" tall and spreads up to 9'. The blue-green foliage takes on only a slight purple tinge in winter. '**Mother Lode**' has needles with gold variegation. '**Wiltonii**' ('Blue Rug') is very low growing, with trailing branches and silvery blue foliage. It grows 4–6" tall and spreads 6–8'. (Zones 3–9)

J. procumbens (Japanese garden juniper) is a wide-spreading, stiff-branched, low shrub 12–36" tall and 6–15' wide. '**Greenmound**' is a low, dense spreader with light green foliage. It grows 4–6" tall and spreads about 6'. '**Nana**' is a dwarf, compact, mat-forming shrub 12–24" tall and 6–12' in spread. (Zones 4–9)

J. sabina (Savin juniper) is a variable, spreading to erect shrub. It grows 12–18' tall and may spread 5–20'.

J. conferta 'Emerald Sea'

The blue 'berries' (actually fleshy cones) are used in small quantities to season meat dishes and to give gin its distinctive flavor. They also make a nice addition to potpourri.

J. chinensis behind lower cultivar
J. squamata

Many popular cultivars are available. **'Broadmoor'** is a low spreader with erect branchlets. It grows 24–36" tall and spreads up to 10'. **'Buffalo'** has bright green, feathery foliage that holds its color well in winter. It grows 12" tall and spreads about 8'. CALGARY CARPET ('Monna') is a low, spreading plant with bright green, leathery foliage. It grows about 12" tall and 4–5' in spread. (Zones 3–7)

J. scopulorum (Rocky Mountain juniper) is a rounded or spreading tree or shrub. It grows 30–50' tall and spreads 3–20'. **'Skyrocket'** is a very narrow, columnar tree with gray-green needles. It grows up to 20' tall but spreads only 12–24". **'Tolleson's Weeping'** has arching branches and pendulous, silvery blue, string-like foliage. It grows about 20' tall and spreads 10'. It is sometimes grafted to create a small, weeping standard tree. This cultivar can be used in a large planter. **'Witchita Blue'** is an upright pyramidal cultivar that grows 15–20' tall and spreads about 4'. It has attractive silvery blue foliage. (Zones 3–7)

J. squamata (singleseed juniper) forms a prostrate or low, spreading shrub or a small, upright tree. It grows up to 30' tall and spreads 3–25'. It is rarely grown in favor of the cultivars. **'Blue Alps'** is an upright cultivar with slightly arching branches and silvery blue needles. It grows 12–15' tall and spreads 12–15'. **'Blue Carpet'** forms a low groundcover with blue-gray needles. It grows 8–12" high and spreads 4–5'. **'Blue Star'** is a compact, rounded shrub with silvery blue needles. It grows 12–36" tall and spreads about 3–4'. (Zones 4–7)

J. virginiana (eastern redcedar) is native to Ohio. This tree has a variable habit, ranging from broadly pyramidal to columnar. It grows 40–80' tall and spreads 8–25'. The needles are gray-green. '**Burkii**' is a variable, broad to narrow, pyramidal cultivar. It grows 10–25' tall and spreads 3–8'. '**Emerald Sentinel**' is a narrow pyramidal cultivar that grows up to 20' tall and spreads 3–5'. '**Grey Owl**' is an upright, spreading cultivar boasting silvery needles and abundant, attractive 'berries.' It grows 3–10' tall and spreads 6–12'. (Zones 2–9)

Problems & Pests

Although junipers are tough plants, they may have occasional problems with aphids, bagworm, bark beetles, caterpillars, leaf miners, mites, scale insects, canker, cedar-apple rust and twig blight.

J. virginiana

Juniper was used traditionally to purify homes affected by sickness and death.

J. horizontalis with lower cultivar beneath

Katsura-Tree

Cercidiphyllum

Features: summer and fall foliage, habit **Habit:** rounded or spreading, often multi-stemmed, deciduous tree **Height:** 10–70' **Spread:** 10–70' or more **Planting:** B & B, container; spring **Zones:** 4–8

IT WAS ALWAYS A MYSTERY TO ME WHY SUCH A WONDERFULLY adaptable and trouble-free tree was not more commonly available and frequently used. That situation has changed in recent years. Katsura-tree is now more widely grown and appreciated, and it can be hard to find only because it's often sold out. I have often said that plant trends are similar to clothing fashions: the only constant is change. By the same token, a good classic transcends fashion. All you have to do is lay eyes on a katsura-tree in full form or fall color, or see a specimen like the gorgeous weeper at Spring Grove Cemetery, and you'll be hooked for life.

C. japonicum *is the largest native deciduous tree in Japan and China, growing as tall as 130' in the wild.*

Growing

Katsura-tree can grow well in **full sun** or **partial shade**. The soil should be **fertile, humus rich, neutral to acidic, moist** and **well drained**. This tree will become established more quickly if it is watered regularly during dry spells for the first two to three years.

Pruning is unnecessary. Damaged branches can be removed as needed.

Tips

Katsura-tree is useful as a specimen or shade tree. The species is quite large and is best used in large landscapes. The cultivar 'Pendula' is wide spreading but can be used in smaller gardens than the species.

This tree is native to eastern Asia, and the delicate foliage blends well into Japanese-style gardens.

C. japonicum
'Pendula'

Recommended

C. japonicum grows 40–70' tall, with an equal or sometimes greater spread. It is a slow-growing tree that takes a long time to exceed 40'. The heart-shaped, blue-green leaves turn yellow and orange in fall and develop a spicy scent. **'Pendula'** is one of the most elegant weeping trees available. It is usually grafted to a standard and grows 10–25' tall, with an equal or greater spread. Mounding, cascading branches sweep the ground, giving the entire tree the appearance of a waterfall tumbling over rocks.

Katsura-tree is generally free of pest and disease problems.

Kerria
Japanese Kerria
Kerria

Features: mid- to late-spring flowers, habit **Habit:** mounding or arching, suckering, deciduous shrub **Height:** 3–10' **Spread:** 3–10' **Planting:** B & B, container; spring or fall **Zones:** 4–9

KERRIA IS OCCASIONALLY CALLED SUMMER FORSYTHIA BECAUSE it has abundant, bright golden yellow flowers and they appear later than those of true forsythia. This plant always stands out in the shade. When in flower its golden yellow blooms draw attention, and when not flowering its bright green stems draw the eye, especially in winter. The cultivar 'Picta' has cream-variegated leaves that seem to jump out of the light-shade areas in which it thrives. There are so many shady places, especially in older land-scapes, and kerria makes a wonderful light, airy addition to them.

Growing

Kerria prefers **light or partial shade** but adapts to other light levels. The soil should be of **average fertility** and **well drained.** Fewer flowers will appear on a plant grown in soil that is too fertile.

Prune after flowering is complete. Cut flowering shoots back to young side shoots or strong buds, or cut them right to the ground. The entire plant can be cut back to the ground after it blooms if it becomes overgrown and needs rejuvenating.

Tips

Kerria is useful in group plantings, woodland gardens and shrub or mixed borders.

Most of the flowers emerge in spring, but some may appear sporadically in summer, especially if the shrub is watered regularly.

Recommended

K. japonica grows 3–6' tall and spreads 3–8'. It has yellow single flowers. **'Albiflora'** ('Albescens') bears light yellow or creamy white single flowers. **'Golden Guinea'** bears large single blooms over a long period. **'Picta'** has grayish blue-green foliage with creamy margins. **'Pleniflora'** ('Flora Pleno') bears double flowers. It grows 10' tall, with an equal spread, and has a more upright habit than that of the species. **'Shannon'** has larger single flowers than those of the species.

Problems & Pests

Canker, leaf blight, leaf spot, root rot and twig blight may occur but are not serious problems.

'Albiflora' (above)

'Golden Guinea'

Kerria flowers can resemble old-fashioned yellow roses, and this plant is indeed a member of the rose family.

K. japonica

Larch

Larix

Features: summer and fall foliage, cones, habit **Habit:** pyramidal, deciduous conifer **Height:** 50–100', or determined by graft height **Spread:** 10–40'
Planting: B & B, container; early spring **Zones:** 3–7

IT'S ONLY NATURAL THAT WHEN A LANDSCAPE designer describes many plants to a client all at once, much is forgotten. When the consultations are over, the contract is signed, the work is done and the bill is paid, the designer will get at least one more phone call from the client in the first fall if any larches have been planted. The tree looks for all the world like an evergreen until then, when it turns a lovely light golden yellow and defoliates. A 'come quick, my tree is dying' call is almost inevitable. It is always fun to state with confidence over the phone that all is well; that's what these trees are supposed to do.

Growing

Larches grow best in **full sun**. The soil should be of **average fertility, acidic, moist** and **well drained**. Though tolerant of most conditions, these trees don't like dry or chalky soils. Pruning is rarely required.

Tips

Larches make interesting specimen trees. They are among the few conifers that lose their foliage each year. In fall the needles turn golden yellow before dropping, and in winter the cones stand out on the bare branches.

The low, weeping cultivars grow to an appropriate size for most residential gardens.

Recommended

L. decidua (European larch) is a large, narrow, pyramidal tree. It grows 70–100' tall and spreads 12–30'. '**Pendula**' has a weeping habit and is usually grafted to a standard. Specimens vary greatly from the bizarre to the elegant. (Zones 3–6)

L. kaempferi (Japanese larch) grows 50–100' tall and spreads 15–40'. It has pendulous branchlets. The summer color of the needles is bluer than that of European larch. Fall color is excellent. (Zones 4–7)

L. x marschlinsii (*L. x eurolepsis;* Dunkeld larch, hybrid larch) is a hybrid of *L. decidua* and *L. kaempferi*. It is a fast-growing tree with a narrow, pyramidal habit. It grows up to 100' tall and spreads about 20'. The needles are grayish green in summer, turning yellow in fall. '**Varied Directions**' is an unusual, fast-growing, spreading cultivar that is grafted to a standard to create a spreading, weeping specimen. The new branchlets splay out near the branch ends, eventually becoming weeping as they mature. Height depends on the graft height and spread is variable to at least 10'. This cultivar is sometimes attributed to *L. decidua*. (Zones 3–7)

Problems & Pests

Problems may be caused by aphids, case bearers or other caterpillars, sawflies, needle blight and rust.

L. decidua 'Pendula'

Larches are good trees for attracting birds to the garden.

L. kaempferi

Lilac

Syringa

Features: mid-spring to early-summer flowers, habit **Habit:** rounded or suckering, deciduous shrub or small tree **Height:** 3–30' **Spread:** 3–25' **Planting:** B & B, container; late winter or early spring **Zones:** 2–8

ON AN ABANDONED FARM, I ONCE MEASURED A GROVE OF LILACS that had spread out from a single original plant. It covered an area 52' by 75'. There are so many varieties of lilacs that a few horticulturists and hybridizers have made lifelong studies of them. Even if our interests are not that specific, there seems to be at least one lilac that brings back wonderful memories of a person or place or even of just one bouquet with an unforgettable color or fragrance. By selecting varied species and/or cultivars, you can have lilacs blooming over a very long period, usually ending in mid- to late June with the flowers of the Japanese tree lilac.

Growing

Lilacs grow best in **full sun**. The soil should be **fertile, humus rich** and **well drained**. These plants tolerate open, windy locations, and the improved air circulation helps keep powdery mildew at bay. Clear up leaves in fall to help discourage overwintering pests.

Most lilacs need little pruning. On established French lilac plants, you can cut one-fourth to one-third of the growth right back to the ground each year after the bloom. This treatment will make way for vigorous young growth and prevent the plants from becoming leggy, overgrown and unattractive.

Deadhead lilacs as much as possible to keep plants neat. Remove the flowers as soon as they are finished to give the plant plenty of time to produce next season's flowers.

S. x hyacinthiflora 'Evangeline'

Not all lilac varieties are equally fragrant, so choose your lilac carefully if this feature is important to you.

S. meyeri

S. x *prestoniae* cultivar

S. *meyeri* 'Palibin'

Tips

Include lilacs in a shrub or mixed border or use them to create an informal hedge. Japanese tree lilac can be used as a specimen or small shade tree.

Recommended

S. x *henryi* (Henry lilac) is a rounded shrub that bears loose clusters of pale purple to red flowers in early summer. It grows 6–12' tall, with an equal spread. '**Lutece**' bears mauve or white flowers. (Zones 2–7)

S. x *hyacinthiflora* (hyacinth-flowered lilac, early-flowering lilac) is a group of hardy, upright hybrids that become spreading as they mature. They generally grow 8–12' tall, with an equal spread. Clusters of fragrant flowers appear in mid- to late spring, two weeks earlier than those of the French lilacs. The leaves turn reddish purple in fall. They are resistant to powdery mildew and bacterial blight. '**Anabel**' ('Annabel') bears pink flowers and grows 6–9' in height and spread. '**California Rose**' bears fragrant light pink flowers. '**Dr. Chadwick**' is a dwarf cultivar with blue flowers. It grows 4–6' tall and wide. '**Evangeline**' bears light purple double flowers. This cultivar is nonsuckering. '**Excel**' bears lavender flowers and grows 8–10' tall and wide. '**Maiden's Blush**' bears fragrant pale pink flowers. It is a vigorous grower and may need more regular pruning than some of the other cultivars in this group. '**Mt. Baker**' bears white flowers in large clusters that completely cover the plant. '**Pocahontas**' bears very fragrant reddish purple flowers. (Zones 3–7)

S. meyeri (Meyer lilac, dwarf Korean lilac) is a compact, rounded shrub that grows 3–8' tall and spreads 3–12'. It bears fragrant pink or lavender flowers in late spring and early summer and sometimes again in fall. It does not sucker profusely. The **Fairy Tale Series** is a new group of hybrids developed from crosses between *S. meyeri* and other lilacs. The plants grow 5–6' tall, with an equal spread. In this series, FAIRY DUST ('Baildust') bears fragrant, dusty pink flowers. TINKERBELLE ('Bailbelle') bears fragrant, bright pink flowers that open from dark pink buds. Both hybrids may continue to bloom sporadically over the summer. **'Palibin'** bears clusters of fragrant mauve pink flowers. (Zones 3–7)

S. meyeri TINKERBELLE

The wonderfully fragrant flowers of S. vulgaris *have inspired the development of some 800–900 cultivars.*

S. reticulata 'Ivory Silk' in very early bloom

S. reticulata 'Ivory Silk'

S. patula (Manchurian lilac) is a hardy lilac from Korea and northern China. It grows 5–10' tall, spreads 3–8' and bears small clusters of fragrant, lilac-colored flowers. This species produces very few suckers. **'Miss Kim'** is similar to the species in shape and size but is denser in habit. The dark green leaves turn burgundy red in fall. (Zones 3–8)

S. pekinensis (Pekin lilac) forms a small, multi-stemmed tree. It grows 15–20' tall, with an equal spread, and bears nodding clusters of creamy white flowers in early summer. This species is similar to *S. reticulata*, but with a more delicate appearance. (Zones 3–7)

S. x persica (Persian lilac) is an upright shrub with graceful, arching branches. It grows 6–8' tall and spreads 5–7'. It bears fragrant pale purple flowers in mid-May. (Zones 3–7)

S. x prestoniae (Preston hybrid lilacs) is a group of hybrids developed from crosses between *S. villosa* and *S. reflexa*. These upright shrubs bear nodding clusters of flowers in early summer, two to three weeks after the French lilacs. They grow up to 25' tall, with up to an equal spread. They are generally nonsuckering and can be trained into small trees. **'Alexander's Pink'** bears large pink flowers. **'Hiawatha'** bears pale pink flowers that open from reddish purple buds. **'Isabella'** bears pinkish lilac flowers. **'James MacFarlane'** (*S. x josiflexa* 'James MacFarlane') bears pink flowers. **'Nocturne'** bears lilac pink flowers that open from dark violet buds. **'Olmstead'** bears purple flowers. **'Redwine'** (*S. x josiflexa* 'Redwine') bears vivid magenta flowers. (Zones 2–7)

S. reticulata (Japanese tree lilac) is a rounded large shrub or small tree that grows 20–30' tall and spreads 15–25'. It bears fragrant white flowers in early summer and does not produce many suckers. This species and its cultivars are resistant to powdery mildew, scale insects and borers. **'Ivory Silk'** has a more compact habit and produces more flowers than the species. It grows 10–20' tall and spreads 6–15'. (Zones 3–7)

S. x tribrida 'Larksong' bears many large clusters of very fragrant, single pink flowers in late spring. This hybrid sets few seedpods, reducing the need to deadhead. It grows 6–12' tall, with an equal or slightly lesser spread. This cultivar was developed by Father Fiala near Medina, Ohio. (Zones 3–7)

S. vulgaris (French lilac, common lilac) is the plant most people think of when they think of lilacs. It grows 8–22' tall, spreads 6–22' and bears fragrant, lilac-colored flowers in late spring and early summer. This suckering, spreading shrub has an irregular habit, but consistent maintenance pruning will keep it neat and in good condition. Many cultivars are available, of which the following are but a few good examples. '**Adelaide Dunbar**' features fragrant, purple double flowers. '**Belle de Nancy**' has pink double flowers. '**Charles Joly**' has magenta double flowers. '**Mme. Lemoine**' has large, white double flowers. '**President Grevy**' bears large clusters of cobalt blue double flowers that open from reddish purple buds. '**Sensation**' bears white-margined, purple flowers. '**Wonderblue**' ('Little Boy Blue') bears blue single flowers. '**Yankee Doodle**' bears dark purple flowers on a compact plant that grows 8' tall, with an equal spread. (Zones 3–8)

Problems & Pests
Borers, caterpillars, root-knot nematodes, scale insects, leaf spot, powdery mildew and stem blight are all possible troublemakers for lilacs.

Don't limit your view of lilacs to the common French lilac seen in your grandmother's garden. You have hundreds of beautiful plants to choose from.

S. x *persica* with *S. vulgaris*

Lilacs are frost-loving shrubs that don't flower at all in the warm southern U.S.

S. vulgaris

Linden

Tilia

Features: habit, foliage **Habit:** dense, pyramidal to rounded, deciduous tree
Height: 20–80' **Spread:** 15–60' **Planting:** B & B, bare-root, container; spring or
fall **Zones:** 2–8

I HAVE BEEN WATCHING A LITTLELEAF LINDEN GROW IN THE LATE
Dr. L.C. Chadwick's front yard for more than 40 years. It is now over 60' wide
and has a low silhouette. It makes a terrific complement to the two-story
home situated on a slight rise. The yellow-green bracts that hold the flowers
hang in stark contrast to the dark green leaves. I stopped short of planting a
pair of lindens one time when the client asked, 'Do these flowers attract bees?'
The client's daughter and grandchildren were highly allergic to bee stings.
If you aren't allergic, the delightful fragrance of the flowers is a wonderful
feature, as are the seasonal interest and durability of lindens.

*Basswood has lightweight wood that
is prized for use by carvers.*

Growing

Lindens grow best in **full sun**. The soil should be **average to fertile, moist** and **well drained**. These trees adapt to most pH levels but prefer soil that is **alkaline**. *T. cordata* and *T. tomentosa* tolerate pollution and other urban conditions better than *T. americana.*

Little pruning is required. Remove dead, damaged, diseased or awkward growth as needed. On shrubby specimens, all but the strongest stems should be pruned out.

Tips

Lindens are useful and attractive street trees, shade trees and specimen trees. Their tolerance of pollution and their moderate size make lindens ideal for city gardens.

Linden blossoms exude a dripping honeydew that will coat anything underneath, so don't plant lindens near a driveway.

Recommended

T. americana (basswood, American linden) is rarely used in gardens. It grows 60–80' tall and spreads about half this wide. Fragrant flowers appear in early to mid-summer. This tree is very cold hardy and is native to most of the eastern half of the U.S., including Ohio. The smaller **'Redmond'** is more commonly grown than the species. It becomes a pyramidal tree, more densely branched than the species, and grows about 20–35' tall and 15–25' wide. (Zones 2–8)

T. cordata (littleleaf linden) is a dense, pyramidal tree that may

T. americana (both photos)

Given enough space, lindens will branch all the way to the ground.

become rounded with age. It grows 60–70' tall, spreads 30–45' and bears small flowers with narrow yellow-green bracts in summer. **CORINTHIAN** ('Corzam') is a compact pyramidal cultivar with a strong central leader. It grows about 45' tall and spreads about 15'. 'Greenspire' is a compact cultivar 40–50' tall and 20–25' in spread. Its uniform shape makes it an excellent choice for a street tree. (Zones 3–7)

T. tomentosa (silver linden) is a broad tree with a columnar to pyramidal habit. It grows 50–70' tall, with a spread of 25–60'. The bright green leaves have silvery undersides. Fragrant flowers appear in summer. **SATIN SHADOW** ('Sashazam') grows about 50' tall, with a spread of about 40'. The attractive dark green leaves have silvery undersides, causing the leaves to shimmer and sparkle when they move with the wind. 'Sterling' ('Sterling Silver'), a broad pyramidal

T. cordata (above)

cultivar, grows about 50' tall, with a spread of 25'. The glossy green leaf tops contrast with the silvery undersides. This cultivar is resistant to Japanese beetle and gypsy moth larvae. (Zones 4–7)

Problems & Pests
Occasional problems with aphids, borers, caterpillars, Japanese beetle, leaf miners, mites, anthracnose, canker, leaf spot and powdery mildew can occur.

Lindens are desirable shade and street trees because of their picturesque shape, moderately fast growth and wide adaptability.

Magnolia

Magnolia

Features: flowers, fruit, foliage, habit, bark **Habit:** upright to spreading, deciduous shrub or tree **Height:** 10–40' **Spread:** 5–35' **Planting:** B & B, container; winter or early spring **Zones:** 3–9

MAGNOLIAS ARE BEAUTIFUL, FRAGRANT, VERSATILE PLANTS THAT also provide attractive winter structure. On the downside, they can be messy when the petals drop and disappointing when late frost kills the flowers. Still, the positives far outweigh the negatives. A whole community once banded together and prevented an oil company from destroying a native cucumber magnolia *(M. acuminata)*—90' tall and with a trunk 4' wide—when building a new station. Thousands of dollars were spent on site redesign and on drainage systems to preserve the giant tree's rootzone. On my own property, I once espaliered a sweetbay magnolia *(M. virginiana)* along the back of the house, and it was far more attractive than the barren stucco.

Growing

Magnolias grow well in **full sun** or **partial shade**. The soil should be **fertile, humus rich, acidic, moist** and **well drained**. A summer mulch will help keep the roots cool and the soil moist. Sweetbay magnolia tolerates wet soils and shaded locations.

Very little pruning is needed. When plants are young, thin out a few branches to encourage an attractive habit. Avoid transplanting, but if necessary, transplant in early spring.

Tips

Magnolias make wonderful specimen trees, and the smaller species can be used in borders. Avoid planting magnolias in sunny locations that warm up quickly in late winter and early spring. The early warmth will encourage early flowering, making the sensitive blossoms more likely to be damaged by a late frost or by wind and rain.

Recommended

M. x 'Ann' becomes a small tree or large shrub 10–15' tall, with a slightly lesser spread. Its purple-red flowers are less likely to suffer frost damage because they open later in spring than those of many other magnolias. This cultivar may also bloom sporadically over the summer. (Zones 5–8)

M. x 'Betty' is an upright hybrid that grows about 10' tall and spreads about 5'. Its mid-spring flowers have 12–15 white petals that are dark purple on the outsides. (Zones 5–8)

M. x 'Butterflies' is an upright tree that grows about 15' tall and spreads

M. x 'Ann'

Despite their often fuzzy coats, magnolia flower buds are frost sensitive.

M. stellata 'Royal Star'

M. x *loebneri* 'Merrill'

M. x *soulangiana*

about 20' tall, with an equal spread, and bears pink flowers in spring. (Zones 5–9)

***M.* x 'Galaxy'** is a pyramidal to columnar tree that grows 30–40' tall and spreads 10–25'. It bears purple or pink flowers in spring, usually after the danger of frost damage has passed. (Zones 5–8)

***M.* x 'Jane'** is an upright hybrid that grows about 12' tall, with a spread of 10'. In late spring, it bears white flowers that are reddish purple on the outside. (Zones 5–8)

M. kobus (kobus magnolia) is a rounded, multi-stemmed tree 30–40' tall and 25–35' in spread. It is covered in a cloud of white blooms in early or mid-spring. Though it may take up to 30 years before this tree reaches its full flowering potential, it is stunning when it does. (Zones 5–7)

M.* x *loebneri (Loebner magnolia) was developed from a cross between *M. kobus* and *M. stellata*. This rounded, spreading tree can grow 15–30' tall, with an equal or greater spread. It is one of the earliest magnolias to bloom, bearing white or pink flowers in early to mid-spring. The hybrid and most cultivars are hardy in Zones 5–9. **'Ballerina'** bears fragrant white flowers in late spring. The 30 petals of each flower have pinkish bases. **'Leonard Messel'** bears white flowers with petals that have a pink or purple stripe down the center and pink undersides. This cultivar also doesn't flower as early as the parent. **'Merrill'** bears abundant white flowers. It is fast growing and cold hardy to Zone 3.

about 11'. In mid-spring, it bears yellow, cup-shaped flowers with red stamens. Many other hybrids have yellow flowers, including **'Elizabeth,' 'Golden Endeavor,' 'Golden Sun,' 'Yellow Bird'** and **'Yellow Lantern.'** They all grow 15–25' tall, with spreads of 15–20'. **'Butterflies'** is considered to have the best yellow flowers. (Zones 5–9)

***M.* x 'Forest Pink'** is a rounded, spreading tree or shrub. It grows

M. x *soulangiana* (*M.* x *soulangeana;* saucer magnolia) is a rounded, spreading shrub or tree. It grows 20–30' tall, with an equal spread. Pink, purple or white flowers emerge in mid- to late spring. '**Alexandrina**' can grow as an upright tree or large shrubby form 20–25' tall and 15–25' wide. Its flower petals are pink on the outside and white on the inside. The variability in habit and flower color may have resulted from several cultivars having the same name. (Zones 5–9)

M. stellata (star magnolia) is a compact, bushy or spreading shrub or small tree. It grows 10–20' tall and spreads 10–15'. Many-petaled, fragrant white flowers appear in early to mid-spring. '**Royal Star**' is a vigorous upright cultivar that grows 15–18' tall, with an equal spread. Its pink buds open to many-petaled white flowers. (Zones 4–9)

M. x '**Susan**' is a dense, upright, pyramidal shrub that grows about 12' tall, with a spread of 10'. It bears large, purple-red flowers in mid-spring. (Zones 5–8)

M. virginiana (sweetbay magnolia, swamp magnolia) forms an open, spreading shrub or a small, multi-stemmed tree. It grows 10–30' tall, with up to an equal spread, and bears very fragrant white flowers in late spring or early summer. (Zones 5–9)

Problems & Pests
Possible problems include scale insects, snails, thrips, treehoppers, weevils, canker, dieback, leaf spot and powdery mildew.

M. x *soulangiana*

The yellow-flowered hybrids tend to bear creamy or light yellow flowers in warmer climates.

M. stellata

Maple
Acer

Features: foliage, bark, winged fruit, fall color, habit, flowers **Habit:** small, multi-stemmed, deciduous tree or large shrub **Height:** 6–80' **Spread:** 6–70'
Planting: B & B, container; preferably spring **Zones:** 2–8

WHEN I WAS LITTLE, I OFTEN STAYED WITH MY GRANDPARENTS on their farm. I recall that whenever the silvery undersides of silver maple (*A. saccharinum*) leaves flipped up in a breeze, my grandmother would proclaim that the cornfields would soon get a drink of rain. It seemed that she was always right. I think almost everyone must have a maple story, because these trees have such a broad distribution. I still get a thrill from the flaming orange-red of sugar maple in fall and from the burgundy summer color of 'Crimson King' Norway maple. I chose a reddish, cut-leaved, weeping variety of *A. palmatum* for the entrance to my home because of its lovely structure, even in winter. There is at least one maple for each of us.

Growing

Generally maples do well in **full sun** or **light shade,** though their preference varies from species to species. The soil should be **fertile, moist,** high in **organic matter** and **well drained.**

The amount of pruning needed depends on how much time you have and on what purpose the tree will serve in the garden. Informal and naturalistic gardens will require less pruning, while a formal garden may demand more effort. If maples are allowed to grow naturally, you simply need to remove dead, damaged or diseased branches at any time. These trees respond well to pruning, however, and can even be used to create bonsai specimens. Pruning should take place when maples are fully leafed out, in early to mid-summer.

A. japonicum

Silver maple (A. saccharinum) *is a common native tree that is frequently used for its fast growth and attractive foliage. But it is also messy, prone to breakage and susceptible to a host of pest and disease problems, making it a poor choice for most gardens.*

A. palmatum cultivar

Tips

Maples can be used as specimen trees, as large elements in shrub or mixed borders, or as hedges. Some are useful as understory plants bordering wooded areas; others can be grown in containers on patios or terraces. Few Japanese gardens are without the attractive smaller maples. Almost all maples can be used to create bonsai specimens.

Recommended

A. campestre (hedge maple) forms a dense, rounded tree 25–35' tall, with an equal spread. Its low-branching habit and tolerance of heavy pruning make it popular as a hedge plant. The foliage is often killed by frost before it turns color, but in a warm fall it may turn an attractive yellow. (Zones 4–8)

A. x *freemanii* and its cultivars were developed from crosses between *A. rubrum* and *A. saccharinum*. They vary in habit and fall coloration. They generally grow 40–50' tall, with a spread of 20–40'. **'Armstrong'**

A. saccharum *is the main source of the sap used to make maple syrup, but other maples can also be tapped for their sweet sap.*

is a fairly narrow, upright tree about 45' tall and about 15' wide. This fast-growing tree has attractive smooth gray bark and is suitable for smaller urban gardens and narrow lawns. **AUTUMN BLAZE** ('Jeffersred') has a dense, broad, oval habit. It grows about 50' tall and spreads about 40'. This cultivar is drought tolerant and develops excellent red fall color. **CELEBRATION** ('Celzam') has a broad columnar or pyramidal habit with strong branch crotches. It is a seedless cultivar that grows up to 45' tall and spreads 20–25'. The leaves develop a reddish cast then turn bright gold in fall. (Zones 4–7)

A. ginnala (Amur maple) is both attractive and extremely hardy; it can withstand winter temperatures as low as –50° F. It also adapts to many soil types and a wide pH range. This species grows 15–25' tall, with an equal or greater spread. It can be grown as a large, multi-stemmed shrub or pruned to form a small tree. *A. ginnala* has attractive dark green leaves, bright red samaras and smooth bark with distinctive vertical striping. The fall foliage is often a brilliant crimson. The color develops best in full sun, but the tree will also grow well in light shade. This is a popular tree for patios and terraces because it can be grown in a large planter. (Zones 2–8)

A. griseum (paperbark maple) is attractive and adapts to many conditions. It grows slowly to 20–35' tall, with a width half or equal the height. This maple is popular because of its orange-brown bark that peels and curls away from the trunk in papery strips. Unfortunately, it is difficult to propagate, so it can be expensive and sometimes hard to find. (Zones 4–8)

A. japonicum (fullmoon maple, Japanese maple) is an open, spreading tree or large shrub. It grows 20–30' tall, with an equal or greater spread. The leaves turn stunning shades of yellow, orange and red in fall. '**Aconitifolium**' has deeply lobed leaves that turn deep red in fall. '**Green Cascade**' has finely dissected, bright green leaves that turn bright yellow, orange and red in fall. The weeping, mounding habit gives the plant a waterfall-like appearance. It grows about 8' tall, with an equal spread. '**Vitifolium**' has shallowly lobed leaves that turn bright orange, red and purple in fall. (Zones 5–7)

A. palmatum (Japanese maple) is considered by many gardeners to be one of the most beautiful and versatile trees available. Though many cultivars and varieties are quite small, the species itself generally grows 15–25' tall, with an equal or greater spread. With enough space it may even reach 50'. Because it leafs out early in spring, this tree can be badly damaged or killed by a late-spring frost. (Zones 5–8)

A. platanoides samaras

Maple fruits, called samaras, have wings that act like miniature helicopter rotors and help in seed dispersal.

Two distinct groups of cultivars have been developed from *A. palmatum.* Types without dissected leaves, bred from *A. p.* var. *atropurpureum,* are grown for their deep red to purple foliage, though many lose their purple coloring as summer progresses. They generally grow the same size as the species. **'Bloodgood'** has reddish purple foliage. The color lasts well over the summer then turns red in fall. **'Oshio Beni'** has bright red foliage that turns scarlet in fall.

A. saccharum (center), A. platanoides (below)

Types with dissected leaves, derived from *A. p.* var. *dissectum,* have foliage so deeply lobed and divided that it appears fern-like or even thread-like. The leaves can be green or red. These cultivars are often much smaller than the species, growing 6–15' tall, with spreads up to 15'. **'Crimson Queen'** has a cascading habit and finely dissected red foliage. **'Inaba Shidare'** ('Red Select') is an upright plant with weeping branches. The burgundy leaves turn red in fall. **'Ornatum'** has bronze-green leaves with silvery variegations. The leaves turn red in fall. **'Viridis'** has green leaves that turn yellow-gold to red in fall.

A. saccharum

Maple wood is hard and dense and is used for fine furniture construction and for some musical instruments.

A. platanoides (Norway maple) is a rounded or oval tree 40–50' tall or taller, with an equal or slightly lesser spread. It has very dense growth, so grass may not grow well beneath it. Its fall color can be good unless an early frost hits before the color develops. This maple is a tough city tree, but don't use it near natural wooded areas; the prolific seedlings can outcompete many native plants when given the opportunity. 'Cleveland' is an upright, oval to rounded tree. It can grow as tall as the species but spreads only 30–40'. The dark green leaves turn golden yellow in fall. 'Columnare' is a broad, columnar tree that grows up to 60' tall and spreads 15–20'. 'Crimson King' is

a very common cultivar with dark purple foliage. This dark tree casts a heavy shade. 'Deborah' is a rounded tree that grows about 50' tall and 45' wide. The new leaves are bright red, maturing to dark green over the summer. 'Drummondii' (harlequin maple) has light green foliage with wide creamy margins. Any growth that doesn't develop the variegated foliage should be pruned out. 'Emerald Queen' is a fast-growing, rounded tree that grows about 50' tall and 40' wide. The dark green leaves turn bright yellow in fall. (Zones 4–8)

A. rubrum (red maple) is native to Ohio. This tree is pyramidal in habit when young and becomes more rounded as it matures. It grows 40–70' tall and has a variable spread of 20–70'. Single- and multi-stemmed specimens are available. The cold tolerance of this maple varies depending on where the plant has been grown. Locally bred trees will adapt best to the local climate. Fall color varies from tree to tree, some developing no fall color and others developing bright yellow, orange or red foliage. Choose named cultivars for the best fall color. 'Bowhall' is a narrow, pyramidal tree that grows about 50' tall and spreads about 15'. The leaves turn yellow-orange and red in fall. 'Embers' is a narrow, upright tree that develops a more rounded and spreading habit as it matures. The leaves turn bright red in fall. RED SUNSET ('Franksred') has deep orange to red fall color and good cold tolerance. (Zones 4–8)

A. saccharum (sugar maple) is also native to Ohio. It is considered by many to be the most impressive and majestic of all the maples. It has a rounded pyramidal outline, grows 50–80' tall and spreads 35–50'. The brilliant fall color ranges from yellow to red. This large species does not tolerate restricted, polluted, urban conditions but makes a spectacular addition to parks, golf courses and other large properties.

A. griseum (above)

'**Bonfire**' is fast growing and heat tolerant, with an oval to rounded habit. The leaves turn yellow-orange or sometimes bright red in fall. '**Commemoration**' is a fast-growing cultivar with an oval habit. The leaves turn yellow, orange and red earlier in fall than those of most other sugar maples. '**Endowment**' is a fast-growing columnar cultivar with scarlet fall color. GREEN MOUNTAIN has dark green foliage and is tolerant of drought and small growing spaces. The fall color may be yellow, orange or scarlet. '**Legacy**' is a dense, rounded cultivar that resists drought. The leaves turn red and yellowish orange in fall. '**Sweet Shadow**' is a rounded tree with deeply cut leaves that turn orange in fall. '**Wright Brothers**' is a hardy, fast-growing tree with a conical habit. The leaves turn gold, orange, pink and red in fall. (Zones 3–8)

A. palmatum var. *dissectum*
A. palmatum var. *atropurpureum*

Problems & Pests
Aphids, borers, caterpillars, leafhoppers, scale insects, anthracnose, canker, leaf spot and *Verticillium* wilt can affect maples. Chlorosis (leaf yellowing) caused by manganese or iron deficiency can occur in alkaline soils. Leaf scorch can be prevented by watering young trees during hot, dry spells.

Mock-Orange
Philadelphus

Features: late-spring to mid-summer flowers **Habit:** rounded, deciduous shrub with arching branches **Height:** 6–12' **Spread:** 5–12' **Planting:** container; spring or fall **Zones:** 3–8

ONE OF THE SWEETEST SCENTS I RECALL FROM MY YOUTH CAME from the flowers of an old, bedraggled, leggy mock-orange I passed on my way to and from grade school. On warm spring days its sweetness could be detected from afar on the breeze. The flowers were borne so high on the old branches that I couldn't even snitch a few. Unfortunately, some plants I've seen offered for sale have not been as fragrant as the original. Purchase some of the new cultivars, by name and description, or use your nose to select unknown plants while they are blooming.

Mock-oranges combine well with forsythias and reliably produce abundant blooms each year.

Growing

Mock-oranges grow well in **full sun, partial shade** or **light shade.** The soil should be of **average fertility, humus rich, moist** and **well drained.**

On established plants, each year after the bloom, remove one-third of the old wood. Overgrown shrubs can be rejuvenated by cutting them right back to within 6" of the ground. Established mock-oranges transplant readily, although they have a huge mass of woody roots in relation to the amount of top growth.

Tips

Include mock-oranges in shrub or mixed borders or in woodland gardens. Use them in groups to create barriers and screens.

P. coronarius

P. x *virginalis* 'Minnesota Snowflake'

P. x *virginalis* 'Minnesota Snowflake'

P. *coronarius*

Recommended

P. coronarius (sweet mock-orange) is an upright, broadly rounded shrub that bears fragrant white flowers in late spring or early summer. It can reach 8–12' in height, with an equal spread. '**Variegatus**' has leaves with creamy white margins. It grows 8' tall and spreads 6'. This cultivar grows best in partial shade. (Zones 4–8)

P. x *lemoinei* '**Innocence**' is an upright shrub with arching branches. It grows about 6–8' tall and spreads 5–6'. It bears large, white, very fragrant flowers in late spring. The leaves are irregularly variegated white and yellow. (Zones 4–8)

P. lewisii '**Snow Velvet**' is a rounded shrub that grows about 6' tall and spreads 5–6'. The fragrant semidouble flowers are 3" across and cover the entire plant in late spring. (Zones 4–8)

P. x **'Natchez'** is a handsome upright plant with arching branches. It grows 8–10' tall and spreads about 6–8'. Large, white, scarcely fragrant flowers are borne profusely in late spring. (Zones 4–8)

P. x *virginalis* **'Minnesota Snowflake'** is a hardy, dense, upright shrub 8' tall and 8–10' in spread. It bears fragrant, white double flowers in mid-summer. (Zones 3–7)

Problems & Pests

Mock-oranges may be affected by fungal leaf spot, gray mold, powdery mildew, rust and scale insects, but these problems are rarely serious.

Grow a mock-orange if only for its heavenly fragrance, which is reminiscent of orange blossoms.

P. coronarius 'Variegatus'

P. x 'Natchez'

Mountain Laurel
Kalmia
Kalmia

Features: foliage, late-spring to mid-summer flowers **Habit:** large, dense, bushy, evergreen shrub **Height:** 3–15' **Spread:** 3–15' **Planting:** container; spring or fall **Zones:** 4–9

MOUNTAIN LAUREL IS NATIVE TO THE EASTERN UNITED STATES, but those of us who deal with the dense, alkaline soils of Ohio must go to great lengths to grow it successfully. One client with a south-facing brick house wanted to use a matched pair by her formal front door. I advised her that there was no way the plant could prosper there. I was told, 'We will see.' Holes were dug to the appropriate depth, tile-drained and a full 5' wide. Her special acidified homemade compost was then used to replace all the backfill. I checked back three years later and was overwhelmed by the growth and flowers present. Her response was a predictable 'I told you so.'

Growing
Mountain laurel prefers **light or partial shade,** but it tolerates full sun if the soil is consistently moist. The soil should be of

average to high fertility, moist, **acidic** and **well drained**. A mulch of leaf mold or pine needles will help to prevent the roots of this drought-sensitive plant from drying out.

Little pruning is required, but spent inflorescences can be removed in summer and awkward shoots removed as needed.

K. latifolia cultivar (above)

Tips

Use mountain laurel in a shaded part of a shrub or mixed border, in a woodland garden or combined with other acid- and shade-loving plants, such as rhododendrons.

Do not make a tea with or otherwise ingest mountain laurel foliage or flowers, because both are extremely poisonous.

K. latifolia 'Ostbo Red' (center), *K. latifolia* (below)

Recommended

K. latifolia grows 7–15' tall, with an equal spread. It has glossy green leaves and pink or white flowers. The cultivars are more commonly grown. '**Alpine Pink**' has a very dense habit and dark pink buds that open to light pink flowers. '**Elf**' is a dwarf cultivar that grows to 36" in height and width. It has pink buds, white flowers and quite small leaves. '**Ostbo Red**' is an old cultivar with bright red buds and light pink flowers. '**Silver Dollar**' has large white flowers.

Problems & Pests

Mountain laurel suffers no serious problems, but it can be affected by borers, lace bugs, scale insects, weevils, leaf blight, leaf gall, leaf spot and powdery mildew.

Ninebark

Physocarpus

Features: early-summer flowers, fruit, bark, foliage **Habit:** upright, sometimes suckering, deciduous shrub **Height:** 4–10' **Spread:** 4–15' **Planting:** container; spring or fall **Zones:** 2–8

MY FIRST EXPOSURE TO NINEBARK WAS LONG BEFORE I KNEW anything about plants, and certainly anything about proper pruning. My dad was angry with me because I hadn't pruned the shrub when told. I was angry because I had to do it. So instead of taking out one-third from the base and doing some tip trimming, I thought I would save myself time another year and just cut it all off at the ground. Fortunately, both the plant and I survived. Common ninebark is less frequently grown now, but the cultivar DIABOLO is gaining in popularity. It has purplish foliage that holds fairly well into our cooler summers before greening up in late July.

Growing

Ninebark grows well in **full sun** or **partial shade**. The best leaf coloring develops in a sunny location. The

soil should be **fertile, acidic, moist** and **well drained.**

Little pruning is required, but you can remove one-third of the old growth each year after flowering is finished to encourage vigorous new growth.

Tips
Ninebark can be included in a shrub or mixed border, in a woodland garden or in a naturalistic garden.

Recommended
P. opulifolius (common ninebark) is native to Ohio. This suckering shrub has long, arching branches and exfoliating bark. It grows 5–10' tall and spreads 6–15'. Light pink flowers in early summer are followed by fruit that ripens to reddish green. **DIABOLO** ('Monlo') has attractive purple foliage and reaches 4' in height and spread.

Problems & Pests
Ninebark may have occasional problems with fire blight, leaf spot and powdery mildew.

P. opulifolius (above & below), DIABOLO (center)

Ninebark is an easy-growing shrub that adapts to most garden conditions.

Oak

Quercus

Features: summer and fall foliage, bark, habit, acorns **Habit:** large, rounded, spreading, deciduous tree **Height:** 35–120' **Spread:** 10–100' **Planting:** B & B, container; spring or fall **Zones:** 2–9

WHEN I'M ASKED TO NAME MY FAVORITE SHADE TREE, I ALWAYS give the same answer: oak. Because of my awe of oaks and love for them, my children had a red oak dedicated in my name on the Ohio State University campus several years ago. These trees are generally long-lived and mature into magnificent specimens. Plant them for their individual beauty and for posterity. About the only significant problem oaks have is with changes in grade and raising or lowering of the water table around them. Unless very carefully handled, they should be moved only in spring. Use caution when irrigating; the buttress roots of the trees should not be constantly wetted or it will cause internal decay problems.

Growing

Oaks grow well in **full sun** or **partial shade**. The soil should be **fertile, moist** and **well drained**. *Q. rubra* prefers an **acidic** soil. Do not disturb the ground around the base of an oak; these trees are very sensitive to changes in grade.

No pruning is needed. These trees can be difficult to establish. Transplant only while they are young.

Tips

Oaks are large trees best suited to be grown in parks and large gardens as specimens or in groves. *Q. imbricaria* responds well to pruning and is sometimes used as a hedging plant.

The acorns are generally not edible. Acorns of certain oak species are edible but usually must be processed first to leach out the bitter tannins.

Recommended

Q. acutissima (sawtooth oak) is a dense, rounded tree with wide-spreading branches. It grows 35–70' tall, with an equal or greater spread. The leaves turn golden brown in late fall. (Zones 5–9)

Q. alba (white oak) is a rounded, spreading tree with peeling bark. It grows 50–100' tall, with an equal spread. The leaves turn purple-red in fall. This tree is native to Ohio. (Zones 3–9)

Q. bicolor (swamp white oak) is a broad, spreading tree with peeling bark. It grows 50–70' tall, with an equal or greater spread. The leaves turn orange or red in fall. This species is also native to Ohio. (Zones 3–8)

Q. macrocarpa

Oaks are important commercial trees. The wood is used for furniture, flooring, veneers, boat building and wine and whiskey casks.

Q. bicolor

Q. rubra

Oaks have been held sacred by many cultures throughout history. The ancient Greeks believed these trees were the first ones created, and the Roman poet Virgil said that they gave birth to the human race.

Q. palustris

Q. coccinea (scarlet oak) is another Ohio native. This open, rounded tree grows 70–75' tall, with a spread of 40–50', sometimes more. The glossy dark green leaves turn bright red in fall. (Zones 4–9)

Q. imbricaria (shingle oak, laurel oak) is a broad, spreading tree with smooth bark. This Ohio native grows 50–70' tall, with an equal spread. The leaves turn yellowish brown or sometimes reddish orange in fall. (Zones 4–8)

Q. macrocarpa (bur oak, mossycup oak) is a large, broad tree with furrowed bark. It grows 50–80' tall, with an equal spread, and is native to Ohio. The leaves turn shades of yellow in fall. (Zones 2–8)

Q. muehlenbergii (chinkapin oak, yellow chestnut oak) is an open, rounded tree with scaly bark. This Ohio native grows 40–50' tall, with an equal to greater spread. The leaves turn yellow, orange and brown in fall. (Zones 4–7)

Q. palustris (pin oak, swamp oak) is a fast-growing, pyramidal to columnar tree that is native to Ohio. It grows 60–70' tall and spreads 25–40'. The foliage develops a good red to reddish brown color in fall. CROWNPOINTE ('Crozam') is a hybrid between *Q. palustris* and *Q. coccinea*. It has a good pyramidal form that requires little or no pruning to maintain. (Zones 4–8)

Q. prinus (chestnut oak, basket oak) is a dense tree that has a rounded habit. It grows 60–70' in height, with an equal spread. The foliage turns yellow-orange to yellow-brown in fall. This tree is native to Ohio, and the sweet acorns attract wildlife to gardens. (Zones 4–8)

Q. robur (English oak) is a rounded, spreading tree, growing 40–120' tall and 40–80' wide. The fall color is golden yellow. Narrow, columnar cultivars suitable for a smaller garden are also available. **CRIMSON SPIRE** ('Crimschmidt') is a cross between *Q. alba* and *Q. robur*. This columnar cultivar grows 45' tall and spreads about 15'. The leaves turn red in fall. 'Fastigiata' is an upright, columnar cultivar that grows up to 60' tall and spreads 10–15'. 'Filicifolia' has deeply cut leaves that give the tree a lacy appearance. This slow-growing, pyramidal to rounded cultivar is suitable for smaller gardens. (Zones 3–8)

Q. rubra (red oak) is a rounded, spreading tree that is native to Ohio. It grows 60–75' tall, with an equal spread. The fall color ranges from yellow to red-brown. The roots are shallow, so be careful not to damage them if you cultivate the ground around the tree. (Zones 4–9)

Q. shumardii (Shumard oak, Shumard red oak) is a broad, spreading tree native to Ohio. It grows 40–70' tall and spreads 40–60'. The leaves turn red in fall. This species is drought tolerant. (Zones 5–9)

Problems & Pests

The many possible problems are rarely serious: borers, gypsy moth caterpillars, leaf miners, leaf rollers, leaf skeletonizers, scale insects, canker, leaf gall, leaf spot, powdery mildew, rust, twig blight and wilt.

Q. imbricaria (above)

Q. robur (center), *Q. rubra* (below)

Oregon-Grape
Oregon Grapeholly
Mahonia

Features: spring flowers, summer fruit, late-fall and winter foliage **Habit:** upright, suckering, evergreen shrub **Height:** 2–6' **Spread:** 2–6' **Planting:** B & B, container; spring or fall **Zones:** 5–9

THE OPEN GROWTH AND NATURAL GRACE OF OREGON-GRAPE make it most desirable for landscape use. However, the waxy green to purple winter foliage—one of its primary attributes—will be outstanding only if the plant is properly sited. I have tried breaking the rules and planting this shrub in open sun with wind, and it just doesn't work. One or the other condition the plant may tolerate with browning of the foliage in winter, but sun and wind together will probably kill it. Even in ideal site conditions, harsh winters may brown the plant or kill stems to the ground, but it can tolerate being cut back hard in spring. Even with the potential drawbacks, I think Oregon-grape deserves a try, especially the compact form.

The glossy, holly-like, evergreen leaves of Oregon-grape contrast beautifully with the yellow spring flowers and, later, with the grape-like fruit.

Growing

Oregon-grape prefers **light shade** or **partial shade**. The soil should be of **average fertility, humus rich, moist** and **well drained**. Provide **shelter** from winter sun and wind to prevent the foliage from drying out and turning brown.

Awkward shoots can be removed in early summer. Deadheading will keep the plant looking neat but will also prevent the attractive, edible (though sour) fruit from forming.

M. aquifolium (all photos)

Tips

Use Oregon-grape in a shrub or mixed border or in a woodland garden. Low-growing cultivars can be used as groundcovers.

Recommended

M. aquifolium grows 3–6' tall, with an equal spread. Bright yellow flowers appear in spring and are followed by clusters of purple or blue berries. The foliage turns a bronzy purple color in late fall and winter. **'Compactum'** is a low, mounding shrub with bronzy green foliage. It grows 24–36" tall, with an equal spread.

Problems & Pests

Scale insects, gall, leaf spot and rust may cause occasional problems. Plants in exposed locations may develop leaf scorch or may even be killed in winter.

The juicy berries are edible but very tart. They can be eaten fresh or used to make jelly, juice or wine.

Pieris
Lily-of-the-Valley Shrub
Pieris

Features: colorful new growth, late-winter to spring flowers **Habit:** compact, rounded, evergreen shrub **Height:** 3–8' **Spread:** 3–8' **Planting:** B & B, container; spring or fall **Zones:** 5–8

PIERIS GROWS BEST IN OHIO'S MORE ACIDIC AREAS. STILL, WITH adequate soil preparation, it can grow in protected areas of central Ohio. Once, while coming up with a quote for a relandscaping job, I crawled under some overgrown brush to estimate removal costs. To my overwhelming pleasure, I found a 7' tall, tree-shaped pieris that could be left in position for the new design. What a find for this central Ohioan property! Since then, I have used pieris almost indiscriminately, but only if time and money allow for proper soil preparation. I have one on the north side of my own home. It is 4' tall and a true pleasure to behold all year round.

Growing

Pieris grows well in **partial shade**. Morning sun is preferable to afternoon sun unless soil drainage and acidity are ideal. The soil should be of **average fertility, acidic, humus rich, moist** and **well drained**. Provide pieris with **shelter** from hot sun and drying winds.

Remove spent flowers once flowering is complete. Prune out awkward shoots at the same time.

Tips

Pieris can be used in a shrub or mixed border, in a woodland garden or as a specimen. Try grouping it with rhododendrons and other acid-loving plants. With its year-round good looks, pieris is a great shrub to use in a protected entryway.

All parts of pieris plants, and even honey made from the nectar, are extremely poisonous. Children have died from eating the leaves.

Recommended

P. japonica grows 4–8' tall and wide. It bears white flowers in long, pendulous clusters. The new flower buds form in late summer and provide winter interest. **'Mountain Fire'** has bright red new growth that matures to chestnut brown. The flowers are white. **'Valley Rose'** has dark green foliage and pink flowers. **'Valley Valentine'** grows about 4–6' tall, with an equal spread. The flowers and winter buds are red. **'Variegata'** has white flowers, and its green leaves have creamy white margins. Also available are several dwarf cultivars that grow about 36" tall and wide, including **'Dorothy Wycoff.'**

'Mountain Fire'

Problems & Pests

Lace bugs, nematodes, canker and root rot can cause occasional problems. Plants may suffer dieback if exposed to too much wind.

P. japonica

Pine

Pinus

Features: foliage, bark, cones, habit **Habit:** upright, columnar or spreading, ever-green tree **Height:** 2–120' **Spread:** 2–60' **Planting:** B & B, container; spring or fall **Zones:** 2–8

PINES ARE PLANTS OF MAGNIFICENT BEAUTY, BUT SOME ARE ALSO now causing heartbreak. The two-needled pines, primarily Scotch and Austrian but occasionally mugo, are prone to infection by a fungus that is limiting their numbers. However, there are many others to choose from. At Hartwick Pines State Park in Michigan, I have seen eastern white pines over 4' in trunk diameter and 85–90' tall that bunched together, forming a canopy that created its own weather. It had to be 5–7° cooler underneath, and the surface soil was moist compared with parched earth nearby. I have a lacebark pine specimen in my side yard and an espaliered bristlecone pine on a west-facing, hot brick wall. When properly selected, pines can be very versatile.

Growing

Pines grow best in **full sun**. They adapt to most **well-drained** soils. These trees are not heavy feeders. Fertilizing will encourage rapid new growth that is weak and susceptible to pest and disease problems.

Generally, little or no pruning is required. Hedges can be trimmed in mid-summer. Pinch up to one-half the length of the 'candles,' the fully extended but still soft new growth, to shape the plant or to regulate growth.

Tips

Pines find use as specimen trees, hedges or windbreaks. Include smaller cultivars in shrub or mixed borders.

Austrian pine *(P. nigra)* and Scotch or Scots pine *(P. sylvestris)* have been recommended as the pines most tolerant of urban conditions. Unfortunately, overplanting of these species has led to severe disease problems, some of which can lead to a tree's death within a single growing season.

Recommended

P. aristata (bristlecone pine) is a fairly small, slow-growing pine with a conical or shrubby habit. It grows 8–30' tall and spreads 6–20'. It is not pollution tolerant but survives in poor, dry, rocky soil. The needles may dry out in areas exposed to winter winds. (Zones 4–8)

P. bungeana (lacebark pine) develops a bushy, multi-stemmed form that is pyramidal, columnar or rounded. This slow-growing tree

P. aristata

Most pine seeds are edible, though many are too small to bother with. Commercially available 'pine nuts' come from P. pinea *and other species.*

P. cembra

P. mugo
P. flexilis

reaches 30–50' in height and spreads 15–35'. The smooth, reddish bark flakes off in scales to reveal creamy or pale green bark below, giving the tree a multi-colored appearance. (Zones 4–8)

P. cembra (Swiss stone pine) has a dense, columnar habit. It grows 30–70' tall and spreads 15–25'. This slow-growing pine is resistant to white pine blister rust. (Zones 3–7)

P. densiflora (Japanese red pine) is a variable open, conical or rounded, spreading tree. It grows 40–80' tall and spreads 15–60'. The bark of younger trees is orange or reddish orange. **'Umbraculifera'** (Tanyosho pine) is a multi-stemmed, spreading cultivar that develops an umbrella-like appearance. It grows 10–25' tall, spreading 15–25'. (Zones 3–7)

P. flexilis (limber pine) is pyramidal when young, maturing to a rounded or flat-topped habit. It grows 30–60' tall and 15–35' wide. The branches are very flexible. **'Vanderwolf's Pyramid'** is an upright cultivar with very attractive, twisted blue-green needles. (Zones 3–7)

P. mugo (mugo pine) is a low, rounded, spreading shrub or tree 10–20' tall and 15–20' wide. **Var. pumilio** (var. *pumilo*) is a dense variety that forms a mound 2–8' tall and wide. Its slow growth and small size make it a good choice for planters and rock gardens. (Zones 2–7)

Pines are more diverse and widely adapted than any other conifers.

P. parviflora (Japanese white pine) grows 20–70' tall and spreads 20–50'. It is conical or columnar when young and matures to a spreading crown. This species has been used to create bonsai. (Zones 4–8)

P. strobus (eastern white pine) is native to Ohio. It is a slender, conical tree 50–120' tall and 20–40' in spread, with soft, plumy needles. It is sometimes grown as a hedge. Young trees can be killed by white pine blister rust, but mature specimens are resistant. '**Compacta**' is a dense, rounded cultivar that grows about 4' tall, with an equal spread. '**Fastigiata**' is an attractive, narrow, columnar form that grows up to 70' tall and one-third as wide. '**Pendula**' has long, ground-sweeping branches. It must be trained when young to form an upright leader to give it some height and shape; otherwise, it can be grown as a groundcover or left to spill over the top of a rock wall or slope. It develops an unusual soft, shaggy, droopy appearance as it matures. (Zones 3–8)

Problems & Pests

Borers, caterpillars, leaf miners, mealybugs, sawflies, scale insects, blight, blister rust, cone rust, pitch canker and tar spot can all cause problems. The European pine-shoot moth attacks pines with needles in clusters of two or three.

'Methuselah,' a bristlecone pine that grows high in the White Mountains of California, is more than 4700 years old—the world's oldest known living thing.

P. strobus (above)

P. mugo var. pumilio (center), P. aristata (below)

Potentilla
Cinquefoil
Potentilla

Features: flowers, foliage, habit **Habit:** mounding, deciduous or semi-evergreen shrub **Height:** 4"–5' **Spread:** 1–5' **Planting:** container; spring or fall **Zones:** 2–8

FOR 45 YEARS I'VE BEEN GARDENING, BUT I STILL CAN'T ALWAYS get it right. I have a definite love-hate relationship with potentillas, having struggled for years to figure out what they need to thrive. I am having more success since I found one growing wild in the Rocky Mountains in a crevice between two boulders. Using this as a clue, I recommend a small planting hole in poor but well-drained soil and no fertilizer—ever. Since these plants can become leggy, I am also inclined to cut them back to 6" in early spring every other year. This technique works nicely because the plants flower on new stems. In spite of the difficulties I've experienced, I will continue to use potentillas because of their color and their June-through-frost flowering.

Growing

Potentillas prefer **full sun** but tolerate partial or light shade. The soil should ideally be of **poor to average fertility** and **well drained,** but these plants tolerate most conditions, including sandy or clay soil and wet or dry conditions. Established plants are drought tolerant. Too much fertilizer or too rich a soil will encourage potentillas to develop weak, floppy, disease-prone growth.

On mature plants, prune up to one-third of the old wood each year to keep the growth neat and vigorous. Though they tolerate more severe pruning, potentillas look best if left to grow as informal rounded or mounding shrubs. Shearing them back hard in spring will rejuvenate older, overgrown or ragged plants.

Tips

Potentillas are useful in shrub or mixed borders. The smaller cultivars

P. fruticosa 'Abbotswood'

Potentilla cultivars offer a rainbow of possible colors: white, yellow, pink, orange and red.

P. fruticosa 'Pink Beauty'

P. fruticosa 'Katherine Dykes'

P. fruticosa

can be included in rock gardens and on rock walls. On slopes that are steep or awkward to mow, potentillas can prevent soil erosion and reduce the time spent maintaining a lawn. Potentillas can even be used to create low, informal hedges.

If your potentilla's flowers fade in bright sun or in hot weather, try moving the plant to a more sheltered location. A cooler location that still gets lots of sun or a spot with some shade from the hot afternoon sun may be all your plant needs to keep its color. Colors should revive in fall as the weather cools. Plants with yellow or white flowers are the least likely to be negatively affected by heat and sun.

Recommended

P. fruticosa (shrubby cinquefoil) is the yellow-flowered parent of many, many cultivars. The following are a few popular and interesting ones. The species and its cultivars flower all summer. '**Abbotswood**' is one of the best white-flowered cultivars. It grows 30–36" tall and spreads up to 4'. '**Gold Drop**' ('Farreri') is a bushy dwarf cultivar with small leaves and bright yellow flowers. It grows 18–24" tall and spreads up to 36". '**Goldfinger**' has large yellow flowers and a mounding habit. It grows up to 40" tall, with an equal spread. '**Jackmanii**' ('Jackman's Variety') is a large, mound-forming cultivar that bears lots of large yellow flowers. It grows about 4' tall, with an equal spread. '**Katherine Dykes**' is a smaller cultivar with arching branches that bear yellow flowers. It grows 24–36" tall, with an equal spread. '**McKay's White**' bears creamy white flowers, but it doesn't develop seedheads. It grows 24–36" tall, with an equal spread. '**Pink Beauty**' bears pink semi-double flowers that stand up well in the heat and sun of summer. It grows 24–36" tall, with an equal spread. '**Primrose Beauty**' has gray-green foliage and pale yellow flowers with darker yellow centers. It grows 3–5' tall, with an equal spread. (Zones 2–7)

P. tabernaemontana (*P. neumanniana*; alpine cinquefoil) forms a low, spreading mat or mound of semi-evergreen foliage. It grows about 4" tall, spreads about 12" and bears yellow flowers from mid-spring through much of summer. (Zones 4–8)

Problems & Pests

Though infrequent, occasional problems with spider mites, fungal leaf spot and mildew are possible.

P. fruticosa 'McKay's White'

Potentillas tolerate excess lime in the soil and handle extreme cold very well. Try one of these small shrubs as a low-maintenance alternative to turfgrass.

P. fruticosa 'Abbotswood'

Privet

Ligustrum

Features: adaptability, fast growth, dense growth **Habit:** upright or arching, deciduous or semi-evergreen shrub **Height:** 5–15' **Spread:** 5–15'
Planting: bare-root, B & B; spring or fall **Zones:** 3–8

PRIVETS ARE AMONG THE MOST USED HEDGE PLANTS OF ALL TIME. A friend of mine had a situation in which his neighbors could peer down from their second-story windows into his yard and patio. Privet grew rapidly enough to solve the problem. The matured plants were kept pruned at 6' wide by 12' tall. They were cut with electric pruners once a year in late June, after the flush of growth was over. Two other large hedges I've seen are allowed to grow to 12'. The first March after they reach this height, they are cut to 3' and then start their ascent over again.

Growing
Privets grow equally well in **full sun** or **partial shade**. They adapt to any **well-drained** soil, and they tolerate polluted, urban conditions and winter salt from roads and walkways.

Hedges can be pruned twice each summer. Plants grown in borders or as specimens should be kept neat by removing up to one-third of the mature growth each year.

Tips
Privets are commonly grown as hedges because they are fast growing, adaptable and inexpensive. Left unpruned, a privet becomes a large shrub with arching branches. This form looks quite attractive, especially

when in bloom. Border privet, in particular, has an attractive habit when left unpruned.

Recommended

L. amurense (Amur privet) is a large, multi-stemmed, deciduous or semi-evergreen shrub that is usually pruned to form a dense hedge. It grows 12–15' tall and spreads 8–15'. It bears small white flowers in early to mid-summer, followed by small fruit that ripen to black. The dark green foliage may turn a dark bronzy purple in fall, but the color is not exceptional. (Zones 3–7)

L. obtusifolium (border privet) is a spreading deciduous shrub with arching branches. It grows 10–12' tall, with a spread of 12–15'. Loose, nodding clusters of creamy white flowers appear in mid-summer. The dark green leaves may be tinged purple in fall. **Var.** *regelianum* (regel privet) is a smaller variety with more horizontally spreading branches. It grows up to 7' tall, with an equal to slightly greater spread. Of the various privets, this variety does particularly well in partial shade. (Zones 3–7)

L. x vicaryi (golden vicary privet) is a bushy, rounded, semi-evergreen shrub that grows 10–12' tall, with an equal spread. The golden yellow foliage may become more green during hot weather. Small clusters of white flowers are borne in mid-summer. Plants are sometimes killed back to nearly ground level in winter; prune them back to live wood in spring and be patient for new growth to start before you start trimming. (Zones 5–8)

L. amurense (both photos)

L. vulgare (European privet, common privet) is a bushy, upright, deciduous or semi-evergreen shrub 10–15' tall, with an equal spread. Small clusters of white flowers are produced in early or mid- summer. This species can be prone to twig blight. (Zones 5–7)

Problems & Pests

Problems can occur with aphids, Japanese beetle, leaf miners, scale insects, canker, leaf spot, powdery mildew, root rot and twig blight.

Redbud

Cercis

Features: spring flowers, fall foliage **Habit:** rounded or spreading, multi-stemmed, deciduous tree or shrub **Height:** 20–30' **Spread:** 25–35' **Planting:** B & B, container; spring or fall **Zones:** 4–9

THIS PLANT IS A DELIGHTFUL NATIVE IN MOST OF OHIO, AND YET I rarely use it as the primary ornamental tree on a site. Many do reach 35 years of age and become rustic, gnarled old beauties. However, many don't reach maturity because of pest and disease problems, particularly a vascular blockage disease. I often recommend redbud anyway because it tolerates our clayish and alkaline soils and usually flowers profusely in many shades of red. Frequently, all the flowers don't open at once, so the color season is spread out over several weeks. There is a pearl white flowering form and, as of recent development, a unique raggedly weeping form and a true light pink one as well.

Select a redbud from a locally grown source. Plants grown from seeds produced far to the south are not hardy in northern regions.

Growing

Redbud will grow well in **full sun, partial shade** or **light shade**. The soil should be a **fertile, deep loam** that is **moist** and **well drained**. This plant has tender roots and does not like being transplanted.

Pruning is rarely required. The growth of young plants can be thinned to encourage an open habit at maturity. Remove awkward branches after flowering is complete.

Tips

Redbud can be used as a specimen tree, in a shrub or mixed border or in a woodland garden.

Recommended

C. canadensis (eastern redbud) is a spreading, multi-stemmed tree that bears red, purple or pink flowers in mid-spring, before the leaves emerge. The young foliage is bronze, fading to green over the summer and turning bright yellow in fall. Var. *alba* ('Alba') has white flowers. **'Forest Pansy'** has purple or pink flowers and dark reddish purple foliage that fades to green over the summer. The best foliage color is produced when this cultivar is cut back hard in early spring, but plants cut back this way will not produce flowers that year. This cultivar is less hardy than the species, to Zone 7 or a sheltered location in Zone 6. **LAVENDER TWIST** ('Covey,' 'Covey's Weeping') is a hardy, fast-growing cultivar with a graceful, contorted, weeping habit. The flowers are pale purple.

C. canadensis (both photos)

Problems & Pests

Caterpillars, leafhoppers, scale insects, weevils, blight, canker, dieback, downy mildew, leaf spot and *Verticillium* wilt are potential problems for redbud.

Rhododendron
Azalea
Rhododendron

Features: late-winter to early-summer flowers, foliage, habit **Habit:** upright, mounding, rounded, evergreen or deciduous shrub **Height:** 3–12' **Spread:** 3–9'
Planting: B & B, container; spring or fall **Zones:** 4–8

MY FIRST RAFTING TRIP ON THE NEW RIVER IN WEST VIRGINIA was as enjoyable as I'd expected. What surprised and overwhelmed me were the miles of native rhododendrons running from the waterline right to the top of the hills. I had never seen anything like it before, even where they grow well in Ohio; here they were the entire understory. Close inspection showed that almost the entire rootzone of these 10–12' giants was in the top 6–8" of soil, and the leaf litter was more than 6" deep. Since that trip, I've planted rhododendrons and azaleas higher than ever in a hole no less than three times wider than the root-ball, with plenty of acidifiers, organic matter and a 4" deep, light mulch.

Growing

Rhododendrons prefer **partial shade** or **light shade**. The deciduous azaleas typically perform best in **full sun** or **light shade,** while the evergreen azaleas often like to grow in **partial shade. Shelter** from strong winds is preferable. The soil must be **fertile, humus rich, acidic, moist** and **well drained**. These plants are sensitive to high pH, salinity and winter injury. They must be kept moist, but not wet. Their shallow roots mean that unnoticed summer drying can be their worst enemy.

Shallow planting with a good mulch is essential, as is excellent drainage. In heavy soils, elevate the crown 1" above soil level when planting to ensure surface drainage of excess water. Don't dig near rhododendrons and azaleas; their root systems are shallow and resent being disturbed.

Remove dead and damaged growth in mid-spring. Spent flower clusters should be removed if possible. Grasp the base of the flower cluster between your thumb and forefinger and twist to remove the entire cluster. Be careful not to damage the new buds that form directly beneath the inflorescences. Spent clusters can also be carefully removed with hand pruners or scissors.

Tips

These plants grow and look better when planted in groups. Use them in shrub or mixed borders, in woodland gardens or in sheltered rock gardens. Take care to give them a suitable home with protection from wind and full sun. In a protected

Exbury hybrid (above), hybrid azalea (center)

Mixed rhododendrons & azaleas (below)

PJM hybrid

Both the foliage and flowers of rhododendrons and azaleas are poisonous, as is honey that bees produce from the nectar.

location they should not need an unsightly burlap covering in winter.

Rhododendrons and azaleas are grouped in the genus *Rhododendron*. Although hybridizing is blurring the distinction, in general rhododendrons are robust, evergreen shrubs whose flowers have 10 stamens. Azaleas tend to be smaller, evergreen or deciduous shrubs whose smaller flowers have 5 stamens.

Recommended

R. catawbiense (Catawba rhododendron, mountain rosebay) is a large, rounded, evergreen species. It grows 5–10' tall, with an equal spread. Clusters of reddish purple flowers appear in late spring. **'Album'** has pale purple buds and white flowers. **'Bikini Island'** bears clusters of large red flowers. **'Boursault'** bears rounded clusters of lavender flowers.

'Casanova' has dark pink buds that open to pale yellow flowers with dark copper speckles in the throat. **'Chionoides'** bears domed clusters of yellow-centered white flowers. It grows about 4' tall, with an equal spread. **'Cunningham's White'** bears pink-flushed buds that open to white flowers with greenish yellow spots in the throats. **'English Roseum'** has light pink flowers. This cultivar is heat tolerant. **'Lavender Queen'** bears lavender flowers. **'Lee's Dark Purple'** bears dark purple flowers that open from darker purple buds. **'Maximum Pink'** bears pink flowers late in the season. It grows 6' tall and wide and tolerates sun well. **'Nova Zembla'** has purple-hued red flowers. It is also heat tolerant. **'Roseum Elegans'** bears lavender pink flowers and is tolerant of both hot and cold weather. (Zones 4–8)

R. **Exbury hybrids** are upright deciduous shrubs that grow 8–12' tall, with a spread of 6–9'. The leaves turn yellow, orange or red in fall. Large clusters of flowers in a wide range of colors are borne in mid- to late spring. **'Dawn's Chorus'** has pink buds that open to white flowers streaked with light pink. **'Firefly'** bears bright red flowers. **'Gibraltar'** is a heat-tolerant plant that bears ruffled flowers of scarlet orange. **'Gold Dust'** bears fragrant dark yellow flowers. (Zones 5–7)

R. mucronulatum (Korean rhododendron) is an open deciduous plant with an upright, oval habit. It grows 4–8' tall, with an equal spread. Bright purple flowers are borne in late March and early April before the leaf buds break. (Zones 4–7)

R. **PJM hybrids** are compact, rounded, dwarf, evergreens. They grow 3–6' tall, with an equal spread. Flowers in a range of colors are produced in early to mid-spring. These hybrids are weevil resistant. **'Aglo'** bears pink flowers with reddish throats. **'Elite'** bears light pinkish purple flowers. It grows 6' tall, with an equal spread. **'Olga Mezitt'** bears peachy pink flowers. The leaves turn red in fall and winter. **'PJM Select'** bears lavender pink flowers and grows about 4' tall and wide. **'Regal'** has a spreading habit and bears pink flowers. (Zones 4–8)

PJM 'Aglo' (above)

R. yakushimanum is a dense, mound-forming evergreen species about 36" tall, with an equal spread. Pink buds open to white flowers in late spring. Many cultivars and hybrids of this species are available. **'Crete'** is very hardy and is dense enough to use as a hedge. **'Mist Maiden'** bears pink flowers in larger clusters than those of the species. It grows about 4' tall, with an equal spread. It is considered to be one of the all-around best rhododendrons. Both of these cultivars were developed by the late David Leach. (Zones 5–8)

R. catawbiense (top center)

Problems & Pests

Rhododendrons suffer few problems if planted in good conditions with well-drained soil. When plants are stressed, however, aphids, caterpillars, Japanese beetle, lace bugs, leafhoppers, root weevils, scale insects, vine weevils, whiteflies, leaf gall, petal blight, powdery mildew, root rot and rust can cause problems.

PJM hybrid (bottom center), *P. yakushimanum* (below)

Rose-of-Sharon
Hardy Hibiscus
Hibiscus

Features: mid-summer to fall flowers **Habit:** bushy, upright, deciduous shrub
Height: 8–12' **Spread:** 6–10' **Planting:** B & B, container; spring or fall
Zones: 5–9

NIGHTMARES ABOUT ROSE-OF-SHARON HAUNTED MY YOUTH.
As forced labor in my mother's garden, I felt as though every rose-of-Sharon
seeded twins or triplets. The seeds always germinated and had to be pulled or
dug just as the season turned hot and sticky. I had to crawl around on hands
and knees as the Great Eradicator and yet not disturb any of the favored
annuals and perennials. This was a great test of the wills of mother and son.
I still think the only reason she won was that she was also the cook. Thanks
to the work of the late Dr. Donald Egolf at the National Arboretum, we now
have many beautiful seedless varieties to choose from.

Growing

Rose-of-Sharon prefers **full sun**. Though the plants tolerate partial shade, they become leggy and produce fewer flowers. The soil should be **humus rich, moist** and **well drained**.

Pinch young plants to encourage bushy growth. Train them to form a tree by selectively pruning out all but the strongest single stem and then removing side branches up to the height where you want the plant to bush out. The flowers form on the current year's growth. Prune back tip growth in late winter or early spring for larger but fewer flowers.

The species and some cultivars are heavy seeders and can produce unwanted seedlings. To avoid this problem, shear off and dispose of the seedheads right after blooming finishes.

'Blue Bird'

A well-tended rose-of-Sharon is one of the most beautiful and prolific blooming shrubs for the late-season garden.

BLUE SATIN

'Diana'

Tips

Rose-of-Sharon is best used in shrub or mixed borders. The leaves emerge late in spring and drop early in fall. Plant along with evergreen shrubs to make up for the short period of green.

This plant develops unsightly legs as it matures. Plant low, bushy perennials or shrubs around the base to hide the bare stems.

Recommended

H. syriacus is an erect, multi-stemmed shrub that bears dark pink flowers from mid-summer to fall. It can be trained to form a small, single-stemmed tree. Many cultivars are available. **'Aphrodite'** bears dark pink flowers with red centers. **'Blue Bird'** bears lilac blue flowers with red centers. **BLUE SATIN** ('Marina') is a vigorous plant with rich blue flowers. **BLUSH SATIN** ('Mathilde')

LAVENDER CHIFFON with WHITE CHIFFON

bears light pink flowers with red centers. **'Diana'** bears large white flowers. **'Freedom'** bears reddish pink semi-double flowers. **'Helene'** has white flowers with red or pink petal bases. **LAVENDER CHIFFON** ('Notwoodone') bears lavender flowers with a second ring of small lacy petals in the center. **'Red Heart'** bears white flowers with red centers. **ROSE SATIN** ('Minrosa') bears pink flowers with red centers. **VIOLET SATIN** ('Floru') bears reddish violet flowers. This vigorous cultivar blooms for a long time in summer and fall. **WHITE CHIFFON** ('Notwoodtwo') bears white flowers with a small second ring of lacy petals in the center.

Problems & Pests

Rose-of-Sharon can be afflicted with aphids, caterpillars, mealybugs, mites, scale insects, bacterial blight, fungal leaf spot, root and stem rot, rust, *Verticillium* wilt and viruses.

'Red Heart' (above), 'Freedom' (below)

Rose-of-Sharon attracts birds and butterflies and repels deer.

Serviceberry
Juneberry, Shadbush, Shadblow
Amelanchier

Features: spring or early-summer flowers, edible fruit, fall color, habit, bark
Habit: single- or multi-stemmed, deciduous large shrub or small tree **Height:** 4–30'
Spread: 4–30' **Planting:** B & B, container; spring or fall **Zones:** 3–9

SERVICEBERRIES ARE MY FAVORITE ORNAMENTAL SMALL TREES.
Flowers, fruit, form and color all combine to make these plants outstanding.
I have three multi-stemmed forms growing together in a mass on an exposed
corner of my home. To emphasize the mass, I have the plants in one continu-
ous bed mulched with coarse-chunk bark. During fruit-
ing time, the birds provide entertainment as good as a
circus. Few sights are more humorous than a robin,
tipsy from eating the partially fermented fruit, trying to
walk along a small twig to get at even more. The
birds don't get all of the fruit, but any seedlings that
sprout from the remaining berries are easy to spot
and remove in my mulched bed.

Serviceberry fruit can be used in
place of blueberries in any recipe,
having a similar but generally
sweeter flavor.

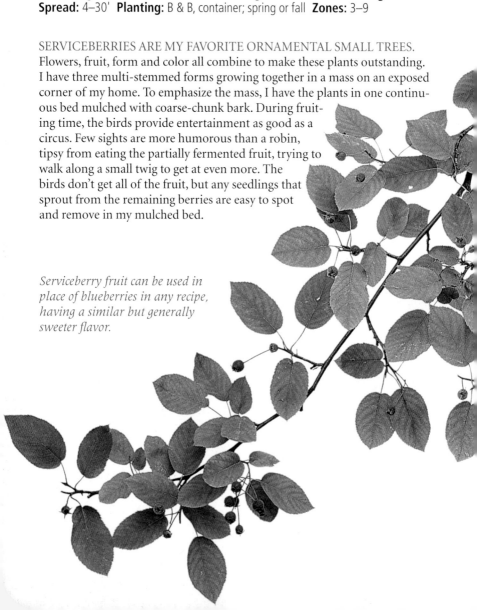

Growing

Serviceberries grow well in **full sun** or **light shade**. The soil should be **fertile, acidic, humus rich, moist** and **well drained**. *A. canadensis* tolerates boggy soil conditions.

Very little pruning is needed. Young plants, particularly multi-stemmed ones, can be pruned after flowering is finished to encourage healthy, attractive growth. Only the strongest, healthiest stems should be allowed to remain. Dead, damaged, diseased and awkward branches can be removed as needed. If you prefer, some of the lower and interior branches can be removed to better display the structure and attractive bark.

A. canadensis (top & bottom photos)

Tips

Serviceberries make beautiful specimen plants or even shade trees in small gardens. Spring flowers, edible fruit, attractive fall color and an often artistic branching habit make these excellent ornamental trees all year long. The shrubbier forms can be grown along the edges of a woodland garden or in a border. In the wild, serviceberries are sometimes found growing near water sources, and they can make beautiful pondside or streamside plants in a garden.

Recommended

A. arborea (common serviceberry, Juneberry) forms a small single- or multi-stemmed tree. This Ohio native grows 15–25' tall and spreads 15–30'. Clusters of fragrant white flowers are borne in spring. The edible fruit ripens to reddish purple in summer. The fall foliage turns to shades ranging from yellow to red. (Zones 4–9)

A. x *grandiflora* PRINCESS DIANA
A. arborea

A. canadensis (shadblow serviceberry, downy serviceberry, Canadian serviceberry) forms a large, upright, suckering shrub. It grows 6–20' tall and spreads 5–15'. White spring flowers are followed by edible dark purple fruit in summer. The foliage turns orange and red shades in fall. **RAINBOW PILLAR** ('Glenform') is a narrow, upright cultivar that develops excellent fall color. It grows 8–15' tall, with a spread of about 5'. (Zones 3–8)

A. x *grandiflora* (apple serviceberry) is a small, spreading, often multi-stemmed tree. It grows 20–30' tall, with an equal spread. The new foliage is often a bronze color, turning green in summer and bright orange or red in fall. White spring flowers are followed by edible purple fruit in summer. The parent hybrid and most cultivars are hardy in Zones 4–8. **AUTUMN BRILLIANCE** is a fast-growing cultivar that reaches 25' in height and about 20' in spread. The leaves turn brilliant red in fall. This cultivar is hardy to Zone 3. '**Ballerina**' has bright red fall color. '**Cole's Select**' ('Cole') consistently develops bright red fall color. **CUMULUS** has an oval habit, growing 20–30' tall, with a spread of 15–20'. Fall color is yellow, orange and scarlet. **PRINCESS DIANA** may be single- or multi-stemmed. It flowers prolifically in spring, and the foliage turns brilliant red in fall. It is hardy to Zone 3. '**Robin Hill**' ('Robin Hill Pink') has pink buds that open to white flowers. It has an upright habit, spreading half as much as the species.

A. stolonifera (running service-berry) is a small, suckering shrub that forms dense thickets. It grows 4–6' tall, with an equal spread. White flowers in late spring are followed by sweet, juicy, dark purple fruit in mid-summer. The leaves turn lovely shades of yellow, orange and red in fall. This Ohio native species is well adapted to streamside use. (Zones 4–8)

Problems & Pests

Problems with borers, leaf miners, fire blight, leaf spot, powdery mildew and rust can occur but are generally not serious.

The alternative common names shadbush and shadblow may have come about because the spring flowers appear about the time shadfish spawn.

A. x *grandiflora* 'Robin Hill'
A. *canadensis*

Seven-Son Flower
Heptacodium

Features: habit, bark, fall flowers **Habit:** upright to spreading, multi-stemmed, deciduous shrub or small tree **Height:** 15–20' **Spread:** 8–15' **Planting:** B & B, container; spring or fall **Zones:** 5–8

I HAVE ALWAYS ENJOYED MY CAREER IN HORTICULTURE AND landscape design because there is no possibility of falling into a mundane routine. There is always something new and different to study or use. This new tree from China, introduced by the Arnold Arboretum, is the current excitement. We don't even know for certain how large it will get on the North American continent. Still, as a smallish tree with fragrant white September flowers followed by red sepals and fruit, it makes a welcome addition to our Ohio plant palette. I have seen it only in nursery plots so far, so let's be patient in finding it on the retail level. Try it, and we'll explore together what develops in the future.

Each flower cluster is made up of seven small blooms, hence the common name.

Growing

Seven-son flower prefers **full sun** but tolerates partial shade. The soil should be of **average fertility, moist** and **well drained,** though this plant is fairly tolerant of most soil conditions, including dry and acidic soil.

Little pruning is required. Remove awkward branches in early spring, and prune out dead or damaged growth as needed. Seven-son flower can be grown as a multi-stemmed shrub or trained to form a small, single-stemmed tree.

Tips

This large shrub can be used in place of a shade tree on a small property. Planted near a patio or deck, the plant will provide light shade, and its fragrant flowers can be enjoyed in late summer. In a border it provides light shade to plants growing below it, and the dark green leaves make a good backdrop for bright perennial and annual flowers.

Seven-son flower's tolerance of dry and salty soils makes it useful where salty snow may be shoveled off walkways in winter and where watering will be minimal in summer.

Recommended

H. miconioides is a large, multi-stemmed shrub or small tree with peeling tan bark. The dark green leaves may become tinged with purple in fall. Clusters of fragrant, creamy white flowers are borne from late summer into fall. The persistent sepals (the outer ring of flower parts) turn dark pink to bright red in mid- to late fall and surround small, purple-red fruit.

Seven-son flower is generally free of problems and pests.

Silverbell

Halesia

Features: late-spring to early-summer flowers, summer and fall foliage
Habit: spreading, rounded, deciduous tree **Height:** 20–40' **Spread:** 20–35'
Planting: B & B, container; spring or fall **Zones:** 5–9

SILVERBELLS ARE SIMPLY NOT USED OFTEN ENOUGH. BUT, LIKE trends in clothing such as the narrow lapel or short hemline, they will come back into fashion eventually. I think that these trees should be brought back immediately. The canopy outline alone is impressive, yet the trees also offer something for nearly every season. For those who want to see them in use, visit the Dawes Arboretum south of Newark. The silverbells there are relatively young trees, but they show the maturing form and the interesting, thread-like, peeling bark. It's well worth visiting this and other arboreta in order to become familiar with trees and shrubs in their prime.

Growing

Silverbells grow well in **full sun, partial shade** or **light shade.** The soil should be **fertile, humus rich, neutral to acidic, moist** and **well drained.** Pruning is rarely required.

Tips

These trees make attractive, small to medium-sized specimens. They can also be used in a woodland garden or as backdrop plants in a shrub or mixed border.

Recommended

H. diptera (two-wing silverbell) is a small, rounded, often multi-stemmed tree that grows 20–30' tall, with an equal spread. It bears white flowers in early summer. In fall the foliage turns yellow. This species is not as common as *H. tetraptera*.

H. tetraptera (snowdrop tree, mountain silverbell) is a rounded, spreading tree. It grows 25–40' tall and spreads 25–35'. The white flowers appear in spring, before the leaves emerge. Fall color is yellow. **'Arnold Pink'** bears pendulous pink flowers that create a striking focal point for the spring garden.

Problems & Pests

Occasional problems with scale insects, root rot and wood rot are possible.

H. tetraptera (both photos)

Depending on the species, two or four narrow 'wings' (ridges) run down the length of each fruiting capsule, giving rise to the specific epithets diptera, *'two-winged,' and* tetraptera, *'four-winged.' The capsules hang from the branches almost all winter.*

Smokebush
Smoketree
Cotinus

Features: early-summer flowers, summer and fall foliage **Habit:** bushy, rounded, spreading, deciduous tree or shrub **Height:** 10–15' **Spread:** 10–15'
Planting: container; spring or fall **Zones:** 4–8

ONE AFTERNOON IN EARLY JULY, WE WERE IN THE CAR AND PASSING an older farm home when my wife exclaimed, 'What is *that?*' I glanced over to be amazed by one of the largest smokebushes I can ever remember seeing. It was almost completely covered in light creamy pink flowers. Even considering all the smokebushes I've seen in the many arboreta I've visited, this one stands out in my mind as the most impressive. The plant appeared to be 14–15' tall, at least two-thirds that wide and full of flower clusters to within 36" of the ground. I envy the people who get to enjoy that incredible specimen every day.

Growing

Smokebush grows well in **full sun or partial shade**. It prefers soil that is of **average fertility, moist** and **well drained**. Established plants adapt to dry, sandy soils.

You have a couple of options where pruning is concerned. Long, lanky growth develops from pruning cuts. To take advantage of this tendency, plants grown for colorful foliage are often pruned back to the ground each spring, encouraging a lush flush of colorful growth. Alternatively, to avoid the long, lanky growth on any smokebush, young plants can be lightly sheared or pruned, then left to develop and mature naturally.

Tips

Use smokebush in a shrub or mixed border, as a single specimen or in a group. It is a good choice for a rocky hillside planting. You can train your smokebush to take a tree form.

Recommended

C. coggygria develops large, puffy plumes of flowers that start out green and gradually turn pinky gray. The green foliage turns red, orange and yellow in fall. **'Daydream'** develops many pink plumes. The habit is more dense than that of the species. **'Grace'** has foliage that emerges a light red and matures to blue-green over the summer. It bears pink flowers in clusters up to 12" long. **'Royal Purple'** (purple smokebush) has dark purple foliage and purple-gray flowers. **'Velvet Cloak'** has purple foliage that keeps its color well over the summer. The leaves turn reddish purple in fall.

C. coggygria (above), 'Royal Purple' (below)

Problems & Pests

Powdery mildew and *Verticillium* wilt are possible problems. Purple-leaved plants are more likely to be affected by powdery mildew.

Snowbell

Styrax

Features: late-spring to early-summer flowers, foliage, habit **Habit:** upright, rounded, spreading or columnar, deciduous tree **Height:** 20–40' **Spread:** 20–30'
Planting: B & B, container; early spring **Zones:** 4–8

THE DOWNSIDE OF LIVING AND WORKING MOSTLY IN CENTRAL
Ohio is that we miss being able to use some really good plants. The dense
calcareous clays here and in much of western Ohio have to be considered
when selecting plants that need well-drained, acidic sites. Sometimes, our
alkaline soils are even beyond amending. So, those of you in the acidic areas,
enjoy snowbells. Meanwhile, horticultural gamblers on our wonderful yellow
and blue-black clays can try their best to prepare a spot for these beautiful
little trees. Those that I have seen doing well around Marietta and up
through Cleveland make me a little envious.

*Snowbells rarely
suffer pest and
disease problems.*

Growing

Snowbells grow well in **full sun, partial shade** or **light shade**. The soil should
be **fertile, humus rich, neutral to acidic, moist** and **well drained**.

Pruning is generally not required. Simply remove damaged branches as needed.

Tips

Snowbells can be used to provide light shade in shrub or mixed borders. They can also be included in woodland gardens, and they make interesting specimens near entryways or patios.

Recommended

S. japonica (Japanese snowbell) is a graceful, upright tree with arching branches. It grows 20–30' tall, with an equal spread. White blossoms dangle from the undersides of the branches in late spring. (Zones 5–8)

S. obassia (fragrant snowbell) is a broad, columnar tree. It grows 20–40' tall and spreads 20–30'. In early summer, white flowers are borne in long clusters at the branch ends. (Zones 4–8)

S. japonica (both photos)

Plant a Japanese snowbell next to your patio so you can admire the flowers as you look up from your lounge chair.

Spirea

Spiraea

Features: summer flowers, habit **Habit:** round, bushy, deciduous shrub
Height: 1–10' **Spread:** 1–12' **Planting:** container; spring or fall **Zones:** 3–9

WHEN I WAS YOUNG, SPIREAS WERE JUST OVERPLANTED SHRUBS
with white flowers. Some people sheared them, and some let them go to
become an unsightly leggy mess. Not anymore! Spireas come in sizes, forms,
flower colors and summer and fall leaf colors to suit almost every sunny area.
I have been using 'Gold Flame' as a divider between my flower and vegetable
beds for more than 15 years. The original plants, cut back to 6" every other
year, are still yielding great spring and summer foliage color and flowers. The
fall color reminds me of a small bonfire. Another great cultivar I grow is
'Shirobori,' which bears both pink and white flowers on the same plant.

Growing

Spireas prefer **full sun**. The soil should ideally be **fertile, moist** and **well drained**. These adaptable plants thrive in a wide range of soils as long as they receive full sun.

Pruning is necessary to keep spireas tidy and graceful. The tight, shrubby types require less pruning than the larger, more open forms, which may require heavy renewal pruning.

The appropriate pruning method depends on the flowering time. Spireas that bloom in spring and early summer usually form flowers the previous year. These plants should be pruned immediately after flowering is complete. Cut out one-third of the old growth to ground level to encourage new, young growth. Spireas that flower later in summer or in fall generally form flowers during the current year. These plants can be cut back to within 12" of the ground in early spring, as the buds begin to swell, to encourage lots of new growth and flowers later in the season.

Tips

Spireas are used in shrub or mixed borders, in rock gardens and as informal screens and hedges.

Recommended

S. albiflora (*S. japonica* var. *albiflora*; Japanese white spirea) is a low, dense, mounding shrub. It grows 24–36" tall, with an equal spread, and bears clusters of white flowers in early summer. (Zones 3–9)

S. betulifolia (birchleaf spirea, white spirea) is a dense, mound-forming

S. thunbergii cultivar

Under a magnifying glass, the flowers of these rose family members indeed resemble tiny roses.

S. betulifolia 'Tor' in fall color

S. nipponica

Spireas are very popular ornamental shrubs because they adapt to many situations and require only minimal care once established.

shrub that grows 2–4' tall, with an equal spread. It bears clusters of small white flowers in early to mid-summer. The foliage turns golden yellow and bronze in fall and provides a long-lasting colorful display. 'Tor' is a compact, rounded plant that grows 24–36" tall and wide and has purple fall foliage. (Zones 3–9)

S. x *bumalda* (Bumald spirea) is a group of hybrid cultivars developed from crosses between S. *albiflora* and S. *japonica*. These hybrids are generally mound forming and grow 2–5' tall and wide. They bear a flush of flowers in late spring and early summer and then flower sporadically through summer. 'Anthony Waterer' grows 3–4' tall and spreads 3–5'. The new foliage is reddish, turning blue-green over summer and red again in fall. This cultivar bears clusters of bright pink flowers. 'Coccinea' is similar to 'Anthony Waterer' but has darker pink flowers. 'Gold Flame' grows 24–36" tall and spreads 2–4'. The new foliage emerges red and matures to yellow-green, with red, orange and yellow fall color. 'Lemon Princess' has bright yellow foliage and bears light pink flowers. This compact plant grows about 24" tall, with an equal spread. (Zones 3–8)

S. *japonica* (Japanese spirea) forms a clump of erect stems 4–6' tall and up to 5' in spread. Pink or white flowers are generally borne in mid- and late summer. Many cultivars and hybrids have been developed from this species. 'Goldmound' has bright yellow foliage. It bears pink flowers between late spring and early summer. 'Little Princess' forms a dense mound 18" tall and 3–6' wide. The flowers are rose pink. MAGIC CARPET grows 12–18" tall, with an equal spread. It has new red growth that stands out above the older gold and lime green foliage. The flowers are dark pink. 'Neon Flash' bears vivid pink flowers and grows up to 36" tall and wide. 'Shirobori' ('Shirobana,' 'Shibori') grows 24" tall and wide. Both pink and white flowers appear on the same plant. (Zones 3–9)

S. *nipponica* (Nippon spirea) forms an upright shrub with arching branches. It grows 3–8' tall, with an equal spread. White flowers appear in mid-summer. 'Halward's Silver' is a compact plant 24–36" tall and wide. It bears abundant flowers and is very hardy. 'Snowmound' (snowmound Nippon spirea) is grown more commonly than the species. The arching, spreading branches are covered with flowers in early summer. This cultivar grows 3–5' tall, with an equal spread. (Zones 3–8)

S. thunbergii (Thunberg spirea) is a dense, arching shrub 3–5' tall and 3–6' wide. Small clusters of flowers appear along the stems in spring, before the leaves emerge. **'Ogon'** (MELLOW YELLOW) has narrow yellow leaves that turn bronzy in fall. (Zones 4–8)

S. x *vanhouttei* (bridal wreath spirea, Vanhoutte spirea) is a dense, bushy shrub with arching branches. It grows 6–10' tall and spreads 10–12'. White flowers are borne in clusters in early summer. The cultivar **'Renaissance'** is more vigorous and disease resistant. (Zones 3–8)

Problems & Pests
Aphids, dieback, fire blight, leaf spot and powdery mildew can cause occasional problems.

S. japonica MAGIC CARPET (above)

S. japonica 'Neon Flash'
S. japonica 'Little Princess'

Spruce

Picea

Features: foliage, cones, habit **Habit:** conical or columnar, evergreen tree or shrub
Height: 2–80' **Spread:** 2–25' **Planting:** B & B, container; spring or fall
Zones: 2–8

AS A KID, I HELPED CUT THE LOWER BRANCHES OFF SOME SPRUCE
trees to clear a sledding hill. At about the same time, just because others were
doing it, I cut my initials in a spruce. I was told the markings would always
be there, but higher up in the tree as it grew older. Well, the tree and I both
lived and grew up. I learned that a tree grows upward only from the tip, and
I gained a whole new respect for the living things I had treated so badly.
Because spruces can grow old while maintaining their lower branches clear
to the ground, I have used hundreds as screens, windbreaks and graceful
specimens. I encourage planting them where their lower branches have
plenty of room to spread, and where they won't be abused by people as
ignorant as I once was.

Growing

Spruce trees grow best in **full sun,** but some, like the dwarf Alberta spruce, also grow well in **light shade.** The soil should be **deep, well drained** and **neutral to acidic.** Pruning is rarely needed.

Spruces are best grown from small, young stock because they dislike being transplanted when larger or more mature.

Tips

Spruce trees are used as specimens and windscreens. The dwarf and slow-growing cultivars can also be used in shrub or mixed borders or even in containers.

Oil-based pesticides such as dormant oil can take the blue out of your blue-needled spruce.

Recommended

P. abies (Norway spruce) is a fast-growing, pyramidal tree with dark green needles. It grows 70–80' tall and spreads about 20'. This species is wind tolerant. **'Little Gem'** is a slow-growing, rounded cultivar that grows about 24" tall, with an equal or greater spread. **'Nidiformis'** (nest spruce) is a slow-growing, low, compact, mounding form. It grows about 3–4' tall and spreads 3–5'. **Forma** *pendula* includes the variable weeping forms of Norway spruce. These trees may need to be trained to form an upright leader. They make interesting and unique specimens. (Zones 2–8)

P. glauca (white spruce) is native to Canada and some northern states. This conical tree has blue-green

P. abies 'Nidiformis'

Try using a dwarf, slow-growing cultivar, such as dwarf Alberta spruce, for plant sculpture and bonsai.

P. abies f. *pendula*

P. glauca 'Conica'

Spruce trees frequently produce branch mutations, or 'witches'-brooms,' which can be propagated to form new cultivars of various sizes, shapes and colors.

P. glauca

needles and grows 40–60' tall, with a spread of 10–20'. It can grow up to 160' tall in the wild. **'Conica'** (dwarf Alberta spruce, dwarf white spruce) is a dense, conical, bushy shrub that grows 6–20' tall and spreads 3–8'. This cultivar works well in planters. Spider mites can be a problem for 'Conica.' (Zones 2–6)

P. omorika (Serbian spruce) is a slow-growing, narrow, spire-like tree with upward-arching branches and drooping branchlets. Two white stripes run the length of each needle. This tree grows 30–50' tall and spreads 10–15'. In restricted spaces it makes a good substitute for the larger spruce species. **'Nana'** is a dwarf cultivar growing 3–8' tall, with a spread of about 36". It has a conical or pyramidal, dense habit. (Zones 4–8)

P. pungens (Colorado spruce) is a conical or columnar tree with stiff, blue-green needles and dense growth.

This hardy, drought-tolerant tree grows 30–60' tall, with a spread of 10–20'. **Var. *glauca*** (Colorado blue spruce) is similar to the species, but with blue-gray needles. Many cultivars have been developed from var. *glauca,* including the following. **'Fat Albert'** is a dense, pyramidal cultivar with bright blue needles. It grows 15–20' tall and spreads 5–10'. **'Hoopsii'** grows up to 60' tall and spreads about 20'. It has a dense, pyramidal form and even more blue-white foliage than var. *glauca.* **'Mission Blue'** is a broad-based, dense form up to 40' tall, with a spread of 20–25'. It has bold blue foliage. **'Montgomery'** forms a dense mound and has bright blue needles. It grows about 5' tall, with an equal spread. (Zones 2–8)

Problems & Pests

Possible problems include aphids, caterpillars, gall insects, nematodes, sawflies, scale insects, spider mites, needle cast, rust and wood rot.

P. abies (above)

P. pungens var. *glauca* 'Mission Blue' (center)

P. pungens var. *glauca* cultivar (below)

St. Johnswort
St. John's Wort
Hypericum

Features: tidy habit, attractive foliage, summer to fall flowers **Habit:** rounded, mounded or spreading, deciduous, semi-evergreen or evergreen shrub
Height: 1–5' **Spread:** 2–5' **Planting:** container; spring **Zones:** 4–9

ST. JOHNSWORTS ARE STURDY, COLORFUL PLANTS THAT SHOULD BE considered for use more often in stressful growing situations. Aaronsbeard St. Johnswort *(H. calycinum)* is used as a groundcover to direct pedestrian traffic through a large area on the campus of Columbus State Community College. Students are guided along two walkways between the primary parking area and the wide pedestrian walks. The plant is dense and tall enough to direct traffic summer and winter. Students occasionally walk on it, and snowplows do their share of scuffing along the edges, yet it continues to look good despite these abuses. Other species can be used as specimens or in mixed borders as well as in mass plantings in large gardens.

The leaves and flowering tops of H. perforatum *(common St. Johnswort) are used in herbal medicine to treat depression. The ornamental species are just what the doctor ordered to cure a dull summer landscape.*

Growing

St. Johnsworts grow best in **full sun** but can tolerate partial shade. **Well-drained** soil of **average fertility** is preferred, but these plants adapt to most soil conditions except wet soils. Once established, they tolerate drought and heavy, rocky or very alkaline soils.

Flowers form on new wood, so any pruning should be done in spring. Little pruning is required, though plants can be cut back to within 6–12" of the ground if they need renewing.

Tips

St. Johnsworts make good additions to shrub or mixed borders, where the late-summer flowers can brighten up a planting that is looking tired or faded in the heat of summer. These durable, easy-to-grow shrubs are also useful for areas where the soil is poor and watering is difficult.

H. frondosum 'Sunburst'

Various medicinal and magical properties have been attributed to species of St. Johnswort. The flowers have also been used to produce yellow or red dyes.

H. 'Hidcote'

H. androsaemum 'Albury Purple'

Sprigs of St. Johnswort were once hung above pictures to keep evil spirits away. The genus name Hypericum, *from the Greek* hyper, *'above,' and* eikon, *'picture,' reflects that superstition.*

H. kalmianum cultivar

Recommended

H. androsaemum (tutsan) is a bushy, spreading, deciduous shrub. It grows 24–36" tall, with an equal spread. It bears clusters of light yellow flowers in mid-summer. **'Albury Purple'** has purple-flushed leaves and grows 18–30" tall, with a spread of 36". (Zones 6–8)

H. calycinum (Aaronsbeard St. Johnswort, rose-of-Sharon) is a low, wide-spreading, evergreen to semi-evergreen shrub. It grows 12–24" tall, spreads 24" or more and bears bright yellow flowers from mid-summer to first frost. (Zones 5–8)

H. erectum **'Gemo'** is a dense, mounded, deciduous shrub that grows 3–4' tall, with an equal spread. It has willow-like leaves and bears small, bright yellow flowers in summer. The fall color is yellow. Plants can be pruned each spring with a lawn mower or hedge shears to encourage new growth. This cultivar is sometimes attributed to *H. kalmianum*. (Zone 4–8)

H. frondosum (golden St. Johnswort, cedarglade St. Johnswort) forms a rounded, upright mound. This deciduous species grows 2–4' tall, with an equal spread. Bright yellow flowers are borne in mid- and late summer. The long, dense stamens give each flower a fuzzy, bushy appearance. **'Sunburst'** is a more compact cultivar with blue-green foliage. It grows up to 36" tall, with an equal spread. The flowers are larger, up to 2" in diameter, and are produced longer into fall than those of the species. (Zones 5–8)

H. '**Hidcote**' (*H. patulum* 'Hidcote') is a dense, bushy, evergreen to semi-evergreen shrub. It can grow up to 5' tall, with an equal spread. However, it is often killed back in winter, resulting in a plant that stays closer to 36" in height and spread. It bears large, golden yellow flowers with a main flush in late spring and early summer and sporadic blooms over the remainder of the summer. (Zones 5–9)

H. kalmianum (Kalm St. Johnswort) is a bushy evergreen shrub that is native to Ohio. It grows 24–36" tall, with an equal spread. Yellow flowers are borne from mid- to late summer. (Zones 4–7)

Problems & Pests

Occasional problems may occur with scale insects, thrips, leaf spot and rust.

H. androsaemum 'Albury Purple' with *Thalictrum*

H. calycinum

Stewartia

Stewartia

Features: mid-summer flowers, summer and fall foliage, exfoliating bark
Habit: broad, conical or rounded, deciduous tree **Height:** 20–35' **Spread:** 20–35'
Planting: B & B, container; spring or fall **Zones:** 5–7

STEWARTIA IS ANOTHER REASON THAT MANY CENTRAL AND western Ohioans dream of having less dense, more acidic soils. With four-season interest provided by its dark green foliage, summer flowers, multi-colored fall leaves and beautiful exfoliating bark, stewartia could easily become my favorite small tree. Early in my career, I thought I could beat Mother Nature by preparing the soil well and by situating stewartia in a sheltered area. I was beaten badly and often, and I finally gave up on success-fully growing this plant. So, those of you who live on the acidic soils of Ohio, give this beautiful small tree a place in your landscape and remember to send pictures to those of us who can't.

Stewartia is rarely affected by pests or diseases.

Growing

Stewartia grows well in **full sun** or **light shade**. The soil should be of **average to high fertility, humus rich, neutral to acidic, moist** and **well drained**. Provide **shelter** from strong winds. Pruning is rarely required.

Stewartia does not transplant easily. The largest balled-and-burlapped tree to try to plant should be no bigger than 4–5' tall. Larger container-grown specimens may be planted, but only in spring. Be sure you have chosen the best location for this tree when you first plant it, because it will probably not survive being moved.

Tips

Stewartia is used as a specimen tree and in group plantings. It makes a good companion for rhododendrons and azaleas because all of these plants enjoy growing in similar conditions.

Don't be concerned if the bark doesn't put on a display when you first plant a stewartia, because it can take several years for the flaking to develop. Stems with a diameter of less than 2" don't exfoliate.

Recommended

S. pseudocamellia (Japanese stewartia) is a broad, columnar or pyramidal tree. It generally grows 20–35' tall, with an equal spread, though it can grow as tall as 60'. Attractive white flowers with showy yellow stamens appear in mid-summer. The leaves turn shades of yellow, orange, scarlet and reddish purple in fall. The bark is scaly and exfoliating,

leaving the trunk mottled with gray, orange, pink and red-brown. Japanese stewartia may survive in Zone 4 in a sheltered spot. '**Ballet**' has a more spreading habit and bears larger flowers than the species. The flowers may be up to 4" across. '**Milk and Honey**' blooms more profusely than the species and has more intensely colored bark.

Sumac

Rhus

Features: summer and fall foliage, summer flowers, late-summer to fall fruit, habit
Habit: bushy, suckering, colony-forming, deciduous shrub **Height:** 2–30'
Spread: equal to or greater than height **Planting:** container; spring or fall
Zones: 3–9

SUMACS ARE UNDERVALUED PLANTS THAT ARE VERY USEFUL IN
tough, rocky, dry sites where maintenance is sporadic or difficult. Because
some are coarse textured, I use them where close-up aesthetics are not an
issue. Unless a sumac has a lot of room and can be left to its own devices, I
make sure the client is aware of the suckering habit and the need to manage
it. 'Gro-low' is an excellent waist-high groundcover that grows well in full
burning sun and under trees where medium light is available. I had one
under a witchhazel tree for more than 10 years and it never faltered in
growth. However, the good fall color was sacrificed with the lower light
levels. 'September Beauty' closely resembles Japanese tree lilac but blooms in
August rather than late spring.

Growing

Sumacs develop the best fall color in **full sun** but tolerate partial shade. They prefer soil that is of **average fertility, moist** and **well drained**. Once established, sumacs are very drought tolerant.

These plants can become invasive. Remove suckers that come up where you don't want them. Cut out some of the oldest growth each year and allow some suckers to grow in to replace it. If the colony is growing in or near your lawn, you can mow down any young plants that pop up out of bounds.

Tips

Sumacs can be used to form a specimen group in a shrub or mixed border, in a woodland garden or on a sloping bank. Both male and female plants are needed for fruit to form.

When pulling up suckers, be sure to wear gloves to avoid getting the unusual, onion-like odor all over your hands.

Poison-sumac (Toxicodendron vernix, *formerly called* Rhus vernix) *can be difficult to distinguish from other sumacs. Its sap may cause severe skin reactions. To identify a poison-sumac, carefully crush a fresh leaf on a piece of white paper. The juice stains of poison-sumac will turn black over about 24 hours.*

R. aromatica 'Gro-Low'

R. typhina

R. typhina cultivar

Recommended

R. aromatica (fragrant sumac) is native to Ohio. It forms a low mound of suckering stems 2–6' tall and 5–10' wide. Clusters of small yellow flowers appear in spring, followed in late summer by fuzzy fruit that ripens to red. The aromatic foliage turns red or purple in fall. This species tolerates hot, dry, exposed conditions. It can be used to prevent erosion on hills too steep for mowing. **'Green Globe'** is a dense, rounded cultivar that grows about 6' tall, with an equal spread. **'Gro-Low'** ('Grow-low') is a groundcover growing about 24" tall and spreading up to 8'. (Zones 3–9)

R. chinensis (Chinese sumac, nutgall tree) forms an upright, suckering small tree or large shrub. It grows 20–25' tall, with a spread of 15–25'. Yellowish white flowers appear in late summer and early fall. In fall, the fuzzy fruit ripens to orange or red and the bright green leaves turn yellow, orange or red. **'September Beauty'** bears large flower clusters and has more dependably attractive fall color. (Zones 5–8)

R. copallina (flameleaf sumac, shining sumac, dwarf sumac) is another Ohio native. It is a dense and compact grower when young, becoming more open and irregular as it matures. It grows 20–30' tall, with an equal spread. The clusters of creamy flowers in mid- to late summer are followed by fuzzy red fruit in fall. The dark green, glossy leaves turn vivid shades of red in fall. This species tolerates dry and rocky sites but can spread rampantly, making it a poor choice for a small garden.

PRAIRIE FLAME ('Morton') is a slow-growing dwarf cultivar. It grows about 4' tall and spreads 4–6'. The leaves turn brilliant red in fall. (Zones 4–9)

R. typhina (*R. hirta*; staghorn sumac) is also native to Ohio. This suckering, colony-forming shrub has branches covered with velvety fuzz. It grows 15–25' tall and spreads 25' or more. Fuzzy, yellow, early-summer flowers are followed by hairy red fruit. The leaves turn stunning shades of yellow, orange and red in fall. '**Dissecta**' has finely cut leaves that give the plant a lacy, graceful appearance. This cultivar is more compact than the species, growing 6' high and spreading 10'. (Zones 3–8)

R. typhina

Problems & Pests
Caterpillars, scale insects, canker, dieback, leaf spot, powdery mildew, wood rot and *Verticillium* wilt can afflict sumacs.

The fruit is edible. For a refreshing beverage that tastes much like pink lemonade, soak the ripe fruit in cold water overnight and then strain and sweeten to taste.

R. aromatica

Summersweet
Clethra, Sweet Pepperbush, Sweetspire
Clethra

Features: fragrant summer flowers, habit, fall foliage **Habit:** rounded, suckering, deciduous shrub **Height:** 2–8' **Spread:** 2–8' **Planting:** B & B, container; spring **Zones:** 3–9

SUMMERSWEET IS A HIGHLY DESIRABLE SHRUB, BOTH FOR ITS fragrant July blooms and for its ability to thrive in a moist or even wet, lightly shaded garden. I have a drainage swale along the south side of my yard that keeps a 6–7' wide area of soil wet all spring and into early summer. I needed a casually shaped, medium-height shrub tolerant of shade from the overhanging serviceberry. A group of three summersweet plants, placed 36" apart, suckered modestly to fill in this area nicely. During the first flush of July flowers, the fragrance of these plants is outstanding, especially when a light evening breeze invites you to find the source.

Growing
Summersweet grows best in **light or partial shade.** The soil should be **fertile, humus rich, acidic, moist** and **well drained.** Summersweet adapts to most moist soils.

Summersweet is useful in damp, shaded gardens, where the mid-season flowers are much appreciated.

Prune up to one-third of the growth back to the ground in early spring. Deadhead if possible to keep the plant looking neat. Dwarf cultivars typically require little if any pruning.

Tips

Although not aggressive, this shrub tends to sucker, forming a colony of stems. Use it in a border or in a woodland garden. The light shade along the edge of a woodland is an ideal location.

Recommended

C. alnifolia is a large, rounded, upright, colony-forming shrub. It grows 3–8' tall, spreads 3–6' and bears attractive spikes of fragrant white flowers in mid- to late summer. The foliage turns yellow in fall. **'Hummingbird'** is a compact cultivar that grows 24–40" tall, with a spread similar to that of the species. **'Pink Spires'** bears pink flowers. It grows up to 8' tall and wide. **'Rosea'** bears pink flowers that fade to white. It grows 3–6' tall, with an equal spread. **'Ruby Spice'** bears deep pink, fade-resistant flowers on densely branched plants. This cultivar grows 6–8' tall and spreads 4–6'. **'September Beauty'** bears large white flowers later in the season than other cultivars or the species. **'Sixteen Candles'** is a dense dwarf form that grows 24–30" tall and 24–36" wide. This cultivar can be hard to locate.

Problems & Pests

Summersweet is generally trouble free, though some fungal infections such as root rot can occur.

'Ruby Spice'

Try one of the new dwarf cultivars at the front of a border, to better enjoy the lovely fragrance.

'Hummingbird'

Sweetgum
Liquidambar

Features: habit, fall color, spiny fruit, corky bark **Habit:** pyramidal to rounded, deciduous tree **Height:** 60–80' **Spread:** 40–50' **Planting:** B & B; spring **Zones:** 5–9

I HAVE ENJOYED THE MANY ATTRIBUTES OF SWEETGUM OVER THE years. Its ability to grow in fairly low-lying, wettish areas is often appreciated. The fall color varies widely from tree to tree, from season to season on the same tree, and even from one type of soil to another. Whatever the case, it is always exciting to watch the fall display: a tree usually starts out in shades of yellow then progresses through orange and various shades of red and burgundy. Because of past successes, I suggest sweetgum for wettish background areas where people won't have to walk much on the spiny fruit pods if they develop. Keep in mind that if the growing conditions are too stressful, this plant can be winter injured or even killed.

Sweetgum is native in the U.S. from southern Ohio to northern Florida.

Growing

Sweetgum grows equally well in **full sun** or **partial shade,** but it develops the best color in full sun. The soil should be of **average fertility,** slightly **acidic, moist** and **well drained.** This tree requires lots of room for its roots to develop. The foliage may develop late after excessively cold winters.

Little pruning is required. Remove dead, damaged, diseased or awkward branches in spring or early summer.

Tips

Sweetgum is attractive as a shade tree, street tree or specimen tree, or as part of a woodland garden. The spiny fruit makes sweetgum a poor choice near patios, decks, walkways or other areas where people may walk in bare feet or get hit by the falling fruit.

Recommended

L. styraciflua is a neat, symmetrical, pyramidal or rounded tree with attractive star-shaped leaves. Spiny, capsular fruit drops off the tree over the winter and often into the following summer. The fall color of the glossy dark green leaves varies, often from year to year, from yellow to purple or brilliant red. Corky ridges may develop on young bark but eventually disappear. 'Brotzman #1' is a cold-hardy cultivar with very corky branches. 'Brotzman #2' is also a cold-hardy cultivar. It is a vigorous grower and develops excellent fall color. 'Moraine' is a fast-growing, cold-hardy cultivar. Fall color is brilliant red. These cultivars are hardy to the warmer parts of Zone 4. Many

L. styraciflua (above), cultivar (below)

other cultivars are available; your local nursery dealer will probably offer only those that grow well in your area.

Problems & Pests

Occasional problems can occur with borers, caterpillars, scale insects, leaf spot and rot. Iron chlorosis (leaf yellowing) can be a problem in too alkaline a soil.

Sweetspire
Virginia Sweetspire
Itea

Features: habit, fragrant flowers, fall color **Habit:** upright to arching, deciduous shrub **Height:** 2–10' **Spread:** 3–10' or more **Planting:** container; spring preferable, but early fall acceptable **Zones:** 5–9

SWEETSPIRE HAS LONG BEEN AN EXCELLENT LANDSCAPE PLANT, especially for low-lying, wetter areas. It can be used individually or in small groups on residential properties, and it can be planted in masses in larger areas. Since the development of the named cultivars, the plant has become so popular that it is frequently sold out. Be patient, because it is well worth waiting for. The long-lasting fall color is so outstanding, especially in sunny areas, that the spikes of fragrant flowers in late spring are just an added bonus. For those of us who deal with the heavier alkaline soils, I suggest using acid fertilizers and/or simply sprinkling sulfur into the planting soil and on the surface thereafter.

Growing

Sweetspire grows well in all light conditions from **full sun to full shade**. Plants grown in full sun develop the best fall color. The habit will be more upright in shade and more arching in sun. The soil should be **fertile** and **moist**,

though sweetspire is fairly adaptable and well-established plants are quite drought tolerant.

One-third of the older growth can be removed to the ground each year once flowering is finished. Do not prune in early spring or you will lose the current season's flower buds.

Tips

This shrub is excellent for low-lying and moist areas of the garden. It grows well near streams and water features. It is also great for plantings near decks, patios and pathways, where the fragrant flowers can be fully enjoyed.

LITTLE HENRY (above), 'Henry's Garnet' (below)

Recommended

I. virginica is an upright to arching, suckering shrub native to Ohio and the southeastern U.S. It usually grows 3–5' tall but can grow up to 10' tall, with an equal or greater spread. Spikes of fragrant white flowers appear in late spring or early summer, and the leaves turn shades of purple and red in fall. '**Henry's Garnet**' bears many long, white flower spikes and consistently develops dark red-purple fall color. It grows 3–4' tall, with an equal or greater spread. **LITTLE HENRY** ('Sprich') is a compact cultivar 24–36" tall and 36" wide, with a low, mounding habit. It bears bright white flower spikes and develops bright red fall color. '**Sarah Eve**' has red new growth that matures to bright green then turns red again in fall. Its flowers are pink. This cultivar is the same size as the species but is slower growing.

Problems & Pests

Sweetspire may suffer infrequent problems with aphids or leaf spot.

Thornless Honeylocust

Gleditsia

Features: summer and fall foliage, habit **Habit:** rounded, spreading, deciduous tree **Height:** 15–100' **Spread:** 15–70' **Planting:** B & B, container; spring or fall **Zones:** 4–8

I HAVE PLANTED A THORNLESS HONEYLOCUST TO EVENTUALLY overhang the patio at each of my homes, so I have lived next to this tree for 40 years now. I chose it because I didn't want a heavy-headed, dense tree close by. In 26 years, the current tree has reached 35' in height and 65' in spread. I do have to sweep up the flower buds and skim the small leaflets out of the little fishpond under it. I have also occasionally had to pick up fruit under the tree in the middle of winter. These few tasks seem inconsequential because I so enjoy the light, airy nature of the tree.

Growing

Thornless honeylocust prefers **full sun.** The soil should be **fertile** and **well drained,** though this tree adapts to most soil types. Little pruning is required. Prune young plants in late winter or early spring to establish a good branching pattern.

Tips

Use thornless honeylocust as a specimen. It is often used as a street tree but is a poor choice for narrow streets because the vigorous roots can break up pavement.

Recommended

G. triacanthos var. *inermis* is a spreading, rounded tree up to 100' tall and up to 70' wide. The fall color is a beautiful warm golden yellow. The flowers are inconspicuous, but the long, pea-like pods that occasionally develop in late summer persist into fall and sometimes still dangle from the branches after the leaves have fallen. This variety is thornless and is the parent of many cultivars, often smaller and better suited for the home garden. The cultivars listed here generally do not bear fruit in Ohio. Abnormal spring weather occasionally encourages some pods to form, but it is very rare for these trees to become problematic because of persistent fruiting. 'Elegantissima' is a dense, shrubby cultivar 15–25' tall and 15–20' wide. 'Emerald Kaskade' is a small, weeping tree with dark green foliage. It grows about 16' tall, with an equal spread. HALKA has a rounded habit with less pendulous branches than the species. It grows about 40' tall, with an equal spread. IMPERIAL ('Impcole') has a spreading habit with graceful branching. It grows up to 35' tall and wide. 'Moraine' was developed in southwestern Ohio. It grows 40–50' tall and wide. The dark green foliage turns golden yellow in fall. This tree resists webworm damage. SKYLINE ('Skycole') is an upright cultivar that grows about 45' tall, with a spread of 35'. SUNBURST

SUNBURST

('Suncole') is a fast-growing, broad-spreading tree 30–40' tall and 25–30' wide. The foliage emerges bright yellow in spring and matures to light green over the summer.

Problems & Pests

Aphids, borers, caterpillars, mites, webworm, canker, heart rot, leaf spot, powdery mildew and tar spot can cause problems.

G. triacanthos var. *inermis*

Tulip Tree
Tulip Poplar
Liriodendron

Features: early-summer flowers, foliage, fruit, habit **Habit:** large, rounded, oval, deciduous tree **Height:** 70–100' **Spread:** 33–50' **Planting:** B & B; spring **Zones:** 4–9

AN AGING CLIENT OF MINE WAS ADAMANT ABOUT SYMMETRY IN all things. One fall day she spotted several young, symmetrical trees at the edge of a wooded area. She contacted me and demanded I determine what they were and then get some for her. I identified them as tulip trees, but I strenuously objected to obtaining them for her because of the trees' mature size. She was determined. I managed to persuade her to plant only a single tree, and only when the two existing 'ugly' trees were removed. The client has now passed away, but the maturing tulip tree persists, still with its youthful symmetry because it has no competition. I have learned from this experience that it can be entirely appropriate in some circumstances to satisfy one's immediate desires.

Growing

Tulip tree grows well in **full sun** or **partial shade.** The soil should be **average to rich,** slightly **acidic** and **moist.** This tree needs plenty of room for its roots to grow. Frequent periods of drought may eventually kill it.

Little pruning is required. Remove dead, damaged or diseased growth as needed, and prune awkward growth in winter.

Tips

This beautiful, massive tree needs lots of room to grow. Parks, golf courses and large gardens can host this tree as a specimen or in a group planting, but its susceptibility to drought and need for root space make it a poor choice as a specimen, shade or street tree on smaller properties.

Recommended

L. tulipifera is native to Ohio and throughout the eastern U.S. It is known more for its unusually shaped leaves than for its tulip-like flowers because the blooms are often borne high in the tree and go unnoticed until the falling petals litter the ground. The foliage turns golden yellow in fall. The leaves of '**Aureomarginata**' have yellow-green margins.

Problems & Pests

Aphids and sooty mold can be common. Borers, leaf miners, scale insects, leaf spot and powdery mildew may also afflict tulip tree. Drought stress can cause some of the leaves to drop early.

L. tulipifera (both photos)

The genus name Liriodendron *comes from the Greek and means 'lily tree.'*

Viburnum

Viburnum

Features: flowers (some fragrant), summer and fall foliage, fruit, habit
Habit: bushy or spreading, evergreen, semi-evergreen or deciduous shrub
Height: 2–20' or more **Spread:** 2–15' **Planting:** bare-root, B & B, container;
spring or fall **Zones:** 2–9

THE GENUS *VIBURNUM* IS ONE OF THE MOST VERSATILE, WITH
plants in a wide range of sizes. Many species are fragrant, making them popular as specimens near doors or walkways. Some have foliage that looks good
all year, while others have spectacular fall color. I came into possession of
some large, unkempt blackhaw viburnum in an old nursery. I spent several
days with pruners, loppers and saws transforming them into sizable multi-
stemmed trees of 8–15'. They were all used as specimens, single or grouped,
in full sun or as understory trees. Pruning and training young plants can create the same effects. Flowers, fruit, structure, shape and fall color are about
everything that can be asked of a plant, and viburnums grant it all.

*The edible but very tart fruits of
V. trilobum are popular for
making jellies, pies and wine.
They are sweeter if frozen or if
picked after a frost.*

Growing

Viburnums grow well in **full sun,
partial shade** or **light shade**. The
soil should be of **average fertility,
moist** and **well drained**. Viburnums
tolerate both alkaline and acidic
soils.

Little pruning is necessary. Remove
awkward, dead, damaged or diseased branches as needed.

Tips

Viburnums can be used in borders
and woodland gardens. They are
good choices for plantings near
patios, decks and swimming pools.
Fruiting is better when more than
one plant of a species is grown.

Recommended

V. x *burkwoodii* (Burkwood viburnum) is a rounded semi-evergreen
shrub. It grows 6–10' tall and
spreads 5–8'. Clusters of fragrant
pinkish white flowers appear in
mid- to late spring, followed by red
fruit that ripens to black.
'Chenaultii' ('Chenault') has pink
buds that open to white flowers. It
grows about 8' tall, with an equal
spread. The leaves turn bronze in
fall. 'Mohawk' is a compact cultivar
with dark pink buds that open to
spicy, clove-scented white flowers.
The glossy dark green leaves turn
bright red in fall. This cultivar
resists leaf spot and powdery
mildew. (Zones 4–8)

V. x *carlcephalum* (fragrant viburnum) is a bushy deciduous shrub
6–10' tall, with an equal spread.
Clusters of fragrant white flowers
open from pink buds in late spring.
(Zones 6–8)

V. dilatatum cultivar

*Viburnums look lovely in the shade of
evergreen trees. Their richly textured
foliage complements other flowering
shrubs and perennials.*

V. opulus

V. sargentii 'Onondaga'

V. dentatum *has long, straight stems that have been used to make arrow shafts, giving rise to the common name arrowwood.*

V. carlesii (Korean spice viburnum) is a dense, bushy, rounded deciduous shrub. It grows 3–8' tall, with an equal spread. White or pink, spicy-scented flowers appear in mid- to late spring. The fruit is red, ripening to black. The foliage may turn red in fall. '**Aurora**' grows about 4' tall, with an equal spread. Deep pink buds open to pinkish white flowers. '**Cayuga**' bears large flower clusters with pink buds that contrast with fragrant white flowers. It grows 4–5' tall, with an equal spread. This culti-var is disease resistant. '**Compacta**' is a dwarf cultivar about 36" tall, with an equal spread. It resists leaf spot. (Zones 5–8)

V. dentatum (southern arrowwood) is an upright, arching deciduous shrub that is native to Ohio. It grows 6–15' tall, with an equal spread. Clusters of white flowers appear in late spring or early summer, fol-lowed by dark blue fruit in fall. This shrub is hardy and durable and adapts to almost any soil conditions. **AUTUMN JAZZ** ('Ralph Senior') has arching branches. It grows 10–12' tall and wide. In fall the leaves turn yellow, orange, red and burgundy. **CHICAGO LUSTRE** ('Synnestvedt') boasts glossy dark green foliage. (Zones 2–8)

V. dilatatum (linden viburnum) is an open, upright deciduous shrub 8–10' tall and 6–10' wide. Clusters of white flowers appear in late spring or early summer, followed by bright red berries in fall. The foliage turns bronze, red or burgundy in fall. '**Erie**' bears fluffy, white, late-spring flowers, followed by lots of coral red fruit that persists over winter into early spring. The leaves turn yellow, orange and red in fall. (Zones 5–7)

V. x juddii (Judd viburnum) is a rounded deciduous shrub. It grows about 7' tall and spreads 5–7'. Clus-ters of pink buds open to fragrant white flowers in late spring. The red fruit turns black and contrasts with the leaves, which turn red or purple in fall. This hybrid resists leaf spot. (Zones 4–8)

V. lantana (wayfaringtree) is a large, multi-stemmed deciduous shrub or small tree 10–20' tall and 10–15' wide. Clusters of white flowers are borne in late spring and early summer, fol-lowed by green fruit that ripens to orange and red before it finally turns black in fall. 'Mohican' is a compact cultivar 10–12' tall, with a spread of 10–15'. The fruit stays red longer than that of the species. (Zones 3–8)

V. lentago (nannyberry, sheepberry) is an open, suckering deciduous shrub or small tree that is native to Ohio. It grows 12–20' tall and spreads 6–10'. Clusters of creamy white flowers appear in mid-spring, followed by green, yellow and pink fruit that eventually ripens to black. The glossy green leaves may develop some purple coloring in fall. (Zones 2–8)

V. nudum (smooth witherod) is a bushy, spreading deciduous shrub 12–15' tall and about 6' wide. It bears clusters of white, musk-scented flowers in early summer, followed by pink fruit that ripens to blue and then black. The pink and blue fruit are present at the same time, creating a striking contrast. 'Winterthur' flowers and fruits prolifically, and the foliage turns bright red in fall. (Zones 5–9)

V. opulus (*V. opulus* var. *opulus*; European cranberrybush, guelder-rose) is a rounded, spreading deciduous shrub that grows 8–15' tall and spreads 8–12'. The flower clusters consist of an outer ring of showy sterile flowers surrounding inner fertile flowers, giving the plant a lacy look when in bloom in late spring. The fall foliage and the fruit are red. 'Compactum' ('Nanum') is dense and slow growing, reaching 2–5' in both height and spread. 'Xanthocarpum' has golden yellow fruit. (Zones 3–8)

V. plicatum var. tomentosum cultivar

Viburnums are generally easy to grow and adapt to most soils.

V. plicatum (Japanese snowball viburnum) is a bushy, upright deciduous shrub with arching stems. It grows 10–15' tall and spreads 12–15'. Ball-like clusters of white flowers appear in late spring. Fall color is reddish purple. **Var. *tomentosum*** (doublefile viburnum) has graceful, horizontal branching that gives the shrub a layered effect. It grows 8–10' tall and spreads 8–12'. The leaves have fuzzy undersides. Clusters of inconspicuous fertile flowers surrounded by showy sterile flowers blanket the branches. Doublefile viburnum can be killed back in winter, but it is usually quick to recover. This variety is the parent of several cultivars. 'Kern's Pink' ('Roseace')

V. plicatum var. tomentosum cultivar

V. carlesii

features clusters of pink flowers. 'Mariesii' has more distinctly layered branches than the parent variety. NEWPORT ('Newzam') is a dense, mound-forming cultivar 5–6' tall, with an equal spread. 'Popcorn' is covered in many small clusters of flowers when in bloom. 'Shasta' is a spreading shrub that grows about 6'

tall, spreads up to 12' and bears plentiful clusters of white flowers. The showy sterile flowers are scattered throughout each cluster rather than forming only an outer ring. 'Summer Snowflake' ('Fujisanensis') bears large clusters of white flowers from late spring until fall. This compact cultivar grows about 6' tall, with a similar spread. (Zones 5–8)

V. x *pragense* (Prague viburnum) is a rounded semi-evergreen shrub with glossy leaves. It grows about 10' tall, with an equal spread. Clusters of pink buds open to fragrant white flowers in late spring. (Zones 5–8)

V. prunifolium (blackhaw viburnum, blackhaw) is an upright, rounded deciduous small tree or large shrub native to Ohio. It grows 12–15' tall and spreads 8–12'. Flat-topped clusters of white flowers appear in late spring. The mildew-resistant foliage turns bronze then bright red in fall. (Zones 3–9)

V. x *rhytidophylloides* (lantana-phyllum viburnum) is a spreading, arching semi-evergreen shrub 8–12' tall and 12–15' wide. It bears clusters of creamy white flowers in mid- to late spring. 'Alleghany' is a dense, rounded cultivar with very dark green leaves that resist leaf spot. It bears more plentiful clusters of creamy white flowers. The fruit eventually ripens to black but is red for several weeks in fall, contrasting attractively with the foliage. (Zones 4–8)

V. sargentii (Sargent viburnum) is a large, bushy deciduous shrub. It grows 10–15' tall, with an equal spread. The early-spring blossoms consist of clusters of inconspicuous fertile flowers surrounded by showy sterile flowers. The fall color is yellow, orange and red. '**Onondaga**' has purple stems and red to pink fertile flowers ringed with showy, pinkish white sterile flowers. The purple-green foliage turns red in fall. (Zones 3–7)

V. sieboldii (*V. sieboldi*; Siebold viburnum) is a deciduous large shrub or small tree that grows 15–20' tall, or taller, and spreads 10–15'. It produces masses of creamy white flowers in late spring or early summer. The leaves may turn purple-red in fall. '**Seneca**' bears larger clusters of flowers, followed by bright red fruit borne on red stems. The fruit eventually ripens to black and falls off. (Zones 4–7)

V. trilobum (*V. opulus* var. *americanum*; American cranberrybush, highbush cranberry) is a dense, rounded deciduous shrub native to Ohio. It grows 8–15' tall, with a spread of 8–12'. Early-summer clusters of showy sterile and inconspicuous fertile flowers are followed by edible red fruit. Fall color is red. This species is resistant to aphids. '**Compactum**' is a smaller, more dense shrub 5–6' in height and width. '**Wentworth**' was selected for its large edible fruit. (Zones 2–7)

Problems & Pests

Aphids, borers, mealybugs, scale insects, treehoppers, weevils, dieback, downy mildew, gray mold, leaf spot, powdery mildew, *Verticillium* wilt and wood rot can affect viburnums.

V. opulus cultivar (above)

V. opulus (center), *V. nudum* 'Winterthur' (below)

The showy fruit comes in colors ranging from bright yellow to bright pink, rich red and deep blue.

Weigela
Weigela

Features: late-spring to early-summer flowers, foliage, habit **Habit:** upright or low, spreading, deciduous shrub **Height:** 1–9' **Spread:** 1–12' **Planting:** bare-root, container; spring or fall **Zones:** 3–8

MANY PLANT NAMES GIVE PEOPLE PAUSE WHEN IT COMES TO pronunciation, but I think weigela is one of the trickiest. Try *why-jee-lee-a.* It gets you there almost every time, and you do need to ask for this beautiful old-timer. A well-pruned, well-maintained old plant or a rampant young one will bloom well for four to six weeks, making quite a show. The trumpet-shaped flowers are appealing, and hummingbirds love them too. New types with wine red or bright gold leaves make a wonderful addition to any sunny border.

Growing

Weigela prefers **full sun** but tolerates partial shade. For the best leaf color, grow purple-leaved plants in full sun and yellow-leaved plants in partial shade. The soil should be **fertile** and **well drained**. Weigela adapts to most well-drained soils.

Once flowering is finished, cut flowering shoots back to strong buds or branch junctions. One-third of the old growth can be cut back to the ground at the same time.

Weigela is one of the longest-blooming shrubs, with the main flush of blooms lasting as long as six weeks. It often reblooms if sheared lightly after the first flowers fade.

Tips

Use weigela in a shrub or mixed border, open woodland garden or informal barrier planting.

Recommended

W. florida is a spreading shrub with arching branches. It grows 6–9' tall and spreads 8–12'. Clusters of dark pink flowers appear in late spring and early summer. **BRIANT RUBIDOR** ('Olympiade,' 'Rubidor') has yellow foliage and red flowers. It grows 4–7' tall and wide. **'Bristol Ruby'** bears dark ruby red flowers. **CARNAVAL** ('Courtalor') bears red, pink and white flowers on the same plant. **FRENCH LACE** ('Brigela') has lime green to yellow leaf margins. The flowers are dark reddish pink. **MIDNIGHT WINE** ('Elvera') is a dwarf plant up to 12" tall and 12–18" wide. The foliage is purple and the flowers are pink. **'Minuet'** is a compact, spreading shrub 24–36" tall and about 3–4' wide. The dark pink flowers have yellow throats. The foliage is a purplish green that matures to dark green over the summer. This cultivar is hardy in Zones 3–7. **'Pink Princess'** grows 5–6' tall, with an equal spread, and bears profuse pink flowers over a long period in summer. **'Red Prince'** is an upright shrub. It grows 5–6' tall, spreads about 5' and is hardy in Zones 4–7. Bright red flowers appear in early summer, with a second flush in late summer. **'Rumba'** is low and spreading, with purple-edged yellow-green leaves and dark red, yellow-throated flowers. It grows about 36" tall, with an equal or greater spread. **'Suzanne'** grows about 7' tall and wide and features white-variegated foliage. It bears

WINE AND ROSES (below)

white to pinkish flowers in late spring. **'Variegata'** is a compact plant about 5' tall and wide. The flowers are pale pink and the leaves have creamy white margins. It is hardy to Zone 5. **'Victoria'** grows about 4' tall and wide. The foliage is burgundy green and the flowers are rose pink. Some sources claim this is the same plant as **WINE AND ROSES**. **WINE AND ROSES** ('Alexandra') grows 4–5' tall and wide. It has dark purple foliage and vivid pink flowers.

Problems & Pests

Foliar nematodes, scale insects, twig dieback and *Verticillium* wilt can occur but usually aren't serious.

White Forsythia
Korean Abelialeaf
Abeliophyllum

Features: fragrant late-winter or early-spring flowers **Habit:** suckering, deciduous shrub **Height:** 3–5' **Spread:** 3–5' **Planting:** container; spring or fall **Zones:** 5–8

HAVING PLANTS IN BLOOM FOR AS MUCH OF THE YEAR AS POSSIBLE is a goal of many gardeners. Ohio landscapes are pretty drab by winter's end, and we welcome the flowers of early witchhazel and cornelian cherry dogwood. We can make another spectacular addition to the early-season landscape with white forsythia. When we are wishing for nearly any sign of spring, it provides a bright dash of color and hope for more. I have only recently become fully aware of this plant's potential, and I am working to clear a space for it. White forsythia tends to develop tangled, twiggy growth. It can be controlled by cutting the stems to the ground after flowering is finished each spring.

White forsythia rarely suffers from any insect or disease problems.

Growing

White forsythia prefers **full sun** but tolerates very light shade. The soil should be of **average fertility** and **well drained**. This shrub adapts to most well-drained soils.

Prune in spring as soon as flowering is complete. Cut plants right back to within 6" of the ground every two or so years to keep them looking their best.

Tips

White forsythia tends to form a mass of tangled twigs. The showy early-spring flowers compensate for its deficiencies when not in bloom. Though it's not ideal in a small garden, gardeners with a bit more space can include this plant in a corner with true forsythia, witchhazel and crocuses to create a wonderful early-season show. White forsythia can also be included in a sunny border or in a naturalized garden.

Recommended

A. distichum is a spreading, suckering shrub that bears creamy white flowers in late winter or early spring, before the leaves appear. The foliage may turn purple in fall. This plant can survive in Zone 4, but the flower buds may be frost killed during severely cold winters. **'Roseum'** bears light pink flowers.

Despite its common name, this shrub is not a member of the genus Forsythia. *It is an unrelated Korean species that has similar flowers and comes into bloom at about the same time.*

'Roseum'

A. distichum

Wisteria

Wisteria

Features: late-spring flowers, foliage, habit **Habit:** twining, woody, deciduous climber **Height:** 15–50' or more **Spread:** 15–50' or more **Planting:** container; spring or fall **Zones:** 4–9

WHEN A WISTERIA IS THRIVING, THERE ISN'T A MORE SPECTACULAR flowering plant. When not flowering, it can be a bane to your gardening existence. I have heard the gentlest gardeners speak with a distinct change in their vocabulary when dealing with wisterias. These plants are finicky bloomers, and they can spread rampantly. Keeping them on the underprivileged side is my custom. No fertilizer—ever; no watering after the first season; significant heading back in late winter; and heavy root pruning, if needed. Abuse is the name of the game, and you may need to be patient for three or four years before you see the first good blooms. It is also important to find a good nursery so you get plants that are started from flowering branches only. I strongly recommend buying wisteria in bloom, when possible.

Growing

Wisterias grow well in **full sun** or **partial shade**. The soil should be of **average fertility, moist** and **well drained**. Vines grown in too-fertile soil produce lots of vegetative growth but few flowers. Avoid planting wisteria near a lawn, where fertilizer may leach over to the vine.

The first two or three years of growth will establish the main framework of sturdy stems. Once the vine is established, side shoots can be cut back in late winter to within three to six buds of the growth that formed the previous year. Trim the entire plant back in mid-summer if the growth is becoming rampant. Grown on a large, sturdy structure, wisterias can simply be left to their own devices, but be prepared for them to escape once they run out of room.

To propagate wisteria, bend a length of vine down and bury it in a pot of good potting soil. Hold the branch

W. sinensis (both photos)

Wisterias look attractive grown against the side of a house, but resist the temptation. The thin young stems can wedge themselves into cracks in the siding, and as the stems mature and enlarge, the cracks are forced to expand with them. Fixing the problem can be time-consuming and expensive.

W. floribunda

You may need to treat your wisteria very badly to get the best blooms. If you have a reluctant bloomer, try pruning the roots and withholding high-nitrogen fertilizer and water.

in place with a rock if required. The buried section will root and can then be cut from the main plant. The roots have taken when you can no longer pull the buried section out of the pot with a gentle tug.

Tips
These vines require something to twine around, such as an arbor or other sturdy structure. You can also train a wisteria to form a small tree. Try to select a permanent site; wisterias don't like being moved once established.

These vigorous vines will send up suckers and can root wherever the

branches touch the ground. Regular and frequent pruning will help prevent your wisteria from getting out of hand.

Wisterias develop long, bean-like pods after flowering. The seeds from these pods, and all other parts of wisteria plants, are poisonous.

Recommended
W. floribunda (Japanese wisteria) grows 25–50' or more in height and spread. Long, pendulous clusters of fragrant blue, purple, pink or white flowers appear in late spring before the leaves emerge. '**Macrobotrys**' bears very fragrant flowers in clusters that may be up to 4' long. '**Rosea**' ('Hon Beni,' 'Honey Bee Pink,' 'Pink Ice') bears clusters of fragrant pink flowers. '**Royal Purple**' bears clusters of darker purple flowers. (Zones 4–9)

W. frutescens var. *macrostachya* (*W. macrostachya*, *W. macrostachys*; Kentucky wisteria) grows 15–25' tall and wide. The pendulous clusters of fragrant purple flowers appear after other wisterias are finished flowering. '**Aunt Dee**' is a popular cultivar with light purple flowers. This cultivar may survive in a sheltered location in Zone 4. (Zone 5–8)

W. sinensis (*W. chinensis*; Chinese wisteria) can grow 20–30' or more in height and spread. It bears long, pendent clusters of fragrant blue-purple flowers in late spring. '**Alba**' has white flowers. (Zones 5–8)

W. venusta '**Alba**' (silky wisteria) can grow about 30' in height and spread, but it is often grafted to form a small tree 6–8' tall, with an equal spread. The fragrant white flowers appear in early summer. The blooms are the largest of any of the wisterias, though the clusters are smaller. (Zones 5–9)

Problems & Pests

Aphids, leaf miners, mealybugs, crown gall, dieback, leaf spot and viral diseases may cause occasional problems for wisterias.

Wisterias can be trained up a pipe to form a small tree.

W. sinensis (both photos)

Witchhazel

Hamamelis

Features: flowers, foliage, habit **Habit:** spreading, deciduous shrub or small tree
Height: 6–20' or more **Spread:** 6–20' **Planting:** B & B, container; spring or fall
Zones: 3–9

I PURPOSELY PLANTED A FALL-BLOOMING WITCHHAZEL WEST OF A
blue spruce in my garden. At around the time of my birthday in October, the
afternoon sun highlights the witchhazel blooms against that light blue background. What a stunning visual birthday present! Because of the desirable
attributes and genetic malleability of witchhazels, breeders are working to
bring out new growth forms and, especially, new flower colors. The Holden
Arboretum northeast of Cleveland is one of the leaders in this endeavor.
Their work has now been combined with that of the late Dr. David Leach,
and I expect we will see some beautiful new trees soon. A visit to this arboretum is a must—take your lunch, you'll need the whole day.

*Witchhazel branches have been used as
divining rods to find water and gold.*

Growing

Witchhazels grow well in **full sun** or **light shade**. The soil should be of **average fertility, neutral to acidic, moist** and **well drained**.

Pruning is rarely required. Remove awkward shoots once flowering is complete.

Tips

Witchhazels work well individually or in groups. They can be used as specimen plants, in shrub or mixed borders or in woodland gardens. As small trees, they are ideal for space-limited gardens.

H. x intermedia 'Jelena'

The unique flowers have long, narrow, crinkled petals that give the plant a spidery appearance when in bloom. If the weather gets too cold, the petals will roll up, protecting the flowers and extending the flowering season.

Early-blooming witchhazels are a welcome sight in late winter and early spring, signaling that a long winter is coming to an end.

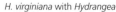

H. virginiana with *Hydrangea*

H. x *intermedia* 'Arnold Promise' (above)

H. virginiana (center)

Recommended

H. x *intermedia* is a vase-shaped, spreading shrub. It grows 10–20' tall, with an equal spread. Clusters of fragrant yellow, orange or red flowers appear in mid- to late winter. The leaves turn attractive shades of orange, red and bronze in fall. **'Arnold Promise'** has large, fragrant, bright yellow or yellow-orange flowers. **'Diane'** ('Diana') bears dark red flowers in late winter, and its fall foliage is yellow, orange and red. **'James Wells'** bears prolific bright yellow flowers. **'Jelena'** ('Copper Beauty') has a horizontal branching habit. The fragrant flowers are coppery orange and the fall color is orange-red. **'Primavera'** bears profuse, very fragrant, bright yellow flowers that have reddish purple petal bases. **'Ruby Glow'** is a vigorous, upright shrub with deep orange flowers. (Zones 5–9)

H. vernalis (vernal witchhazel, Ozark witchhazel) is a rounded,

upright, often suckering shrub. It
grows 6–15' tall, with an equal
spread. Very fragrant yellow, orange
or red flowers are borne in early
spring. The foliage turns bright yellow in fall. (Zones 4–8)

H. virginiana (common witchhazel,
American witchhazel) is a common
Ohio native. It is a large, rounded,
spreading shrub or small tree 12–20'
or more in height, with an equal
spread. Yellow fall flowers are often
hidden by the foliage that turns yellow at the same time, but this
species is attractive nonetheless.
(Zones 3–8)

Problems & Pests
Aphids, leaf rollers, scale insects, leaf
spot, powdery mildew and wood rot
are possible, but rarely serious,
problems.

H. vernalis

*The branches of spring-blooming
witchhazels can be cut in winter and
forced into bloom indoors.*

H. virginiana

Yellowwood
Cladrastis

Features: summer and fall foliage, spring flowers, bark, habit **Habit:** rounded, low-branching, deciduous tree **Height:** 30–50' **Spread:** 30–55' **Planting:** B & B; spring **Zones:** 4–8

TWENTY-SEVEN YEARS AGO, I SOUGHT OUT, PURCHASED AND planted a beautiful triple-stemmed yellowwood. Contrary to my understanding of its brittle nature, I planted it next to the edge of the family room window on the ground floor and our master bedroom window upstairs. I spent 16 years gradually heading the tree up over these windows. Not unexpectedly, the center stem got pinched out by growth of the other two stems. Two stems were quite acceptable, but in the 21st year, one of the other stems suddenly cankered and died. Oh well, one stem was still okay. Unfortunately, it, too, has now cankered and died and was just removed as I started this writing. None of us is immune to the periodic ravages of Mother Nature.

Yellowwood is lovely in all seasons and is rarely afflicted by pest or disease problems.

Growing

Yellowwood grows best in **full sun**. The soil should be **fertile, moist** and **well drained**. Alkaline soil is preferable, but yellowwood adapts well to acidic soil. Plant trees when they are young and don't move them again because they resent root disturbance.

Remove dead, diseased, damaged or awkward growth in summer. The sap tends to run profusely if yellowwood is pruned in winter or spring.

Tips

Yellowwood is a beautiful flowering shade tree appropriate for large properties. Do not plant it close to houses or other buildings because the wood is fairly weak and can break in a strong wind.

Recommended

C. kentukea (C. lutea; American yellowwood, Kentucky yellowwood) is native to Ohio. This attractive, wide-spreading tree has bright yellowish green leaves. In late spring and early summer, the branches are covered with long, drooping clusters of white or pink, pea-like flowers. In

fall the leaves turn bright yellow. The bark is smooth and gray, much like beech bark, and provides winter interest. The bean-like pods and seeds within are not edible.

C. kentukea (foreground) with *Crataegus*

Yew

Taxus

Features: foliage, habit, red seed cups **Habit:** evergreen; conical or columnar tree or bushy or spreading shrub **Height:** 1–70' **Spread:** 1–30' **Planting:** B & B, container; spring or fall **Zones:** 4–7

TAXUS HAS BEEN CALLED 'THAT DUMB GREEN BALL YOU SEE everywhere,' usually as part of a rant about gardeners' lack of imagination. It's also been called 'the Cadillac of plants.' I agree with both comments. Yews have been grossly overused and are very rarely pruned correctly to maintain a natural form. They are, however, the only reliable evergreens for deep shade. Given appropriate siting and hand pruning to enhance their natural form, they are beautiful and necessary plants. But prune you must, because unchecked yews can become very large. I hand prune mine every other year, and at 27 years of age, they are still below waist height and look natural. Do be aware of deer browsing, black vine weevils and excessive soil water, as these conditions seem to be the only real impediments to yew longevity.

All parts of yews are poisonous, except the pleasant-tasting, fleshy red cup that surrounds the inedible hard seed.

Growing

Yews grow well in any light conditions from **full sun to full shade**. The soil should be **fertile** and **moist** and must be **well drained**. Yews will tolerate soils of any acidity, most urban pollution and windy or dry conditions. They dislike soil contaminated with road salt and soil that is very wet. Do not plant them near downspouts or other places where water collects.

Hedges and topiary can be trimmed back in summer and fall. Yews can be cut back very hard during their dormant period to reduce their size or to rejuvenate them. New growth will sprout from old wood after a hard pruning.

Tips

Yews can be used in borders or as specimens, hedges, topiary and groundcovers. Male and female flowers are borne on separate plants. Plants of both genders must be present in order for the attractive red arils (seed cups) to form.

T. baccata (above), *T.* x *media* cultivar (center)

T. x *media* 'Densiformis'

T. *cuspidata* cultivar

T. x *media* cultivar

Recommended

T. baccata (English yew) is a broad, conical tree with attractive flaking bark. It grows 30–70' tall and spreads 15–30'. The foliage can become discolored in winter and the roots can rot in wet soil, so wind protection and excellent drainage are essential. '**Repandens**' is a spreading, mounding shrub. It grows 2–4' tall and spreads 12–15'. (Zones 5–7)

T. cuspidata (Japanese yew) is a slow-growing, broad, columnar or conical tree. It grows 30–50' tall and spreads 20–30'. '**Capitata**' is a pyramidal form that can grow up to 50' tall if left unpruned. (Zones 4–7)

T. x *media* (English Japanese yew), a cross between *T. baccata* and *T. cuspidata*, has the vigor of English yew and the cold hardiness of Japanese yew. It forms a rounded to pyramidal tree or rounded to spreading shrub. '**Brownii**' has a globe-shaped habit, generally growing about 5' tall and wide. '**Chadwick**' is a low, spreading cultivar. It grows 2–4' tall and spreads 4–6'. '**Densiformis**' is a wide, dense, rounded shrub 3–4' tall and 6–8' in spread. ERIE SHORES ('Ershzam') is a smaller, spreading cultivar. It grows about 24" tall and about 5' wide. '**Everlow**' is a low spreader with dark green needles. It grows 12–24" tall and spreads up to 5'. '**Hicksii**' is an open, columnar tree 15–25' tall and 5–10' in spread. '**L.C. Bobbink**' is a rounded to mound-forming cultivar. It grows about 6' tall and spreads 6–8'. '**Sebian**' is a larger, spreading cultivar that grows about 6' tall and spreads up to 12'. **'Viridis'** is a narrow, columnar cultivar that grows 10–12' tall and spreads 12–24". The foliage emerges yellow green and matures to light green. **'Wardii'** is a dense, spreading culti- var that grows about 6' tall and spreads about 20'. (Zones 4–7)

Problems & Pests

Black vine weevils, mealybugs, mites, scale insects, dieback, needle blight and root rot are possible but not serious problems. Deer brows- ing can be a problem in some areas.

T. baccata (above)

Taxol, a drug for treating ovarian, breast and other cancers, was originally derived from the bark of T. brevifolia *(western yew).*

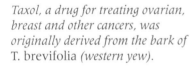

T. x *media* cultivars (center & below)

Yucca
Adam's Needle
Yucca

Features: summer flowers, foliage, habit **Habit:** rounded rosette of long, stiff, spiky, evergreen leaves with tall flower stalk **Height:** 24–36"; up to 6' in flower **Spread:** 24–36" **Planting:** container; spring or fall **Zones:** 5–9

AFTER 45 YEARS IN HORTICULTURE AND LANDSCAPE DESIGN, I STILL don't know exactly how I feel about yucca. It seems like an Arizona desert plant; yet, when used in groups and in appropriate combinations with other species, it can add great interest to Ohio land-scapes. After all, what else gives us a 5–6' tall flower stalk? For those of us who enjoy varied textures, the leaves and stems are unique and appealing, as are the occasional fruit pods that develop from June into winter. Improperly used, however, yucca can be pretentious—and, if you aren't careful to keep it out of walkways, painful. In mixed bor-ders, large bed plantings and masses it often looks great, but let's all take care to follow good design principles.

If you consider yourself to have a brown thumb, try growing yucca for almost certain success.

Growing

Yucca grows best in **full sun** but will tolerate partial shade. Almost any **well-drained** soil is suitable. This plant is very drought tolerant.

Pruning is not needed, but the flower spikes can be removed when blooming is finished, and dead leaves can be removed as needed.

Tips

Yucca is used as a specimen, usually in groups or in planters, to give a garden a southern appearance. In pots, planters and urns this plant also makes a strong architectural statement.

Yucca fruit rarely develops in Ohio. The yucca moth, which pollinates the flowers, is uncommon outside of the plant's native range in the southern U.S.

Recommended

Y. filamentosa has long, stiff, finely serrated, pointed leaves with threads that peel back from the edges. It is the most frost-hardy *Yucca* species available. **'Bright Edge'** has leaves with yellow margins. **'Golden Sword'** has leaves with yellow centers and green margins. **'Hofer's Blue'** has attractive blue-green leaves and is salt tolerant.

Problems & Pests

Cane borers, scale insects and fungal leaf spot can cause problems.

The striking white flowers are edible raw or cooked and are said to taste like Belgian endive. Try adding them to a salad.

'Golden Sword' (above), 'Bright Edge' (below)

Zelkova
Japanese Zelkova
Zelkova

Features: habit, summer and fall foliage **Habit:** vase-shaped to broadly spreading, deciduous tree **Height:** 50–80' or more **Spread:** up to 50–80' **Planting:** B & B; spring or fall **Zones:** 5–9

I PLANTED TWO ZELKOVA TREES TO SCREEN THE AFTERNOON SUN that danced off the white house north of my property. One of the two trees cankered and abruptly died in the seventh year, but the other individual persisted and has continued to do a good job of screening the upper portion of the house. The death of the first tree gave me room to plant a lacebark pine, which does a much better screening job at the lower levels. I enjoy the combination year round. I'm particularly pleased with the dull, rusty burgundy fall color of the zelkova, which holds its leaves quite late to continue the screening job.

Growing

Zelkova grows well in **full sun** or **partial shade**. The soil should be **fertile, humus rich, moist** and **well drained**. Young trees are sensitive to wind, drought and cold, but established plants tolerate these conditions. Prune in fall or winter to encourage neat, even growth.

Tips

Zelkova is a medium-sized tree with an attractive habit and foliage. It is well suited as a residential shade tree or for street plantings.

Recommended

Z. serrata grows 50–80' tall, or taller, with a spread of 50–80'. It is vase shaped when young and develops a broader, more spreading habit as it matures. It also develops exfoliating bark as it matures. Inconspicuous flowers are produced in early spring. The dark green leaves turn yellow or orange and sometimes red in fall. **'Green Vase'** maintains a vase-shaped habit and develops a strong, straight trunk. It grows up to 70' tall and spreads up to 50'. **'Village Green'** is a hardy, fast-growing, pest- and disease-resistant tree. It develops red fall color. This cultivar is hardy to the warmer parts of Zone 4. There is also a dwarf cultivar of *Z. serrata*, but it is currently difficult to find in North America.

Problems & Pests

This tree is in the elm family, but it is resistant to Dutch elm disease. Zelkova may have trouble with elm-leaf beetle, scale insects and canker.

Z. serrata in fall color

The mature, exfoliating bark of zelkova provides interest in the winter landscape.

'Green Vase'

OTHER TREES & SHRUBS TO CONSIDER

AMERICAN HOPHORNBEAM
Ostrya virginiana

This informal tree has an open habit and provides dappled shade. It is small enough for most gardens.

American hophornbeam is a small to medium, pyramidal tree 25–50' tall and 20–50' wide. It becomes rounded as it matures and may be single- or multi-stemmed. The bark peels away from the trunk in narrow, shaggy strips. Papery cones contrast nicely with the dark green foliage. The fall foliage is yellow or brown. (Zones 4–9)

This tree grows well in **full sun** or **partial shade** with **fertile, moist, well-drained** soil. It tolerates rocky or dry soil once established, but it can be slow to do so and needs supplemental watering until then. This native species makes an excellent shade tree for a small property or woodland garden and can be used as a street tree. Shade tolerant, it can be used where buildings or existing trees block some sunlight.

Ostrya virginiana (above)

Fraxinus americana
F. pennsylvanica

ASH
Fraxinus species

Emerald ash borer has recently become a serious problem for ashes in some parts of the northeastern U.S. If you choose to grow an ash, be aware it will need to be removed if attacked by this pest.

F. americana (white ash) is an oval to rounded, open tree 50–80' tall and wide. Fall color ranges from yellow to purple. *F. pennsylvanica* (green ash, red ash) is an upright to spreading, irregular tree 50–70' tall and wide. Fall color is usually yellow but can range through shades of orange and red. (Zones 3–9)

Ashes prefer **full sun** with **fertile, moist, well-drained, neutral to acidic** soil, but they adapt to most soil conditions. These popular, fast-growing trees are often used as street and shade trees. Some pests and diseases are becoming troublesome because of the widespread use of ashes. Choose resistant male cultivars, and keep trees stress free. Female trees produce many seeds that linger on the branches before sprouting enthusiastically in the garden.

Bald-Cypress
Taxodium distichum

Bald-cypress is a grossly underused tree, frequently and falsely associated only with standing water and a southern climate.

This conical coniferous, deciduous or semi-evergreen tree grows 50–130' tall and 20–30' wide. It becomes more open and asymmetrical with age. The bright green foliage turns orangy brown in fall. In or near swampy areas, the tree forms gnome-like 'knees' (pneumatophores), knobby roots that poke up out of the water and are thought to help the roots breathe. (Zones 4–9)

Bald-cypress prefers **full sun** or **partial shade** and **moist, acidic** soil but adapts to many soil conditions. Alkaline soil can cause the foliage to turn yellow (chlorotic). Bald-cypress has a deep taproot but transplants easily when young. This tree can be a bit large for most home gardens but makes a good choice in waterlogged soils. Use it as a large specimen individually or in groups.

Taxodium distichum

Black Tupelo
Nyssa sylvatica

When this tree establishes in your garden, be ready for a spectacle in all seasons.

Black tupelo is a pyramidal to rounded, deciduous tree that grows 30–50' tall and 20–30' wide. The glossy dark green leaves of this Ohio native turn brilliant shades of yellow, orange, red and purple quite early in fall. Black tupelo is not frequently found in cultivation owing to transplanting difficulties, but availability should improve as more nurseries produce container-grown stock. (Zones 4–9)

Grow black tupelo in **full sun** or **partial shade** and in **average to fertile, neutral to acidic, well-drained** soil. Plant trees when they are young, because the roots resent being disturbed. This beautiful specimen tree is suitable for a medium-sized property, but it resents polluted conditions and shouldn't be used as a street tree.

Black tupelo fruit attracts birds but is too sour for human tastes.

Nyssa sylvatica cultivar

U. americana

U. parvifolia *and* U. pumila *have both been called Chinese elm.* U. pumila *is an undesirable, weak-branched species susceptible to leaf beetle damage.*

U. glabra 'Camperdownii' (center & below)

ELM
Ulmus species

I almost caused a traffic accident once when I stopped suddenly to look at a beautiful old 35' by 35' Camperdown elm on the grounds of an abandoned estate. What a pleasure to behold!

U. americana (American elm) is a vase-shaped native tree with arching branches. It grows 60–100' tall and spreads 30–80'. Once very popular as a shade and street tree, it has been ravaged by the fungal Dutch elm disease. Disease-resistant culti-vars such as '**Valley Forge**' should be grown instead. (Zones 2–9)

U. carpinifolia (smoothleaf elm) is a columnar tree 70–90' tall and about 70' wide. This species and its many cultivars resist Dutch elm disease. '**Wredei**' (golden elm) is a dense, conical tree about half the size of the species. Its bright golden foliage keeps its color all summer. (Zones 5–7)

U. glabra '**Camperdownii**' (Camper-down elm) is a trailing or spreading culti-var that is often grafted to a standard to create a broadly spreading or weeping tree up to 25' in height and spread. (Zones 4–7)

U. parvifolia (lacebark elm, Chinese elm) is an upright, rounded to spreading tree that grows 40–60' in height and spread. Exfoliating bark gives the trunk a colorful, mottled appearance. This species and its many attractive cultivars are highly resistant to Dutch elm disease. Cultivars are less variable in habit than seed-grown species plants. (Zones 5–9)

Elms grow well in **full sun** or **partial shade**. They adapt to most soil conditions but prefer a **moist, fertile** soil. Smaller species and cultivars make attractive speci-men and shade trees, while larger trees look attractive where given plenty of room to grow, on larger properties and in parks.

Dutch elm disease has reduced the pres-ence of elms dramatically. The introduc-tion of resistant species and cultivars should encourage their use once again.

ENKIANTHUS
Enkianthus campanulatus

The lucky one-third of Ohioans who garden on fairly well-drained, acidic soil have a real gem here.

This large, bushy, deciduous shrub or small tree grows 10–15' tall and wide. It bears small, white, red-veined, pendulous, bell-shaped flowers in spring. The foliage turns fantastic shades of yellow, orange and red in fall. (Zones 4–7)

Enkianthus grows well in **full sun, partial shade** or **light shade,** with a **fertile, humus-rich, moist, acidic, well-drained** soil. It is generally free of pest and disease problems. A perfect shrub for the understory of a woodland garden, enkianthus also makes a good companion for rhododendrons and other acid-loving plants.

Enkianthus campanulatus

NORTHERN BAYBERRY
Myrica pensylvanica

Northern bayberry is a wonderful shrub that can stand alone as a specimen or blend easily into a mixed border. I have also trained it to grow as a small tree.

This dense, rounded, suckering shrub grows 5–12' tall, with an equal or greater spread. Inconspicuous male and female flowers are borne on separate plants in early to mid-spring. The small, waxy gray fruit persists through winter on female plants. (Zones 3–7)

Northern bayberry grows well in **full sun** or **partial shade** and adapts to most soil conditions, from poor sandy soil to heavy clay soil. It tolerates salty conditions, making it useful where road spray and runoff occur. Northern bayberry forms large colonies and can be used for mass plantings in underused areas.

The waxy fruit of northern bayberry is used to make bayberry-scented candles.

Myrica pensylvanica

Pyrus calleryana cultivar

Pear trees, like apples, are popular for use as espalier specimens.

Corylopsis spicata

PEAR
Pyrus calleryana

When the full moon and full flowering of callery pear cultivars coincide on a cloudless spring night, the glowing white flowers suggest an earthly Milky Way.

P. calleryana is a conical tree with thorny branches. It grows 30–50' in height and spread. Plentiful clusters of white flowers appear in mid-spring. The glossy green foliage turns red in fall. The species is rarely grown, but the many attractive cultivars include ARISTOCRAT, BURGUNDY SNOW, CLEVELAND PRIDE and REDSPIRE. 'Bradford' was a popular cultivar but is no longer recommended because of serious problems with branch and tree breakage. (Zones 5–8)

This tree grows well in **full sun** and in **fertile, well-drained** soil. It adapts to most well-drained soils. The size and pollution tolerance of pear makes it useful as a specimen in small and medium-sized city gardens.

SPIKE WINTERHAZEL
Corylopsis spicata

Spike winterhazel will furnish you with branches for fragrant indoor forcing, and it looks good outdoors, too. It thrives in moist, shady areas.

This open, wide-spreading, deciduous shrub grows 4–10' tall and 6–10' wide. It bears 6" long tassels of fragrant pale yellow flowers in mid-spring, before the leaves emerge. (Zones 5–8)

Spike winterhazel grows well in **full sun, partial shade** or **light shade**. It prefers **fertile, humus-rich, moist, well-drained** soil and should be given **shelter** from winter winds. This attractive shrub is useful in borders or as a specimen.

WILLOW
Salix species

As a child I grew up thinking there were only pussy willows and weeping willows. Now I know that these fast-growing deciduous shrubs or trees can have colorful or twisted stems or foliage, and they come in a huge range of growth habits and sizes.

S. alba 'Tristis' (golden weeping willow) is a graceful weeping tree with long, flexible, trailing young branches. It grows 50–70' in height and width. The young growth and fall leaves are bright yellow. (Zones 4–8)

S. x *grahamii* (Graham's willow) is a shrubby dwarf hybrid that grows 18–24" in height and spread. 'Moorei' is a low, trailing plant that grows about 12" tall and spreads 36" or more. (Zones 3–8)

S. integra 'Hakuro Nishiki' (dappled willow, Japanese dappled willow) is a spreading shrub with supple, arching branches that appear almost weeping. It grows 3–8' in height and spread. The young shoots are orange-pink in color and the leaves are dappled green, cream and pink. This cultivar is often grafted to a standard to create a small tree form. (Zones 5–8)

S. SCARLET CURLS (*S.* 'Sarcuzam') is an upright shrubby tree with curled and twisted branches and leaves. It grows up to 30' tall and spreads 15–25'. The young stems are reddish and become redder after a frost, creating an attractive winter display of twisted red shoots. This cultivar is often pruned back hard each year or two to encourage the young twisted growth. (Zones 5–8)

Willows grow best in **full sun**, with **moist, well-drained** soil. *S. alba* 'Tristis' tolerates wet soil, while the smaller shrubby willows are more drought tolerant. *S.* x *grahamii* and 'Moorei' grow well in exposed sites with rocky, well-drained soil. Large tree willows should be reserved for large spaces and look particularly attractive near water features. Smaller willows can be used as small specimen trees or in shrub and mixed borders. Small and trailing forms can be included in rock gardens and along rock retaining walls.

S. integra 'Hakuro Nishiki'

Be careful where you plant a willow tree. Some willows aggressively seek water sources and can invade water and sewage pipes.

S. alba 'Tristis'

TREE HEIGHT LEGEND: Short: < 25' • Medium: 25–50' • Tall: > 50'

SPECIES by Common Name	FORM							FOLIAGE							
	Tall Tree	Med. Tree	Short Tree	Shrub	Groundcover	Climber		Evergreen	Deciduous	Variegated	Blue/White	Purple/Red	Yellow/Gold	Dark Green	Light Green
Aralia			•	•					•	•				•	
Arborvitae		•	•	•				•					•	•	
Aronia				•					•					•	
Barberry				•	•				•	•	•	•	•	•	
Beautyberry				•					•						
Beauty Bush				•					•						
Beech	•	•							•	•		•	•	•	
Birch	•	•							•			•			•
Black Jetbead				•					•						
Boxwood				•				•						•	
Buckeye	•	•	•	•					•						
Butterfly Bush			•	•					•						
Caryopteris				•					•		•		•	•	•
Cherry	•	•	•	•					•			•		•	•
Cotoneaster			•	•	•			•	•					•	
Crabapple		•	•						•						
Dawn Redwood	•								•					•	
Deutzia				•					•						
Dogwood			•	•					•	•	•		•	•	•
Elder				•					•	•	•	•	•	•	
Euonymus			•	•	•	•		•	•	•	•		•	•	•
False Cypress	•	•	•	•				•		•	•		•	•	
False Spirea				•					•						
Filbert		•	•	•					•			•	•	•	
Firethorn			•	•	•	•		•	•					•	
Flowering Quince				•					•						
Forsythia				•	•				•	•	•		•		•
Fothergilla				•					•		•			•	

| | FEATURES | | | | | | | | BLOOMING | | | | | SPECIES by Common Name |
Form	Flowers	Foliage	Bark	Fruit/Cones	Scent	Spines	Fall Color	Winter Interest	Spring	Summer	Fall	Zones	Page Number	
	•	•		•		•				•		4–8	76	Aralia
•		•	•	•	•			•				2–9	78	Arborvitae
	•			•			•	•	•	•		3–8	82	Aronia
	•	•		•			•	•	•			4–8	84	Barberry
				•						•		5–10	88	Beautyberry
	•								•			4–8	90	Beauty Bush
•		•	•				•					4–9	92	Beech
•	•	•	•	•			•	•	•			3–9	96	Birch
•	•			•					•	•		4–8	100	Black Jetbead
•		•			•			•				4–9	102	Boxwood
	•	•		•			•		•	•		3–9	106	Buckeye
•	•	•			•					•	•	5–9	110	Butterfly Bush
•	•	•			•					•	•	5–9	112	Caryopteris
•	•	•	•	•	•		•	•	•	•		2–9	114	Cherry
•	•	•			•		•	•		•		4–9	120	Cotoneaster
•	•	•	•	•	•		•	•	•			4–8	124	Crabapple
•		•	•	•			•	•				4–8	130	Dawn Redwood
•	•						•			•		4–9	132	Deutzia
•	•	•	•	•			•	•	•	•		2–9	134	Dogwood
•	•	•		•					•	•		3–9	138	Elder
•		•	•				•	•				3–9	142	Euonymus
•		•		•				•				4–8	146	False Cypress
	•	•								•		2–8	150	False Spirea
•	•	•		•				•	•			4–8	152	Filbert
•	•	•		•		•	•			•		5–9	156	Firethorn
	•			•	•	•			•			5–9	160	Flowering Quince
•	•	•							•			4–9	162	Forsythia
•	•	•			•		•		•			4–9	166	Fothergilla

TREE HEIGHT LEGEND: Short: < 25' • Medium: 25–50' • Tall: > 50'

SPECIES
by Common Name

Species	Tall Tree	Med. Tree	Short Tree	Shrub	Groundcover	Climber	Evergreen	Deciduous	Variegated	Blue/White	Purple/Red	Yellow/Gold	Dark Green	Light Green
Fringe Tree			•	•				•					•	
Ginkgo	•	•						•						•
Golden Rain Tree		•	•					•						•
Hawthorn		•	•					•					•	
Hemlock	•	•	•	•	•		•		•	•			•	
Holly		•	•	•			•	•					•	
Honeysuckle			•			•	•	•		•		•	•	•
Hornbeam	•	•	•					•						
Hydrangea		•	•			•		•	•			•	•	•
Japanese Hydrangea Vine						•		•	•		•			
√ Juniper	•	•	•	•	•		•		•	•		•	•	•
Katsura-Tree	•	•	•					•	•		•			
Kerria			•					•	•					•
Larch	•	•	•					•						•
√ Lilac (3)		•	•					•	•				•	•
Linden	•	•						•					•	
Magnolia		•	•	•				•						
Maple	•	•	•	•				•	•		•	•	•	•
Mock-Orange			•					•	•					
Mountain Laurel			•				•						•	
Ninebark			•					•			•			
Oak	•	•						•					•	
Oregon-Grape			•	•			•						•	
Pieris			•				•		•		•			
Pine	•	•	•	•			•		•			•	•	•
Potentilla			•	•				•						
Privet			•				•	•				•	•	
Redbud		•	•					•			•		•	•

| | FEATURES | | | | | | | | BLOOMING | | | | | SPECIES by Common Name |
Form	Flowers	Foliage	Bark	Fruit/Cones	Scent	Spines	Fall Color	Winter Interest	Spring	Summer	Fall	Zones	Page Number	
•	•		•	•				•		•		4–9	168	Fringe Tree
•		•	•	•	•		•	•				3–9	170	Ginkgo
•	•	•		•			•			•		5–8	172	Golden Rain Tree
•	•	•	•	•		•	•	•	•	•		3–8	174	Hawthorn
		•		•				•				3–8	178	Hemlock
		•		•		•		•				3–9	180	Holly
•	•			•	•				•	•	•	3–9	186	Honeysuckle
•		•					•					3–9	190	Hornbeam
•	•	•	•				•	•		•	•	3–9	192	Hydrangea
•	•	•								•		5–8	198	Japanese Hydrangea Vine
•		•		•	•	•		•				2–9	200	Juniper
•		•			•		•	•				4–8	206	Katsura-Tree
•	•		•				•	•	•			4–9	208	Kerria
•		•		•			•					3–7	210	Larch
•	•	•			•		•		•	•		2–8	212	Lilac
•	•	•								•		2–8	218	Linden
•	•	•	•	•				•	•			3–9	222	Magnolia
•	•	•	•	•			•	•	•			2–8	226	Maple
	•				•				•	•		3–8	232	Mock-Orange
	•	•						•	•	•		4–9	236	Mountain Laurel
•	•	•	•	•			•	•	•	•		2–8	238	Ninebark
•		•	•	•			•					2–9	240	Oak
•	•	•		•		•	•	•	•			5–9	244	Oregon-Grape
•	•	•					•	•	•			5–8	246	Pieris
•		•	•	•	•			•				2–8	248	Pine
•	•	•		•						•	•	2–8	252	Potentilla
•		•										3–8	256	Privet
•	•	•					•		•			4–9	258	Redbud

TREE HEIGHT LEGEND: Short: < 25' • Medium: 25–50' • Tall: > 50'

SPECIES by Common Name	FORM						FOLIAGE							
	Tall Tree	Med. Tree	Short Tree	Shrub	Groundcover	Climber	Evergreen	Deciduous	Variegated	Blue/White	Purple/Red	Yellow/Gold	Dark Green	Light Green
Rhododendron				•			•	•					•	•
Rose-of-Sharon			•	•				•	•					
Serviceberry			•	•				•					•	
Seven-Son Flower			•	•				•						
Silverbell		•	•					•						•
Smokebush			•	•				•			•		•	
Snowbell		•	•					•						
Spirea				•				•			•	•	•	•
Spruce	•	•	•	•			•			•			•	•
St. Johnswort				•			•	•		•	•			
Stewartia		•	•					•						
Sumac			•	•	•			•						
Summersweet				•				•						
Sweetgum	•							•					•	
Sweetspire				•				•			•		•	•
Thornless Honeylocust	•	•	•					•				•		
Tulip Tree	•							•	•				•	
Viburnum			•	•			•	•						
Weigela				•				•	•		•	•	•	•
White Forsythia				•				•						
Wisteria				•		•		•						
Witchhazel		•	•					•					•	
Yellowwood		•						•				•		•
Yew		•	•	•			•						•	
Yucca				•			•			•	•			•
Zelkova	•	•						•					•	

	FEATURES								BLOOMING					SPECIES by Common Name
Form	Flowers	Foliage	Bark	Fruit/Cones	Scent	Spines	Fall Color	Winter Interest	Spring	Summer	Fall	Zones	Page Number	
•	•	•			•		•	•	•	•		4–8	260	Rhododendron
	•	•								•	•	5–9	264	Rose-of-Sharon
•	•	•	•	•			•	•	•	•		3–9	268	Serviceberry
•	•		•	•			•	•		•	•	5–8	272	Seven-Son Flower
•	•	•		•			•		•	•		5–9	274	Silverbell
•	•	•					•			•		4–8	276	Smokebush
•	•	•							•	•		4–8	278	Snowbell
•	•	•		•			•			•		3–9	280	Spirea
•		•		•	•	•		•				2–8	284	Spruce
•	•	•					•			•	•	4–9	288	St. Johnswort
•	•	•	•				•	•		•		5–7	292	Stewartia
•	•	•		•			•			•		3–9	294	Sumac
	•	•			•		•			•		3–9	298	Summersweet
•		•	•	•		•	•					5–9	300	Sweetgum
•	•				•		•		•	•		5–9	302	Sweetspire
•		•		•			•					4–8	304	Thornless Honeylocust
•	•	•		•			•			•		4–9	306	Tulip Tree
•	•	•		•	•		•	•	•	•		2–9	308	Viburnum
	•	•							•	•		3–8	314	Weigela
	•	•			•		•	•	•			5–8	316	White Forsythia
•	•	•		•	•		•		•	•		4–9	318	Wisteria
•	•	•			•		•	•	•		•	3–9	322	Witchhazel
•	•	•	•	•	•		•	•	•			4–8	326	Yellowwood
•		•		•				•				4–7	328	Yew
•	•	•						•		•		5–9	332	Yucca
•		•	•				•					5–9	334	Zelkova

GLOSSARY

B & B: abbreviation for balled-and-burlapped stock, i.e., plants that have been dug out of the ground and have had their rootballs wrapped in burlap

Bonsai: the art of training plants into miniature trees and landscapes

Bract: a modified leaf at the base of a flower or flower cluster; bracts can be showy, as in flowering dogwood blossoms

Candles: the new, soft spring growth of needle-leaved evergreens such as pine, spruce and fir

Crown: the part of a plant at or just below the soil where the stems meet the roots; also, the top of a tree, including the branches and leaves

Cultivar: a cultivated plant variety with one or more distinct differences from the species; e.g., *Hedera helix* is a botanical species, of which 'Gold Heart' is a cultivar distinguished by leaf variegation

Deadhead: to remove spent flowers in order to maintain a neat appearance, encourage a longer blooming period and prevent the plant from expending energy on producing fruit

Dieback: death of a branch from the tip inwards; usually used to describe winter damage.

Dormancy: an inactive stage, often coinciding with the onset of winter

Double flower: a flower with an unusually large number of petals, often caused by mutation of the stamens into petals

Dripline: the area around the bottom of a tree, directly under the tips of the farthest-extending branches

Dwarf: a plant that is small compared to the normal growth of the species; dwarf growth is often cultivated by plant breeders

Espalier: the training of a tree or shrub to grow in two dimensions

Forma (*abbrev.* f.): a naturally occurring variant of a species; below the level of subspecies in biological classification and similar to variety

Gall: an abnormal outgrowth or swelling produced as a reaction to sucking insects, other pests or diseases

Genus: a category of biological classification between the species and family levels; the first word in a scientific name indicates the genus, e.g., *Pinus* in *Pinus mugo*

Girdling: a restricted flow of water and nutrients in a plant caused by something tied tightly around a trunk or branch, or by an encircling cut or root

Heartwood: the wood in the center of a stem or branch consisting of old, dense, nonfunctional conducting tissue

Hybrid: any plant that results from natural or human-induced cross-breeding between varieties, species or genera; hybrids are often sterile but may be more vigorous than either parent and have attributes of both. Hybrids are indicated in scientific names by an *x*, e.g., *Forsythia* x *intermedia*

Inflorescence: a flower cluster

Leader: the dominant upward growth at the top of a tree; may be erect or drooping

Nodes: the places on the stem from where leaves grow; when cuttings are planted, new roots grow from the nodes under the soil

pH: a measure of acidity or alkalinity (the lower the pH below 7, the greater the acidity; the higher the pH between 7 and 14, the greater the alkalinity); soil pH influences nutrient availability for plants

Pollarding: a severe form of pruning in which all younger branches of a tree are cut back virtually to the trunk to encourage bushy new growth

Procumbent, prostrate: terms used to describe plants that grow along the ground

Rhizome: a modified stem that grows horizontally underground

Rootball: the root mass and surrounding soil of a container-grown or dug-out plant

Semi-evergreen: describes evergreen plants that in cold climates lose some or all of their leaves over winter

Single flower: a flower with a single ring of typically four or five petals

Species: the original plant from which cultivars are derived; the fundamental unit of biological classification, indicated by a two-part scientific name, e.g., *Pinus mugo* (*mugo* is the specific epithet)

Standard: a shrub or small tree grown with an erect main stem; accomplished either through pruning and training or by grafting the plant onto a tall, straight stock

Subspecies (*abbrev.* subsp.): a naturally occurring, regional form of a species, often geographically isolated from other subspecies but still potentially able to interbreed with them

Sucker: a shoot that comes up from a root, often some distance from the plant; it can be separated to form a new plant once it develops its own roots

Topiary: the training of plants into geometric, animal or other unique shapes

Variegation: describes foliage that has more than one color, often patched or striped or bearing differently colored leaf margins

Variety (*abbrev.* var.): a naturally occurring variant of a species; below the level of subspecies in biological classification

RESOURCES

Dirr, M.A. 1997. *Dirr's Hardy Trees and Shrubs: An Illustrated Encyclopedia.* Timber Press, Portland, Oregon.

Dirr, M.A. 1998. *Manual of Woody Landscape Plants.* 5th ed. Stipes Publishing, Champaign, Illinois.

Dirr, M.A. and C.W. Heuser, Jr. 1987. *The Reference Manual of Woody Plant Propagation.* Varsity Press, Athens, Georgia.

Ellis, B.W. and F.M. Bradley, eds. 1996. *The Organic Gardener's Handbook of Natural Insect and Disease Control.* Rodale Press, Emmaus, Pennsylvania.

Fiala, J.L. 1988. *Lilacs: The Genus* Syringa. Timber Press, Portland, Oregon.

Flint, H.L. 1997. *Landscape Plants for Eastern North America.* 2nd ed. John Wiley and Sons, New York.

Galle, F.C. 1997. *Hollies: The Genus* Ilex. Timber Press, Portland, Oregon.

Kelly, J. and J. Hillier, eds. 1997. *The Hillier Gardener's Guide to Trees and Shrubs.* Reader's Digest Association, Pleasantville, New York.

Sydnor, T.D and W.F. Cowen. 2000. *Ohio Trees.* Ohio State University Extension, Columbus.

Tripp, K.E. and J.C. Raulston. 1995. *The Year in Trees: Superb Woody Plants for Four-Season Gardens.* Timber Press, Portland, Oregon.

• BuckeyeGardening.com
http://buckeyegardening.com/

• Buckeye Yard & Garden onLine
http://bygl.osu.edu/

• Ohio State University Extension
'Ohioline'
http://ohioline.osu.edu/lines/hygs.html

• International Society of Arboriculture
http://www.isa-arbor.com/

• Chadwick Arboretum, Ohio State University
http://chadwickarboretum.osu.edu/

• Franklin Park Conservatory
http://www.fpconservatory.org/

INDEX OF PLANT NAMES